To ▬▬▬▬
from ▬
London, 1958

THE STORY OF THE NURSERY

Nurses and Sucklings. From M. S. J. Quichirat's *Costumes in France*

The Story
of
the Nursery

by

MAGDALEN KING-HALL

Routledge & Kegan Paul
LONDON

First published 1958
by Routledge & Kegan Paul Ltd.
Broadway House, Carter Lane, E.C.4
Printed in Great Britain
by Wyman & Sons Ltd.
London, Reading and Fakenham

With love to my great-nephews,
NICOLAS, OLIVIER AND DOMINIQUE BARRAUD
AND CHARLES MAVOR

Contents

❖▸❖

ILLUSTRATIONS

ILLUSTRATIONS

ACKNOWLEDGMENTS

MY grateful thanks for the very kind help given me, as well as for permission to reproduce portraits, etc., are due to:

The Earl and Countess of Belmore for Nos. 9a and 11 (the 18th century cradle and Victorian pram at Castlecoole); Mrs. W. E. D. Allen for Nos. 3 and 7 (the 17th-and 18th-century portraits from her collection at Whitechurch House, Cappagh, Co. Waterford); Major and Mrs. Montgomery for No. 10 (the portrait at Greyabbey, Co. Down, of the three Montgomery children, William Edward born 1847, later a Major-General, Scots Guards, Robert born 1848, later Major-General and Colonel Commandant of the Royal Artillery, and their sister Lucy, born 1849); Major and Mrs. Perceval Maxwell of Finnebrogue, Co. Down, for No. 15b (the 18th-century child's chair), Nos. 12, a, b and c and 13 a, b (the photographs of Victorian children), No. 14 (the little boy of the 1870's—later the Rt. Honbl. Lt.-Colonel R. D. Perceval Maxwell, D.S.O., P.C., D.L.); No. 15a (the Nursery Party, which shows the Cherry family and their Terry cousins, also Nanny Mercy Bullimore, the nursery maid Edith and the Terry Nanny); No. 16 (the author's husband in a pram, and his eldest brother, now Major Perceval Maxwell, B.L., D.L., playing croquet).

This is to say 'thank you' to the authors, past and present whose books (given in a list at the end) I have consulted while writing this story of the Nursery. I must also acknowledge my particular indebtedness to the authors and publishers concerned for permission to quote from the following books:

Miss Weeton, ed. Squadron Leader Edward Hall; *The Child in Fashion*, Doris Langley Moore, Messrs. B. T. Batsford Ltd.; *The Elizabethan Home*, ed. Mary St. Clare Byrne, Messrs. Methuen & Co. Ltd.; *Report on the MSS. of Lord de L'Isle and Dudley*, by courtesy of the Controller of Her Majesty's Stationery Office; *John Evelyn and his Family Circle*, W. G. Hiscock, Messrs. Routledge & Kegan Paul Ltd.; *Lives of the Norths*, Dr. Jessop, Messrs. G. Bell & Sons, Ltd.; *Caroline Clive*, ed. Mary Clive, The Bodley Head; *The Amberley Papers*,

ACKNOWLEDGMENTS

Bertrand and Patricia Russell, The Hogarth Press, Ltd.; *The Diary of Lady Frederick Cavendish*, Lucy Cohen, Messrs. John Murray & Sons, Ltd.; *Life in the Middle Ages*, ed. G. G. Coulton, Cambridge University Press; *Memoirs of the Verney Family*, Frances P. Verney, Messrs. Longmans Green & Co., Ltd.; *Admiral's Wife*, Cecil Aspinell-Oglander, Messrs. Longmans Green & Co., Ltd.; *Left Hand, Right Hand!* Sir Osbert Sitwell, Messrs. Macmillan, Ltd.; *The Wynne Diaries*, ed. Anne Fremantle; Oxford University Press (Royal Classics) *Elizabeth Ham by Herself*, ed. Eric Gilbert, Messrs. Faber & Faber.

Introduction

❖❖❖

EVERYONE who is interested in history must have wished that they could visit a past epoch, through some magical process of vision or dream. I say 'visit' because I fancy that there are few people, however disillusioned they may be with the present age, who would have the courage, when it came to the point, to cut themselves adrift from their familiar mooring in time.

It would be a fascinating and disturbing experience, perhaps as intimidating in its way as one of those trips to the blanched and eerie reaches of the Moon promised by scientists. No doubt a great many preconceived ideas and illusions would have to be jettisoned. But what bewitchment to the enquiring mind, of *knowing* instead of merely imagining how our ancestors lived! Perhaps one day science will be able to project us backwards in time as well as through the immensities of space. Till then we must be content to guess.

This book is a modest attempt to reconstruct the English scene, from the Middle Ages to Victorian times, as it seemed to the eyes of its youngest denizens—the very small children of nursery age.

If we could take an imaginary expedition into the past, we would, I suppose, find ourselves more at home with the children than with the adults, for child nature in its pristine simplicity hardly alters throughout the centuries. New to the world, the young child is as much an alien in its particular era as any traveller returned from the future would be.

'There cometh from the child thus born a wailing and weeping that must about midnight make thee to waken', is as true of the modern infant as of the medieval babe.

It is the nature of young children of every century to play mysterious absorbed games with objects such as pebbles and buttons that were never intended to be used as toys, and to put them in their mouths to the clucking dismay of mothers and nurses. They discover a world of enchantment in the cup of an acorn; a crumpled coverlet in a darkened room assumes a hideous shape of nightmare terror. Griefs and joys are acutely felt and soon forgotten; time flows with deceptive slowness like a broad river, featureless except for meals and bedtime.

But the pressure of their environment and of the adult society around them soon closes in on them, moulding them into some semblance of the accepted contemporary type. This process was very much speedier, more ruthless as it seems to us, in former than in present times. It is only comparatively recently, broadly speaking within this present century, that childhood has come to be regarded as a state of existence complete in itself, a kingdom with its own laws and privileges.

The study of child psychology, spreading in widening circles from the library and the psychiatrist's consulting room to the correspondence columns of the women's magazines, the dwindling size of the average family, inevitably making each little arrow in the parental quiver more important if not necessarily more loved, have combined to invest childhood with an almost sacrosanct atmosphere that would have amazed and outraged our ancestors.

'They say don't give them chips, but my children have always loved chips. When they were quite tiny we had only to rustle a newspaper and say "chips" and they stopped crying' was a striking piece of practical experience (rather reminiscent of the late Professor Pavlov's experiments with dogs;) proffered to Mass Observation by a mother, and deemed not unworthy by them to be included in their findings relating to child welfare.

Compare this with the brisk medieval: 'The more the father loveth his child the more busily he teacheth and chastise him.'

This changed attitude towards the young was summed up plaintively by a modern grandfather: 'I was born into an unfortunate generation. When I was a child I had to knuckle under to the grown-ups, and now that I am a grown-up I have to knuckle under to the children.'

Sir Basil Henriques, formerly chairman of East London Juvenile Court, told the Royal Empire Society in an address, that everybody today was afraid of the child. One might qualify this by saying that nearly everyone is afraid of what they may do to the child. The more well-meaning the adult, the more they are dogged by the fear that some lack of wisdom or understanding on their part may cause irreparable harm to the tender young plant. It has been said that there never has been an age in which more was known about children, but in which parents had less confidence in their powers to handle their own children. Grown-up people in the 'old days' were comfortably free from any such qualms. The child was regarded as a troublesome little adult in embryo, chock-full of original sin (though we shall find many gleams of tenderness towards children in our excursion through the centuries, only poets like Traherne or Wordsworth regarded them with sentiment) who must be induced by constant precept, admonition and discipline to fit as speedily as possible into the surrounding adult world. The background of this adult world then must be sketched in lightly if the child's life is to be understood.

It would be highly presumptuous of me to claim that I have written a complete and fully documented history of the Nursery. Such a book would have been quite beyond my powers, and perhaps would have been an equally great strain on the patience and time of my readers. I regard this book as an imaginative excursion or voyage of exploration, and hope that there may be some interest and entertainment in the reading as well as in the writing of it.

For my readers' sakes as well as for my own, I have confined myself to the English scene, though naturally much of what I have written, particularly in the part dealing with the Middle Ages, applies to Western Europe as a whole.

It soon occurred to me when I was planning this book that its scope must necessarily be limited in a class sense. The word 'nursery' implies some special care and attention, and though the children of the poor have been no less loved throughout the ages, neither cherishing in a physical sense nor segregation came their way. It would be heartless irony to apply the word 'nursery' to the barefooted children scaring crows in the fields, or to the piteous little slaves toiling in the mines and factories of the Industrial Age.

A medieval writer blandly asserted that rich men's children being habitually overfed, had less chance of survival than the children of the poor. The argument sounds familiar, and is not very convincing. Against his description of the pampered lordling crying and tossing his little limbs, may be set that of Piers Plowman's 'babes that continually cry for food'. But overfeeding apart, the children of the 'commyn peple' certainly scored in some important points. Not for them the starched ruffs, buckrammed skirts and padded breeches that give the portraits of the aristocratic Tudor young the air of wizened little men and women, and that make it hard to believe that they would ever run around in play. They escaped too, the iron discipline of the tutor with his busy rod, while the pernicious custom of child marriage, based as it was on the ambition or cupidity of parents and guardians, greedy for family aggrandizement or financial gain was, by its nature more common in the higher than in the lower ranks of society.

It is conceivable then that a child's existence may have been less constricted even—in spite of great hardships—more carefree in the wattle and daub cottage than in the manor house. But the lives of these children are unrecorded, merging, in the grim fight for survival, into the struggling lives of their parents.

The dictionary defines the word 'nursery' as, (1) Room assigned to children and their nurses, (2) Practice, institution, sphere, place in or by which qualities or classes of people are fostered and bred. It is, of course, with the second broader meaning of the word that we are concerned. The nursery in the first sense as a room with a definite purpose of its own, gradually emerged towards the close of the Middle Ages, when the communal pattern of domestic life with its astonishing lack of privacy, began to disintegrate before the wish for greater comfort and seclusion, but it only came to its full blossoming in the Victorian Age. To say the word 'Nursery' is to conjure up the picture of what we now think of as an 'old-fashioned nursery' of that period. Its size and proportions may be nebulous, but it *must* have a high, polished fire guard, a rocking chair and a rocking horse with scarlet nostrils, a doll's house, a screen covered with glossy, coloured picture 'scraps', a cuckoo clock, and of course presiding over it all, stout, comfortable yet superb in her cap with streamers and her voluminous white apron, that unique institution, the British Nanny.

But all this belongs to the last chapter of our story. Hundreds of years must pass, countless children be born and reared before the Nursery develops into Nanny's impregnable citadel, the little kingdom where she reigns supreme.

Now we must go far back in time to an age when adults often behaved like children, and when children were soon thrust out of the dubious security of childhood into the rough and tumble of the adult world.

I

✦✦✦

The Middle Ages

'They love an apple more than gold.'

I

An authority on the Middle Ages, the late Professor G. G. Coulton, has said: '. . . we cannot understand the Middle Ages unless we are willing to bear in mind two complementary truths; first the essential similarity of human nature in all ages; and secondly the dissimilarity of men's environment . . . at that distance in time.'

These are good words to carry in our minds as we set out on our journey of exploration to an age that seems strangely vivid and yet remote. It is like peering through the wrong end of a telescope. The colours are fresh and bright, the figures life-like, yet so far removed from us that to establish any real contact with them is a difficult proposition.

It is not only another world, but another universe that we have to contemplate. How cosy—if one may use the word—that medieval universe must have been, in spite of superstitious terrors, with earth hanging like a crystal ball (or rather one should say like a plate off which the unwary navigator might fall into limbo) suspended between heaven and hell, compared to the unthinkable immensities of space in which science has obliged us to dwell.

The civilized medieval world is small, its walled cities and towns, castles, monasteries, villages, fields, forests and swamps

B   I

surrounded by uncharted seas and by lands inhabited by pagans, barbarians, and worse. Sir John Mandeville (alias Jean d'Outremeuse) that *'menteur à triple etages'*, (as a French writer unkindly termed him) was an entertaining, but hardly a reassuring travel-author, describing with the utmost non-chalance men with heads like hounds, others who had no heads at all and kept their eyes in their shoulders, and pigmies who lived on the smell of raw apples (precursors surely of Jean de Brunhoff's engaging monster Polomoche?). All this and much more Sir John Mandeville's readers swallowed, we must believe, without a blink. To them it was as credible as Marco Polo's account of the hitherto fabled land of Cathay. We must admire the robust appetite of our medieval ancestors for marvels, an appetite, judging by the popularity of space thrillers, which the children of the atomic age have not outgrown.

In this medieval world anything may happen outside the fold of Christianity. Satan is always on the prowl, or hovering on his dark and terrible wings waiting to destroy the heedless soul. The regions of cold and ice and perpetual storm are his; yet below in hell his attendant fiends stoke up the everlasting fires.

It is forbidden, as well as desperately unsafe, to wander beyond the sheltering mantle of Mother Church. But ancient beliefs from primeval, half-forgotten cults still survive, manifesting themselves in an offering by a well or a fairy-haunted tree, or in the more sinister outlet of witchcraft.

A passionate longing for unity (which we are in a better position than our immediate predecessors to understand) was the mainspring of medieval thought, inspiring some of its finest aspirations and its most repulsive cruelties.

So the medieval world begins to take shape before us, in its beauty and squalor, its compassion and cruelty, its exuberant, childish gaiety and morbid gloom, its violent passions and unrestrained impulses and pranks.

It is the contrasts in medieval life that strike us most forcibly. Its discomfort would appal us, its squalor and dirt nauseate us. It was the golden age of the scavenger. In the towns kites, so tame that they ate from the children's hands, fed on the garbage in the streets; in the castle hall where ladies and knights banqueted, stately in their robes of velvet and cloth of gold and fur, dregs of wine and scraps of food were thrown down into the rushes on the floor (rushes that sometimes were sprinkled with flowers). Leprosy, beggars exhibiting their revolting sores, filth, lack of sanitation, obscene jests and atrocious tortures, this is part of the medieval scene. Its other aspect is portrayed in the tapestries in the Musée de Cluny. It is true that snow-white unicorns, bearing standards or pennons, two of them sitting on their haunches like performing dogs, are in attend-ance on the exquisite ladies with golden hair and gauzy veils who are the central figures in at least three of the tapestries, but this need not detract from the authenticity of the vision. How ravishingly beautiful these roseate tapestries are, with their delicate perfection of detail, the fruit-ladened trees, the grass embroidered with flowers, the little beasts and birds! It is the essence of medieval poetry, only to be compared in its joyous freshness to *Aucassin and Nicolette*.

I realize the presumption of trying to compress the Middle Ages, a period which for the purpose of this book, I have taken to mean from the 12th to the end of the 15th century, into a single section, as though oblivious of the great changes, political, economic and social that took place during those three hundred years. But the information available about the lives of young children during those centuries is, compared to later periods, so scanty that I have had no alternative. Moreover though the 'feel' of each century differs sharply from that of its predecessor and successor, a difference that is expressed subtly in the appearance of its clothes and architecture, the word 'medieval' does denote an outlook and way of living common to them all, while the attitude of parents to their children, and the lives of the children themselves hardly altered during that long stretch of time. So I hope I shall be excused if I range to and fro among those three centuries without paying too much regard to chronological order.

2

A picture from an illuminated manuscript—Lydgate's metrical 'Life of St. Edmund'—shows the birth of the saint and gives a vivid idea of a medieval nursing chamber. The clothes of the ladies—one of them wears a horned head-dress, another a U-shaped one, showing the fretted nets over her ears—their graceful, fitted dresses, as well as the elegant and even luxurious furnishings of the room, show that the scene dates from the later Middle Ages, in fact the 15th century, when privacy and comfort were valued more than they were in the early part of the period.

The room is one in which one would not mind sleeping oneself. The mother of the newly-born saint sits up in bed, receiving the ministrations of three female attendants, while another one, the lady in the horned head-dress, is seated before a blazing log fire. The mother appears to be fully clothed and is wearing a veil, complete with halo, on her head. The head covering is what one would expect, for up till comparatively modern times people were careful to protect their heads from the night air. But it was the usual custom in the Middle Ages to sleep naked in bed. (A woodcut from the *Roman de Melusine* shows a married couple in bed, wearing nothing but night caps, intently watching a lady who from the text I take to be Melusine, suckling one of a pair of twins.) Whether some kind of garment was worn during childbirth, I do not know. It seems more likely that the illustrator thought it more decorous to clothe the mother of a saint even in bed.

The bed itself, probably a feather one, is handsome, with a richly patterned canopy and curtains, the sheet neatly folded over a coverlet of the same design. The walls appear to be painted in a floral pattern; the floor is tiled in small squares, and there is a decorative looking rug in front of the fire, and gold candlesticks, cups and other vessels in recesses over the fireplace and on top of an open cupboard.

There is an air of indescribable well-being and cosiness about the scene, and of that triumphant joyfulness which was summed up once and for ever in the words; 'but as soon as she is delivered of the child, she remembereth no more the anguish for joy that a man is born into the world.'

One of the sculptures on the columns of the Hôtel de Ville in Brussels shows another mother, also belonging to the latter part of the 15th century. She wears a turban-like head-dress and is

4

seated at the foot of a solid-looking cradle. She has a wistful expression as though she were reflecting more on the cares than on the delights of motherhood, and no wonder, for not only has she a child lying in the cradle, but is suckling a smaller infant who lies naked on her lap. She seems to be meditating on the apparent unfairness of Providence in allotting to women so much the larger share in the production and rearing of children. This theme was the subject of a charming sermon by St. Bernadino da Siena.

St. Bernadino admonished husbands thus: 'Wherefore as thou seest that thy wife endureth travail on every side, therefore thou, O husband, if she falls into any need be sure thou help her to bear the pain. If she be with child or in child-birth, aid her in so far as in thee lieth, for it is thy child also. Let all help her whereinsoever they may. Mark her well, how she travaileth in childbirth, travaileth to suckle the child, travaileth to rear it, travaileth in washing and cleaning by day and by night . . .' He goes on to say: 'All this travail seest thou, is of the woman only, and the man goeth singing on his way.'

Then comes this engaging anecdote: 'There was once a baron's lady who said to me, "Methinks the dear Lord our Master doeth as He seeth good, and I am content to say that He doeth well. But the woman beareth the pain of the children in many things, bearing them in her body, bringing them into the world, ruling them, and all this oftentimes with grievous travail. If only God had given some share to man. If only God had given him the child-bearing!"'

Did St. Bernadino rebuke the baron's lady for impiety? No, good man that he was, he merely replied, 'Methinks there is much reason on thy side.'

3

The everyday miracle is accomplished. The thin, protesting wail of the new-born babe is heard in the birth chamber. The midwife receives the child. It's mouth and gums are rubbed with a finger dipped in honey, its little limbs washed and rubbed with salt and honey, or oil of myrtle and roses before being tightly swaddled in swaddling bands, for it is supposed that

without these its limbs will not grow straight. Then it is put in
a dark place to sleep for, as a Franciscan monk, Barthelemy
l'Anglais, pointed out in a book he wrote, about 1350, babies
need a great deal of sleep. (He also warned parents to protect
the baby's eyes against too strong a light, and against the
danger of impure milk.) If it is a child of royal or noble birth
it may have a gilded cradle with a fur coverlet.

Now the child must be baptized, for the belief is held that if
it dies without baptism, its soul will never reach Heaven, but
will be consigned to limbo. What this state of being implied
was a questionable point. Some theologians believed that it
entailed an eternity of physical torment. Others, like St.
Thomas Aquinas, who were unable to accept this atrocious
perversion of the teaching of the Saviour who said; 'Suffer the
little children to come unto me', claimed that the limbo of the
unbaptized though falling far short of course, of the ineffable
bliss of Heaven, was a place of relative happiness. Others again
(I think they may well have been parents) cherished the tender
belief that these little lost souls were baptized at the feet of
Christ. Popular superstition said that they were changed into
Gabble or Gabriel hounds, who hunted their despoiler the
Devil throughout eternity. When the wind moaned round the
house on stormy nights, people told one another that it was the
Gabble hounds howling for their prey. It was not surprising
that theologians wrote with abhorrence of those priests or midwives who by their negligence robbed the dying infant of its
chance of salvation. It may seem astonishing, in the circumstances, that the infant was not usually baptized till the day
after its birth, but it must be remembered that in an emergency,
and in the absence of a priest, anyone could administer baptism
to the dying child, a woman, or even a heretic or a pagan.
Medieval theologians held that three circumstances supple-
mented the actual rite itself—if a child died on its way to
church, if it died in the presence of the priest who was about to
baptize it, or if it was an abortion born of pious parents who
had prayed for its salvation.

Some care had to be exercised in choosing a godmother, for
there was a superstition that if a pregnant woman stood as godmother, either her godchild or her own child would die prema-

turely. (To invite the first poor person met with on the way to church, to act as godfather was thought to bring long life to the baby.) Altogether it was a tricky time. St. Augustine said: 'All diseases are to be ascribed to demons, chiefly so they torment the fresh baptized, yea, even the guiltless new-born infant.' Women were inclined to rely for protection on obscure and ancient beliefs, forbidden by the Church. There were appropriate spells for each state—pre-natal, and before and after the christening.

A woodcut dating from about 1450 shows a baptism. The baby is being held over the font by a woman, while the Bishop holds up his hand in blessing.

The baby's soul having been thus cared for, the next consideration was to keep its body alive. The death rate among young children was cruel throughout the Middle Ages, and for centuries to come, and this is hardly to be wondered at when one considers the elementary state of medical science and of sanitation.

After the break-up of the Roman Empire, the art of medicine fell upon bad times. Surgery, physiology and medicine itself made hardly any progress, in the earlier part of the Middle Ages at any rate (though the flame of knowledge was kept alight at such centres of medical learning as Salerno and Padua). Disease was generally considered to be a punishment for sin. The Black Death, before whose appalling ravages the physicians were helpless, was popularly ascribed to such diverse causes as Divine Wrath at the introduction of long, pointed shoes, and to the malice of the Jews.

Superstition dictated a number of remedies—'This charme brought Angel Gabriel to Sanctus William for to charm cristen men from worm, from venom, fro goute, fro festyn and fro rankyl.' Others were a mixture of exorcism and herbalism: 'If a mad hound hath bitten a man, take the seed of flex and stampe it and temper it with holy water and give it him to drink.' Others contained fearsome ingredients: 'the grease of a rat', 'the hair of a dog', 'snails that creep in' (i.e. slugs). 'A good ointment for the gout. Take an owl . . .' and so on.

There is a masterly simplicity that must be admired about

the following: 'Give him to drink cristal' (ice water?) 'and if he spew it he shall be dyed.'

One wonders how many children who were backward at talking were dosed with this one: 'For him that may not speak well give him to drynke houndstongue.' Or when they had a toothache underwent this treatment: 'Take a candle of mutton fat mingled with seed of sea holly; burn the candle as close as possible to the tooth, holding a basin of cold water beneath it. The worm' (which was gnawing the tooth) 'will fall into the water to escape the heat of the candle.'[1]

It is consoling to reflect on the immense number of herbs that were used for medicinal purposes in the Middle Ages. One hopes that quite a number of them may have done good.

The medieval baby's chance of survival might have been even slimmer, if it had not been for the fact that breast-feeding was the accepted custom. In the higher ranks of society, the mother usually delegated this important duty to a wet-nurse, and the reluctance of fashionable women to feed their children was fulminated against by both doctors and theologians. There were three reasons, according to one male authority why these ladies shirked their maternal duties; first because it was not the fashion to give suck; secondly because they were afraid of losing their figures; and thirdly because they wished to frolic with their husbands (which, the writer added severely, is incontinence).

There were some women of rank however who did their duty in this respect. St. Bernard, who was the son of a noble knight, was first fed with his mother's milk, and afterwards 'nourished with greater meats'. Then there is the story about the Countess of Boulogne, which not only conveys one in imagination right into the solar or lady's chamber in a medieval castle, but shows the almost mystical significance attached to the act of breast-feeding, and the belief that with the woman's milk the child imbibed something of the woman's characteristics. The close tie that existed between foster-mothers and their fosterlings, and between foster-brothers is too well known to need emphasizing.

[1] Here, as in the other prescriptions I have drastically modernized the spelling for the reader's convenience.

Count Eustace of Boulogne married a 'good and fair lady' called Yde, whose father had the romantic title of the Knight of the Swan. She became the mother of three sons, Eustace, Godfrey and Baldwin, and being a devoted (one might almost say over-devoted) mother, nourished them all at her own breast. What was more, she made it a strict rule that no waiting maid or damosel should be allowed to deputize for her. However, one day when she was at mass, leaving one of her maidens in charge of her three sons, one of the children woke up and 'wailed sore and howled'. The maiden, unable to soothe it—one can imagine her trying to distract it with a gold or silver rattle hung with bells—called a damosel and told her to suckle the child.

The observant Countess, returning from chapel said, 'Tell me wherefore this child hath wetted his chin?' 'My lady,' the maiden replied, 'he awoke but now; loud and sore were his cries and I bade a damosel give him of her milk.' The Lady Yde's reaction to this was dramatic. 'Her heart shook . . . she fell back upon a seat. . . . Sore gasped her heart under her breast . . . she called herself a poor leper. Swiftly she flew all trembling with rage and caught the child under the arms; the child of tender flesh she caught him in her hands, her face was as black as a coal with the wrath that seethed within. . . . There on a mighty table she bade them spread out a purple quilt and hold the child; then she rolled him and caught him by the shoulders that he delayed not to give up the milk which he had sucked. . . . The maiden stood more benumbed than worm in winter-time. . . . She fled before the bursting of the storm,' and prudently absented herself from the Countess's presence for several months.

'Then the saintly and devoted countess laid the child in the place where he should be, and suckled him so long until she had laid him to rest, and all three were covered with her ermine mantle.'[1]

But her precautions were in vain. The damage had been done, or perhaps she had not been drastic enough when she had rolled Eustace to and fro upon that mighty table (rather in the manner of a German cook making an *appelstrudel*). It was one

[1] *The Middle Ages*, G. G. Coulton.

of the fundamental tenets of the Middle Ages that '*bon sang*', (or in this case '*bon lait*') '*ne peut mentir*'. The chronicler solemnly recounted that as a result of this mishap, Eustace's deeds and renown were the less to the day of his death. His brother Godfrey became Duke of Lorraine, and could, had he wished, have been King of Jerusalem; Baldwin actually became King of Jerusalem, while poor little Eustace never rose above the rank of Count!

One thing that occurs to me about this story is that in the maiden who was left in charge of the children we may dimly perceive the prototype of the latter-day Nanny. (The 'damosel' who dared to offer her inferior milk was evidently a waiting-maid.) But what a difference there is between them. Impossible to imagine the typical Victorian Nanny standing 'more benumbed than worm in winter-time' before her mistress. Rather the other way round!

While on the subject of nurses—a 13th-century MS. shows two nurses carrying their tiny, swaddled charges. They are young, good-looking women, one bare-headed, the other with a veil as a head covering. Their youthful aspect suggests that they are wet-nurses. No doubt the role of wet-nurse and children's nurse (in the more modern sense of the word) were usually combined, particularly as it seems likely that babies were breast-fed for as long as possible. The medieval system of farming whereby most of the cattle were slaughtered and salted down during the winter, owing to the scarcity of fodder, must have led to a serious shortage of milk during those months. In the Countess Yde story, however, the unlucky maiden, acted as a kind of superior nursery maid, as the Countess nursed her children herself.

It is clear from the admonitions addressed to nurses by medieval writers, that the nurse was expected to devote herself entirely to her nursling. In return she occupied a privileged position in the family she served. On the baptismal day, the ladies who were invited to the ceremony, gave her gifts of money. As it was believed that anything that upset her would affect her milk, her comfort and content-ment was a matter of importance. Or as a 14th-century writer put it:

'Les nourisses sont partout
Chières tenues et honnourées.'

Another curious sidelight on the belief in the special properties of breast-feeding is given in a proclamation issued in 1235
by Henry III, prohibiting Christian nurses from serving Jews.
It was believed (as is shown by a letter of Pope Innocent III,
incorporated in Canon Law) that Jews compelled the Christian
nurses in their households to spill their milk for three days after
their Easter communion so that the Jewish nurslings should not
be contaminated by the consecrated Host.

When the breast-fed infant was ill, it was recommended that
it's wet-nurse should take the necessary medicine or diet in its
stead.

The child who did not thrive on either its mother's or foster-
mother's milk, ran a risk of being considered a changling, for it
was an understood thing that the changling drained his nurse
dry 'and yet profiteth not nor cometh to any increase, but
hath a hard inflated belly; yet all the while his belly thriveth
not.'

Yet a 13th-century preacher, complaining of inattentive
congregations, gives a glimpse of two mothers exchanging
nursery grumbles—this child 'is a weariness' and that one
'thriveth not', in a very matter-of-fact way, and it must surely
have been hard to find any mother, even in that superstitious
age, who would admit that she had a changling in *her* cradle.

Milk and pap was the usual diet of the child who, for some
reason or other, could not be breast-fed, and this was given to
it in a pap-boat or with a spoon. The author of *English Children
in the Olden Time* (Elizabeth Godfrey) says that sucking bottles
were not mentioned till the 17th century, but according to
La Vie Privée d'Autrefois (Albert Franklin) they were alluded to
in the 13th-century romance of *Robert le Diable*. A theologian,
writing about the translation of the Scriptures says that 'the
common people be as infants that must be fed with milk and
pap'. The rest of the sentence, 'and if we have any stronger meat
it must be champed afore by the nurse and so put into the babe's
mouth', is a startling commentary on the lack of hygiene in
medieval nurseries.

As I mentioned in the preface, one authority on what would nowadays be called child-welfare, considered that poor men's children stood a better chance of growing to maturity than the children of the rich because the latter were overfed. The passage seems to me to be worth quoting because it gives a striking picture of the haphazard dietary methods of those times; 'Rich men's children' it says, 'grow far more seldom to old age or even to manhood than poor folk's children. That cometh from the overfeeding that men practise on rich folk's children, for none can ever fill them so full that another will believe it is full enough. That ariseth from the tenderness wherewith they are cherished, and also for that there is ever enough and to spare in the house. So the child's sister makes pap and coaxes it into him; now mark! his little cauldron, his little belly is soon filled, and the pap begins to bubble out again, but she coaxes it in and in. Then cometh his aunt and doth likewise, then cometh his nurse and crieth: "Alas! my child hath eaten nought this live-long day!" and she will straightway coax the pap in again as before, for all that the child may cry and toss his little limbs. Thus do all vie with one another in feeding rich men's children, so that few indeed grow to a good old age.'

There are few pictures of young children in the MSS. of the 13th and 14th century, which gives an added interest to a 14th-century woodcut of a man carrying two babies in a canoe-shaped basket slung from a curved pole which he holds with one hand, the basket being tucked under his arm. It is an ingenious arrangement; the babies who lie toe to toe are held in by straps.

Another baby is shown in white wrappings with blue swathes. There is a neat, even snug look about these swaddled babies in their mummy-like wrappings, but what it must have cost the unfortunate little creatures in frustration and discomfort to be bound hand and foot defies imagination. There is another point to be considered. In medieval pictures babies are always shown being held upright to the breast in what appears to be a very uncomfortable position both for the nursing woman and the nursling. (In a woodcut from *Chroniques de France* a lady in a steeple head-dress is shown seated in a field feeding twins. She holds the little cocoon-like figures vertically to her bosom.)

There was none of that soft, contented cuddling of the child against its mother which makes the act of breast-feeding so aesthetically and emotionally satisfying. There is interesting material here for a psychiatrist!

4

The moment has come, perhaps, to consider the surroundings in which these young children's (often too brief) lives were set. For convenience sake I have used the phrase 'medieval nursery', but one realizes what a misnomer it is when one remembers the almost complete lack of privacy of living conditions at that time.

In the great, bare, draughty hall of the castle, or the lesser hall of the manor house, with its heavy, simple furniture, its narrow, unglazed windows, widening towards the inside, protected from the wind and the rain only by shutters, and the louvre in the roof out of which the smoke was hopefully supposed to find its way, the family, their visitors and retainers, ate, drank, danced, sang, played chess and boisterous, naïve games, listened to minstrels, laughed at jugglers and tumblers, and conducted their everyday affairs in what, to modern ideas, would seem intolerable noise and congestion. At night the family retired to the chamber, while the retainers bedded down with the wolf-hounds on the rushes in the hall.

The chamber was the special apartment of the ladies during the daytime, so it is reasonable to suppose that their babies and young children were in there with them. At night the master and mistress of the household and their family slept there, with any guests, regardless of sex, who happened to be staying with them. This of course might mean total strangers in an era when hospitality to the traveller was considered a Christian duty. If the guests were disturbed by the fretful cries of a new-born or teething infant—'There cometh from the child a wailing and a weeping that at midnight maketh thee to waken'—so much the worse for them.

People in the Middle Ages can hardly have suffered from nerves, or if they did their exasperation relieved itself in some forthright manner such as braining one another with a chess board (as in the tale of *Ogier le Danois*). The taste for quietness and privacy is an acquired one, and varies greatly with individuals even nowadays. One household, for instance, has the wireless blaring all day in a way that would drive the members of another family distracted in a matter of hours. The sound of babies crying or of small children squabbling can have made little impression on the general hubbub of a medieval household. One of the duties however of a medieval nurse was to sing her charge to sleep while she rocked the cradle gently with her foot.

As time went on, a first floor solar, or withdrawing room, was built above the chamber. In medieval tales it served as a convenient place for the wife's lover to hide in when the husband arrived home unexpectedly, but its ordinary domestic use was to give the lord and lady of the house some additional privacy. It would have a great stone fireplace built against the wall, a pench for hanging clothes on, some massive chairs and chests, while its plastered walls, painted in brightly coloured patterns or scenes from the lives of saints or from romances, or hung with woven materials and tapestries, gave it an air of comfort. Here, then, would be another room for the small children to live in, and by the 15th century the manor house would also have a winter parlour (afterwards to become a dining-room) as well as the chamber and solar, and other small rooms which could be used as bedrooms. It is easy to see how one of these rooms might be set apart for the children, and gradually evolve into the nursery. More than that cannot be said with certainty.

One may be sure that with this communal way of life, it was not long before the medieval toddler emerged from whatever room did duty as a nursery, and joined, as far as it could, in its elder's activities.

Childhood was so brief. Maturity began so early, according to modern ideas, a youth being considered fit for knighthood and military pursuits at the age of sixteen, a girl for marriage at fourteen or younger. No wonder that children were hustled pitilessly through the preliminary stages of babyhood and early childhood, and sent away from home at the age of seven to be brought up in some great household.

The anxiety of English parents to get rid of their children in this way was unfavourably commented upon as late as the 16th century by an Italian writer, though it does not really seem to have been more reprehensible, and from a parent's point of view was certainly more economical, than our modern system of sending children to preparatory schools.

A few years—seven or eight at the most—are therefore all that we have to consider, but these are the all-important years, according to psychologists, when the child's character is being formed.

Before the toddler is let loose among its elders, here is a passage from a medieval sermon which, whatever the accommodation in a contemporary household, has the ideal nursery spirit of loving protection:

'Let us be as little children learning to walk, who are not downcast or angry with their faults, but who humbly and faithfully stretch out their hands to their loving mother that she may raise them up.'

Children long above all for security—emotional not necessarily physical security. The young are amazingly resilient, and have a disconcerting capacity for surviving and sometimes even enjoying catastrophes. But they must feel that they 'belong' if they are to thrive spiritually.

It seems to me that the children of the Middle Ages did not fare altogether badly in this respect. The castle (and to a lesser degree the manor house) was a little, self-contained world of its own. Within its encircling walls was some degree of safety and stability; outside were wars, robbers, wolves, heretics, witches, infidels and other abominations. From a purely practical aspect it had the satisfying completeness of a small town. In the bailey were the stables, mews and the granary, the carpenter's and the armourer's workshops, the barracks for the men-at-arms. The place was a hive of industry. Scullions ran to and fro in the kitchen, helping to turn the spits and to prepare the vast meals that were borne ceremoniously in to the hall to the sound of trumpets. In the chamber the ladies span and wove and embroidered, while they gossiped in their light, rippling voices. They were skilled in the use of medicinal herbs, and were prepared to attend to wounds received in skirmishes or tourneys, or to childish cuts and grazes.

There must have been so much for a child to watch—the drawbridge being wound up or let down, the falcons being fed and trained; pilgrims, minstrels, wandering friars, pedlars, beggars and other wayfarers coming in and out of the hall; the armourer working at his anvil. The castle workshops must have been favourite playgrounds. Children, very understandably, enjoy the company of those who are too busy with their own tasks to bother them. Among the crowd of retainers, squires, pages, servants and hangers-on, there would always be some-one good-natured or idle enough to romp with a child, to show him how to feather an arrow, and to pick him up when he tumbled down the narrow, circular stair in the angle tower of the keep. There would always be something happening—move-ment, bustle, noise, all things in which the average child rejoices.

The day in a medieval household began at sunrise. Six o'clock was considered late for rising. To be in bed when the cock crowed was the mark of a sluggard. The jingle:

'Lever à cinq, diner à neuf, souper à cinq, coucher à neuf
    Fait vivre d'ans nonante et neuf'

fixes the medieval time-table.

The child's first task, after getting out of its truckle bed with the straw mattress, which it would almost certainly share with a brother or sister, was to comb its hair, wash its hands and face and say its prayers.

How much did people wash in the Middle Ages? It is an interesting and debatable point. There is a tendency nowadays to suppose that personal cleanliness was unknown before the days of Beau Brummel. It would be absurd to pretend that either the sanitation or the personal habits and table manners of the Middle Ages would not offend us (though Professor Coulton says that in the later Middle Ages, some of the larger castles had an elaborate drainage system) but that medieval people did wash and even have baths is proved by numerous allusions. In the history of Fulke Fitz Warine, the lord of Ludlow Castle is described as hearing prayers in his chapel early in the morning, and then 'causing a horn to be sounded for washing'.

16

1. A Medieval Nursing Chamber. From Lydgate's *Metrical Life of St. Edmund*

2. James I (born 1566) as a child. Artist unknown

Washing before meals in a feudal household was carried out with some ceremony, a retainer called a 'ewer' bringing a basin, water and towel to the guests at a signal from the trumpeters or musicians.

Baths are said to have been introduced into England by Edward I's Spanish Queen Eleanor of Castille. It would be optimistic to conclude that daily baths were the custom after that even in aristocratic circles, but there are frequent allusions in medieval romances to people taking baths before and after dinner and before going to bed. It seems to have been usual for a visitor, newly arrived from a journey, to be offered a bath, and in the free and easy manner of the times, the ladies of the castle often escorted him to it. The bath tub in fact was, according to many stories, the starting point for amorous intrigues; a woodcut from the 13th-century MS. of the *St. Graal* shows a lady sitting stark naked in a large bath tub while a knight in full armour, who has evidently just dismounted from a rather oddly shaped horse, leans in a familiar way on the edge of the tub. Another illuminated MS. of the 15th century shows a king in a bath tub, shaped not unlike a modern bath though with a canopy with curtains over it. He is wearing his crown, and I am sorry to say is being speared by a group of armed men.

As far as children were concerned, it must have been a temptation to a lazy nurse to leave an infant too long unwashed in its swaddling clothes, but washing certainly was part of the nursery routine. A writer recommends that babies should often be bathed and anointed with oil of roses, particularly males as their limbs must be harder than those of females. The Emperor Frederick, conducting some curiously modern linguistic experiments on infants, ordered the foster-mothers and nurses to 'suckle, bathe and washe the children, but in no wise to speak or prattle with them'. (In spite of this spartan regime, it is heartening to record that the children 'could not live without clappings of the hands; and gestures and gladness of countenance and blandishments'.)

Soon after rising, the feudal household assembled for service in the private chapel or in church, and the child would join in these devotions at an early age. Children were confirmed before they were three years old (Bishops were apt to be casual about carrying out this rite, and had to be secured when they happened to be passing through the neighbourhood), though probably they did not receive the sacrament of the eucharist before the age of twelve.

Long as the church services and the sermons must have seemed to small children, there was much to occupy their attention; the brilliant colours of the stained glass windows, the lively carvings with which the craftsmen had decorated the carved pillars of the aisle and other parts of the stonework—grotesque faces, knights mounted on snails, hares shooting at dogs. A good-humoured lady might let a small boy or girl caress the pet falcon on her wrist. The behaviour of grown-ups in church for that matter was uninhibited; they chatted and laughed, and sat about on the floor during the sermon.

Breakfast, which came after devotions, was an informal meal, designed as the name suggests, to keep people going till the main meal of the day at nine, or later at ten o'clock. All the same it would be a mistake to conclude that the medieval breakfast invariably consisted of wine or beer and a piece of bread. There were those, like the two heroes of *Huon de Bordeaux* who agreed that 'eating early in the morning brings great health and gives one greater courage and spirit', and breakfasted 'very pleasantly and peacefully' off a very large pasty set on a white napkin. I feel doubtful though if a child would have been invited to share that noble pasty. It is only in recent years that parents have held the view that the choicest food should go to their growing children; formerly the children, even of wealthy households, fared nearly as plainly as the servants.

Medieval cooking was very rich and elaborate. Vegetables were in short supply, and held in poor esteem, perhaps because the medieval palate, vitiated by so much salt meat, craved after highly flavoured food. Alexander Neckham, the 12th-century author of a treatise, 'De Naturis Rerum', wrote of the vegetable garden: 'Let there also be beds enriched with onions, leeks, garlic, melons and scallions. The garden is also enobled by the cucumber which creeps on its belly . . .' One notices that out of the five plants mentioned here, four were useful for flavouring. For the same reason herbs were grown in a variety that would put a modern gardener to shame—parsley, fennel, southernwood, coriander, sage, savery, hyssop, mint, rue, dittany, smallage, pellitary, anise, mustard, herb mercury and white pepper, to give the name of a few.

Practically everything that ran on four legs, swam or flew, featured on the medieval menu, to be dished up in stews flavoured with an immense number of spices and condiments, or made into huge pasties. Here at random are some culinary items—boar's head, roasted veal, baked mallard, rabbits, squirrels, magpies, herons, peacock roasted and served with the skin, cormorants, swan, curlews, partridge, sparrows, pork, liver, minnows, salmon, lampreys, eels, seals, sturgeon . . . one could go on for pages. It would be easier to enumerate what was *not* eaten in medieval times. The following comparatively simple recipe for a syrup for a capon gives an idea of the elaborate methods:

'Take almonds and pound them and mix them with wine till they make a thick "milk", and colour it with saffron and put it into a saucepan, and put into it a good quantity of figs and currants and add ground ginger, cloves, galingale and cinnamon; let all this boil, add sugar and pour it over your capon or pheasant.'

Then there was every kind of sweet dish, tarts, custards, sugared sweetmeats, cakes, and jellies in fantastic shapes. ('Subtlety on the Nativity of St. John' is the description of one confection.) Each course, and a moderate meal would have at least three or four courses, consisted of soup, fish, meat and sweets. When one course was finished, you began all over again.

To what extent did young children join in these gargantuan and elaborate meals? To be honest, I don't know. But my guess is that except on festive occasions, they were kept on a plainer diet. For the sake of their young stomachs, one hopes anyhow, that this was so. But after a feast there must have been treats to be had in the kitchen—caraway cake, nuts and figs and dates, rose sugar, tarts and the quivering ruins of those lordly jellies. One wonders too what part they took in the chief meal of the day—dinner—which beginning with much ceremony at nine or ten o'clock, must have lasted for several hours. In the many pictures of dinner parties from medieval MSS. which I have come across, I have not seen one which shows a child among the adult diners, but this of course does not prove that they were not there, because it is usually the main table on the dais that is depicted where the more important members of the household sat against a background of hangings of tapestry or other rich material. When family and retainers all ate together it seems most improbable that the children, once they had got past the 'milk and pap' stage, should not join in the communal meal. How bored and restless they must have got during the interminable after-dinner performances of harpers and minstrels— one minstrel is described as having recited five thousand lines at a sitting—though they surely enjoyed the jugglers and tumblers and the nimble damsels who danced on their hands.

Here in company, sharing a plate with a companion as a sign of friendship, they learnt the rules of good breeding—not to take their food with unwashed hands, not to touch the bread and wine till the food had been served or to eat till grace had been said, or spit upon the table, or pick their teeth with a knife, or wipe their nose with a clean hand (there were no handkerchiefs then). Hardest rule of all for the child who was fond of animals to observe—'Be careful at table not to handle the cat or the dog.'

When the ladies retired leaving the men to their carousels, they must have taken the children with them. An illumination, dating from the middle of the 14th century, shows four ladies of noble rank wearing gracefully shaped coronets, sitting on a carved settle. Each one holds a small boy by the hand. The children appear to be about four or five years old, and wear little gowns with cowls that reach down to their feet. Another one shows a knight in armour and his lady also seated on a handsome settle, covered with some kind of decorative material, with their young son standing between them. There is evidence here of something resembling the present-day intimacy of family life.

This would seem as good a time as any to say something of the clothes worn by these children. At this time and for centuries to come they differed very little from those worn by grown-ups. A 13th-century MS. shows one small boy snugly dressed for the winter in a dark coat with long sleeves and a hood. Another one wears a kind of pinafore with deep armholes. A third one has a long garment with a cape and wears a little round furred hat. There is quite a modern look about the 'get-up', evidently for warm weather, of a little boy who wears what would be described nowadays as 'jeans', worn with shoulder straps over a long-sleeved vest. A young girl is dressed exactly like an adult woman, except that she wears no head-dress on her hair.

To get back to the dinner. Except on great occasions, it must have been over by midday which left a good deal of the day to dispose of before the household gathered together for supper, after which one supposes that the children were packed off to bed, for the adults themselves, though they sometimes danced and played games after this last meal, went to bed as soon as it grew dark.

How did the young children in a feudal household spend those daylight hours?

5

In Edward IV's family, the children were 'sette to scole' at the age of four. This suggests an impressive regard for learning, but it would be a mistake to conclude that it was widespread throughout the Middle Ages. In a general way (in the earlier part of the period anyhow) the nobles had a deep-rooted contempt for book learning, and took no particular trouble to see that their children acquired it, thus being spared one of the chief anxieties of the modern parent.

Clerkly accomplishments, even such elementary ones, as they seem to us, as reading and writing, were not considered a necessary part of the upbringing of a boy of good birth, who before he could become a knight, underwent a narrow but arduous training in the arts of war (real and mimic), in hunting, falconry, and such important branches of courteous behaviour as learning to sing and dance and carve and wait at table. *The Babee's Boke* written in 1475 for the instruction of 'six enfauntes' at the Court of Edward IV, gives a detailed picture of the behaviour expected from young boys of royal or noble parentage, but as these 'bele Babees' (as the author politely addressed them) would be pages of at least seven years old, it does not really concern us.

More to the point is the treatise written in Norman-French in the year 1300 by Walter de Biblesworth, who was tutor to a young Kentish heiress, Diane de Montchesney. The book which was written for her edification deals with a child's upbringing from the cradle onwards. His little pupil must learn to tie her own shoes, to do up her buttons and cover her head. When she is at mass she must not stare around her. She must give willingly to the poor and love her neighbours. After supper she was to be coiffed, and to work in thread and silk under the eye of her governess or 'tutresse'. On a *jour de fête* she was not to cry but to be merry. 'My gentle child,' he exhorted the little Diane, 'learn well to speak French and listen well to those who talk to you.'

On the whole the women of feudal times were better educated than the men. Though a section of the clergy deplored the spread of knowledge among women, maintaining that the daughters of Eve had caused enough mischief in the world since their mother tasted the fruit of the forbidden tree, medieval ladies, as a change from their needlework and housewifery, were fond of reading the romances and fabliaux that were the equivalent of the modern novel. Some of them were not only literate but actually learned, having studied such erudite subjects as geometry, astronomy, sophistry and 'arsmetrick' i.e. arithmetic, but these were the exception rather than the rule.

The children of the middle and lower classes, with their A.B.C. and grammar schools, were really better provided for than those of the upper classes. The latter seldom went to school, except occasionally to a nunnery school, and these were usually, though not invariably, for girls. (A decree of 1367 allowed a nun to keep one child with her for educational purposes, provided it was not a male child over seven, and even for this the bishop's permission was necessary.)

In a general way the children of knightly and noble families received such sketchy education as came their way at home from the family chaplain or from the nearest chantry priest. A small child of nursery age would learn its A.B.C., its Paternoster,

Ave and Credo, also enough Latin to enable it to take part in the church services. A little girl of four, in the later Middle Ages 'speaketh prattely and French and hath near hand learned her sawter' (psalter). Henry IV bought an A.B.C. book costing 20 pence, for his seven-year-old daughter. Edward III's daughters on the other hand, if one judged by the household accounts, would seem to have escaped lessons altogether. This is nothing to do with education, but the little princesses' names (I like writing them) were Isabella, Joanna, Blanche, Mary and Margaret, and they were dressed in Cyprus and Tripoli silk interwoven with threads of gold. The eldest of them before she was a month old, had a robe of silk richly trimmed and edged with fur.

Horn books, by the way, are said to date from the end of the 15th century. They existed before the invention of printing, and may have originated in the monasteries, as it is known that the monks used layers of horn to protect their precious manuscripts.

If, as we believe, the ultimate purpose of education is to enlighten and broaden the mind, the medieval tot may be thought to have come off badly, but from a practical point of view it learned all that was necessary to enable it to take its part in the vigorous rough and tumble of society around it. It learned, too, that social discipline that was expressed in the favourite medieval word 'courtesy'.

It is a commonplace to say that the child learns from many other sources than its actual lessons, and the medieval child in its games was preparing itself unconsciously for adult life, particularly so because the adults were very childish themselves in their pastimes. Grown-up people as well as children are shown in medieval pictures, playing hot-cockles, hoodman-blind (a rough form of blind-man's-buff with a lot of buffeting and hitting one another with knotted bands), tip and run, frog in the middle, and other games that later were relegated to the nursery. Nor did they consider it beneath their dignity to whip tops or play simple games of throwing and catching balls. (Rubber balls were of course unknown then. Balls were made of the inflated bladders of sheep or goats, of wood, wool, leather and other materials.)

The joke about the father who monopolizes his small son's Meccano or Hornby set must often have had its medieval counterpart in the child who waited impatiently while its elders disported themselves with the only available ball or top. How pleasant, on the other hand, always to have plenty of grown-ups ready to join in your favourite game, not condescendingly as adults do now at a children's party, but with a gusto and an enjoyment equal to your own!

It is impossible to draw a dividing line between adults and children's games in the Middle Ages—the likelihood is that there was no hard and fast division. Everyone joined in the boisterous fun when the trestle tables were cleared away in the great hall, particularly during the junketings at Christmas and other festivals.

Some ball games such as striking a ball with the hand against a wall (the origin of 'fives' i.e. five fingers) and tennis, (not to be confused of course with our 'lawn tennis'), the latter quite a fashionable pastime in Chaucer's day, would be beyond the skill of very small children, nor would they learn to play chess or cards, when these were brought to England towards the end of the Middle Ages, till they were older. One guesses though that they often played with the chess-men—the mounted knights in armour, the kings and queens carved in walrus tooth and ivory would be enticing playthings. A 14th-century MS. shows two fairly small boys playing bandy-ball, a primitive form of golf with a big ball and clubs not unlike hockey sticks, and club-ball, thought to be the origin of cricket, was also played by boys and girls. Games of this kind are said to have been of Celtic origin.

Perhaps the most popular toy of all was the hobby horse. A 15th-century print shows the Christ-child riding a hobby horse with St. Dorethea walking by His side. In another picture of a domestic scene there is a child riding a hobby horse, a toddler learning to walk with the aid of a little platform on wheels, while a baby lies in a cradle on rockers.

From a very early age, little boys were trained in the martial pursuits that were to be the chief aim and occupation of their adult life. The pick-a-back (which I must admit I always imagined was pronounced 'pig-a-back' till I began to write

24

this book) was just a mimic tournament, and little boys 'joust-
ing' with sticks, either on foot or astride hobby horses would be
a familiar sight in the bailey or walled garden of any castle or
manor house. There would be no shortage of 'knights' when
the leaders came to pick sides, for medieval families were large,
even when they had been tragically thinned out by plague and
other diseases, and it was the tolerant custom, we are told, in
knightly families for the illegitimate children of the husband,
and even of the wife, to be reared with the legitimately born
offspring.

All the various forms of military exercises practised by the
knights and squires would be eagerly imitated by their small
sons, brothers and nephews. William the Conqueror at five
years old had a little troop of boys under his 'command'. A
MS. in the Bodleian Museum, dating from 1344, shows small
boys tilting at a water tub. They have to support the heavy
pole between them, and are prepared for a sousing for they have
taken off their clothes.

The toddler, too small for these sports, would have a little
knight on horseback in wood or brass to drag along on a string,
a jointed wooden soldier that could be manipulated with a
cord, a painted cross-bow (such as Edward I gave to his children) or a toy drum or trumpet that some kindly grown-up had
bought off a pedlar or at one of the great fairs held in a neigh-
bouring town. Tiny toy windmills to catch the breeze were sold
at these fairs too, and gingerbreads shaped like dolls or like the
letters of the alphabet. Gingerbread was so popular that a
warrant was granted for gingerbread fairs to be held at Birmingham in the 13th century.

It was considered a shameful thing for a knight to ride in a
cart, for this was the way in which criminals were conveyed to
the gallows, but this would not spoil the very young child's
enjoyment of its toy wagon and horse. If the child travelled with
its mother and the other women of the household, it would be
in a 'char' or wagon drawn by five horses.

There are some toys so ancient that their origins are lost in
the immemorial past. Marbles for instance. They are said to
have come to England with the Romans (though I have also
seen it stated that they were introduced in the Middle Ages from

the Low Countries). The doll is another of these ancient toys. Yet—this may surprise you as much as it did me—the name is comparatively modern. The earliest mention of the word 'doll' in print is in the 1751 edition of *The Gentleman's Magazine*, though the term was probably in current use long before that.

I don't think that anyone really knows much about medieval dolls. Many of them were almost certainly made of wood, but the little girls' latent maternal instinct can transform almost anything into a 'baby'. One pictures an obliging waiting-woman with nimble fingers, turning a ninepin and a kerchief into a doll for the pleasure of the little girl who stands at her knee. The child is dressed in the style of the 13th century, in a *cotte* of green material and over it a scarlet *bliaut* or sleeveless tunic. But as a concession to her tender years, her hair flows loose around her chubby cheeks, confined only by a plain circlet on her head. She holds a crudely shaped sugar doll in her hand, and the dilemma that confronts her is reflected in her round, blue eyes that regard with sadness her sugar baby rapidly diminishing beneath the onslaughts of her own tongue.

As early as the 14th century, the Queen of England had fashion dolls sent to her, so that she might see the newest modes of the French court. These puppets were not dolls in the accepted sense of the word, but when they had served their purpose one cannot doubt that they were handed on to some little girl as a plaything. With time and handling their finery would become shabby, their faces featureless, they themselves beloved.

It is not surprising to learn that in Paris as early as the middle of the 15th century, there were 'charming dolls, marvellously dressed' for sale in the galleries.

But dolls would not be the little girls' only toys. They would have miniature crossbows and bows and arrows, for feudal ladies were ardent sportswomen, and hunted the stag, and shot rabbits and birds, as well as practising archery.

There must have been children in the Middle Ages, just as there are now, who preferred animate to inanimate playthings. It would be useless to gloss over the fact that there was considerable cruelty to animals in the Middle Ages; it was all part of the indifference to suffering that makes us wonder if these ancestors of ours, who were so easily moved to tears and laughter, were actually less sensitive than we are to physical and mental pain. Cockfighting and bear-baiting were considered suitable sports for children to watch, and a common game among the young was to tie a piece of cord to the leg of a bird, and to pull the unfortunate creature in the opposite direction to which it was facing, chanting the jingle:

'Put your foot to the rock,
And out the birds flock.'

These are comparatively mild examples of callousness. One could find far worse barbarities if one searched for them. But there is also evidence of a more humane outlook. The author of a treatise on domestic economy reminded the ladies of the household to look after the 'chamber beasts' and 'chamber birds', as these creatures not having the gift of speech 'could not ask for themselves'. (Which I think is underestimating the powers of dogs in this line.) In fact one writer complained that ladies fed their dogs on delicacies while keeping their servants on short commons.

Another writer says that 'some people delight more in their dogs that are deprived of all possibility of reason than they do in children that are capable of wisdom and judgement. Yea, they oft feed them of the best while the poor man's child at their doors can hardly come by the worst.' One of these pampered creatures, the greyhound of Queen Isabella of France, is shown in an illuminated manuscript, prancing in front of its mistress's palfrey, wearing a little coat embroidered with fleurs-de-lis.

Dogs and birds were the favourite pets. Cats were regarded with disfavour, as they were associated with witches. An illumination from the MS. of the *St. Graal* shows a lady wearing a crown, with her hand resting fondly on the 'smale hounde' or *chiennez* seated on her lap. The dog's expression is smug to a degree, as though it had just heard itself described as 'little and prettie, proper and fine'. Another charming picture from the *Romance of Othea* shows the interior of a lady's chamber. She is receiving a visit from her lover—a gallant-looking young man

27

with two tall feathers in his cap—and she carries a falcon on her wrist. Her greyhound, who wears an ornamental collar, also has that knowing expression peculiar to medieval dogs, and has ostentatiously turned his back on the lovers.

A child's favourite pony would have its caparison of scarlet or green cloth, hung with little jingling bells, and would be fed with carrots by its small owner. (As a Queen of Navarre used to feed her horses.)

Falcons were often cherished pets, and were kept on a perch in the chamber. Moreover it was quite usual for their noble owners to carry them about on their wrist to social gatherings and even to church. It would be a proud moment for a boy or girl when they were given their first hawk, but a small child would hardly be entrusted with so valuable and spirited a bird. They would more likely be given a caged bird to look after, a lark, a parrot or popinjay (a tapestry is described as having a design of roses and popinjays) and magpies which were taught to speak.

There were pet squirrels and pet monkeys too—the latter brought back perhaps from the Crusades?—and Edward III's little daughters were given the present of a young hare.

It is curious to reflect that rabbits in the Middle Ages were preserved in 'coney garths', but less curious now than it would have been before the advent of myxomatosis. The wheel may turn full circle, and a rabbit may once again be a rare present to give a child.

The literature and art of the Middle Ages is permeated with the love of flowers and of the spring.

'A meade, al ful of freshe floures whyte and reade.'

In contrast to the dark, draughty and often squalid discomfort of the indoor scene, one may set a picture of young squires and damsels, dressed in the brilliant colours of the age, with chaplets of fresh flowers on their heads, riding on joyful pilgrimage through the translucent leafiness of the May woods. Or of an enclosed garden with its fruit trees ladened with rosy or golden fruit, its tufted seats, little plots of grass besprinkled with flowers, and trellis fences twined with roses, or rose hedges decorating the harsh outlines of castle battlements.

> 'About the tour was made a walle
> So that betwixt that and the tour
> Roses were sette of sweet savour,
> With many roses that they bore.'

In this walled garden, the ladies in jewelled head-dresses and gauzy veils sit in arbours. They fondle their pet birds and grey-hounds, make garlands of flowers, or walk hand in hand with their knightly admirers, entranced for ever in the sunlight of a summer's day.

How understandable is that intense delight in the sunshine and bird-song after the long, dreary months spent trying to keep warm (one ingenious device was to sit on a stool over a bowl of hot water). when the swiftly falling dusk meant either early bed or the expensive luxury of lamps and candles.

Healthy children love being out of doors, and children in those days must have looked forward even more exuberantly than their elders to the coming of spring and summer. The long daylight hours would not be long enough to hold all their pastimes. There were birds' nests to rifle, apples and cherries to eat, butterflies to catch, and nuts to gather when the days became crisp with autumn. The little girls would help their mothers pick the flowers for the garlands which it was the pleasant custom of both men and women to wear when feeling in a joyous mood. Medieval people were fond of picnics, and there are numerous pictures of these out-of-door meals, the picnickers squatting or kneeling on the grass, the food and wine spread out on a fair white cloth, while one of the company plays the harp or a lute. The children must surely have joined in these alfresco meals, though it must be admitted that they are not shown doing so.

By the way, according to an illustration in the *Roman d'Alexandre*, 1344, adults did not despise butterfly catching as a sport. A man is shown preparing to strike down an outsize butterfly with a large club. The onlookers hold up their hands in understandable amazement. However, as he is looking back over his shoulder, the butterfly does not seem to be in any immediate danger.

The turn of the year would bring with it a revival of those games that are traditionally associated with spring time.

Mysterious games, carrying us back in imagination to the childhood of the race! The author of *Children's Games throughout the Year* (Leslie Daiken) says that the time of the springing-up of seed was celebrated in pre-Christian days by movements of hopping, jumping and skipping.

May brought in the courtship and marriage games that were ancient, generations before the medieval children played them —games of the 'Ring o' Roses' and 'Nuts' (or 'knots' i.e. posies of flowers) 'in May' variety that are believed to derive from the fertility cult, which perhaps explains the Church's hostility towards them.

The author quoted above tells something of the fascinating history of the jingle: 'A rosy apple, a lemon and a pear', which it appears has a parallel in nearly all the Romance languages. An authority gives fifty-nine examples of it!

Then there were the arch games—'Oranges and Lemons' and 'London Bridge' are two examples. It has been supposed that the words, 'London Bridge is falling down' (or 'broken down') alludes to the collapse of the actual London bridge in the 13th century, but the game appears to be much older and more widespread geographically than such a theory supposes.

A medieval woodcut shows grown-ups playing one of these arch games. But long after adults grew too sophisticated for such simple pleasures, the children kept alive, down the centuries, these fragmentary memories of a past buried deep below the dust of time.

6

It was one of the paradoxes of medieval life that adults, though so juvenile themselves in many of their tastes and ways, had scant patience with the foibles of children.

'Marriage fills the earth, virginity fills heaven,' said St. Jerome. The implication is that it would be just as well if children had not been born at all. Having been born, they were obviously heavily tainted with original sin, and only to be saved from hell by baptism.

It was hardly to be wondered at that severity was the key-note of a child's upbringing in the Middle Ages. In an age when it was quite in order for men to beat their wives, children were not spared the rod.

The author of *The Goodwife* advises:

> 'And if thy children be rebel and will not them bow,
> But of any of them misdoeth, neither ban them nor blow'
>   (curse nor cuff)
> 'But take a smart rod and beat them in a row
>   till they cry for mercy and be of their guilt aknow.'

Absolute obedience and deference to the parent was the rule and it was an unusually unruly or high-spirited child who dared defy it. Not surprisingly perhaps this enforced docility did not make for filial devotion in later life, and there are legal records of complaints from parents who had been assaulted by their children.

Too many parents in the upper classes regarded their children as pawns to be moved about on the matrimonial chess-board, for financial or territorial gain. This led to the evil custom of child marriage, by which parents or guardians arranged marriages between children who were often hardly more than babies.

There is both humour and pathos in the glimpse of John Rigmardin, who, at the age of three, was carried to church in the arms of a priest, who had to coax him to repeat the words of the marriage service. Half-way through the little boy announced that he would 'learn no more that day'. (After all these centuries, one can almost see the mutinous little face.) The priest told him, 'You must speak a little more and then go play you'.

Sir William Plumpton, no doubt a fond grandfather, according to his lights, arranged marriages for his little grand-daughters and handed them over to their future 'in-laws' when they were less than four years old.

About the year 1200, a little girl called Grace, daughter of Sir Thomas de Saleby, a great heiress, was given in ward on her father's death to Adam Neville. With blatant unscrupulousness, Neville attempted to marry her himself though she was only four years old. The Bishop vetoed this, so her guardian had the marriage solemnized by a priest during the Bishop's absence in

Normandy. By the age of six, Grace had been sold by King John to his chamberlain for the sum of 200 marks. When this husband died the little widow, then aged eleven, was sold again by the King to 'the third and worst of her husbands' Brian de Lisle. In the end she died childless.

What desolation and fear one senses in this brief account of poor young Grace's matrimonial experiences! It would perhaps have been better for her if she had featured at an early age, as so many little girls did, on one of the monumental brasses to be seen in old churches.

Feudal wards were indeed helpless if they fell into unscrupulous hands. On their father's death they became the wards of his overlord, who could use their dowry and dispose of them in marriage to suit his own advantage. To be guardian to a young heir or heiress was quite a profitable sideline.

The orphans of burghers were better off as they usually became the wards of the mayor and aldermen.

The Church attempted to protect these poor children, but the custom of child marriage was so firmly rooted in the upper classes that the best the ecclesiastical authorities could do was to forbid parents and guardians to dispose of babies in their cradles unless there was some urgent reason for the match, for instance to put an end to a feud. These child marriages or betrothals could, it is true, be nullified at the wish of both parties when the boys were fourteen and the girls twelve, ages at which they were hardly likely to resist their parents' wishes.

Other children were disposed of by their parents in no less arbitrary a way though from less sordid motives. To dedicate a small son or daughter to the Church was considered a sure way of securing the child's salvation and one's own.[1] These children were called 'oblates' and were usually at least seven years old, though there were instances of much younger children entering the Church. For instance one of Edward I's daughters became a novice at the age of five, and another child took the veil at one

[1] There were also cases where children were dedicated to a religious life from shamelessly mercenary motives. One bishop bestowed an archdeaconry on his small nephew, who at his installation was embarrassingly found 'not yet to have outgrown the needful ministrations of his nurse'.

3. A Little Girl of the Stuart Period. Artist unknown

4. The Children of Charles I. After Sir Anthony Vandyck. Mary born 1631, James born 1633, Charles born 1630, Elizabeth born 1635, Anne born 1636-7

year old! These little princess-nuns had a pleasant enough time. The dowry which they brought with them (and a daughter had to be endowed whether she became a nun or a wife) ensured their material comfort, and they were allowed out into the world to go on pilgrimages to shrines, to visit relations and attend family gatherings. The alternate fate would be to be sent off, far from their family and friends, as brides to foreign princes, and the chances are that they were fortunate in their peaceful, sheltered convent life.

But Guibert de Nogent, who was given to the Church by his parents when very young, gives rather a pathetic picture of himself in his *Life*. After saying that he had a 'childish prettiness and a certain vivacity natural to that age', he describes himself 'sitting in his little clerical cloak' watching the other children at their boisterous play 'like some tame animal'.

One modern writer on the social life of the Middle Ages mentions the number of accidents to children that were recorded—an infant burnt in its cradle during its mother's absence, another child aged three who was drowned in a pit full of water, another who was accidentally shot by an archer—and deduces from this that they were not well cared for by their parents. A medieval person reading our newspapers might get exactly the same impression! Hardly a day passes without some poor little creature getting burnt, scalded, drowned, accidentally poisoned, electrocuted or run over.

It would be absurd to suppose that parents in the Middle Ages were devoid of parental love. But it is surely not unfair to say that the tie between parents and children was less intimate and often less enduring than it is nowadays? The whole pattern of life in the Middle Ages was responsible for this. The child's hold on life was so precarious that the mother and the father had to face the possibility that it would not survive its infancy. If it came through those perilous first years, it would almost certainly be sent to foster at the age of seven in some great household, to be trained as a page if it was a boy, or as a *chambrière* or damsel-in-waiting if it was a girl. Town people's children would remain longer under the parental roof. It is significant though that in one medieval romance, the heroine says: 'It is now the custom with many wealthy burghers to

D

caress their children when they are small, but when they grow up they care for them no more.'

I compared this custom of fostering to our modern system of sending children away to boarding school, but of course though there may have been a similarity in the parents' intention—to give the children an upbringing or education in some way superior to that which they would receive at home—the practical result in those days of slow and difficult communications was vastly different. The child once sent away to another household had virtually left its home for ever.

In spite of its morbid preoccupation with death and doom, the Middle Ages was not on the whole an introspective age. The exuberant good spirits and freshness of outlook of those medieval people which we may envy them, was only made possible because like children they were creatures of impulse, living from day to day often with a child's unconscious cruelty and lack of thoughtfulness.

A medieval writer says of children that they lead their lives 'without thought or care, and set their courage only on mirth and liking, and dread no peril more than beating with a rod, and they love an apple more than gold. When they be praised or shamed or blamed they set little thereby.'

Some of this description might have been applied to the writer's contemporaries, who, even when they were kings and nobles, flew into rages, and wept and sulked, and when they were in a good humour delighted in naïve pranks and jests. Perhaps this explains the prevailing severity towards children, for tolerance towards the young is, on the whole, an attribute of maturity rather than of youth itself.

Harsh as the medieval attitude towards children was in a general way, there were those like St. Anselm who had enlightened views on their nurture. He disapproved of children being hemmed in 'on every side with terrors, threats and stripes, so that they can get no liberty whatsoever'.

In the beautiful medieval poem 'Pearl', the poet sees a vision of the soul of his infant daughter clad in the white robes of the redeemed, and adorned with pearls. She tells him to mourn for her no longer, for by God's courtesy she is now a queen in heaven. Marvelling he asks her:

'Not two brief years with us dids't lead
Too young to please thy God or pray,
And yet made queen on thy first day.'

She reminds him of the parable of the labourers in the vineyard:

'More have I joy and bliss herein
Of ladyship great and life's full bloom
Than all the wives in the world might win.
Though night was nigh ere I could begin
(So late was I to the vineyard come)
First of them all my hire did I win
And was paid outright the whole full sum.'

Could one find in any age a more moving example of parental
love?

II

❖❖

The Tudor Age

'The verie infant from his first entry till he be thought fit
to pass to the grammar school.'

I

IN the Earl of Northumberland's household book for the
year 1512 is the entry: 'Breakfast for the nurcery, for my
lady Margaret and Mr. Ingram Percy, a manchet,[1] one
quart of beer, three mutton bones boiled.'

The young Percys dined like puppies, two to a plate. On fish
days they were allotted, 'a manchet, a quart of beer, a dish of
butter, a piece of salt fish, a dish of sprats and three white her-
rings'.

Thus early in the Tudor period, the Nursery emerges as a
separate part of the household with its own room or set of apartments, entailing its own attendants, and its own diet. One may
even suspect that the internecine warfare between the Kitchen
and the Nursery has begun!

But this last is mere fancy. What is certain is that when this
entry was made the Middle Ages had died; the modern world
was in the throes of being born. The whole pattern of feudal life
had dissolved. The Wars of the Roses (it is ironic that this
dreary dynastic struggle should have been so poetically named)
had dealt a fatal blow to the power of the old nobility. A strong
central government, guided by the adroit and crafty hand of

[1] A fine white bread made of wheat.

36

Henry VII, had superseded the rule of the local magnate with his castle dominating the countryside (rendered obsolete in any case by the invention of gunpowder) and his little private army of retainers. The retainers would still be there, though in somewhat diminished numbers, but they would be there primarily to wait on their lord and to contribute to his prestige, not to fight for him. Comfort not security would now be the predominant consideration in domestic architecture, and even the most sincere child-lover must admit that a separate room for the children is an important feature of a really comfortable house.

Further proof of the existence of a nursery—perhaps even a nursery wing—in the 16th-century house is provided by the evidence given in the Darrell-Hungerford divorce case (1568–70). Lady Hungerford was accused by her husband of having committed adultery with William Darrell. A piece of evidence reads: 'Whereupon he called Alice Cleck in the nurcery chamber going to bed'—and 'When Sir Walter hath come in he hath slipt away to his own chamber at a back paier of stayre towards the nurcery.'

Poor Lady Hungerford! Though her honour was cleared she was separated from her children, and her letters to her friends on the subject make piteous reading. To Dorothy Essex she wrote:

'My childrene I have not harde of this xj mountes and more. Y are loste for wante of good plassing (?); Susane is as I hear clen spoilted, she has forgotten to rede and hur complexsione clen gone with a yeche (itch), and she hathe skante to shefte her wt all. Jane is wt a semster in Malboro very evel (do) Surly I wer happy if God wolde take them out of this life. The Savoy, March 25th, 1570.'

Mothers of daughters will be touched by that pathetic complaint; 'her complexsione clen gone'.

To the Duchess of Feria she complained: 'Touching my cheldren, I am as a stranger unto them, which I must suffer praing God to bless them and make them all his servantes for other good by prayer can I not do them. I hear yr ar very evell youssed (?) and no bringer up ye have. Well God comforte and helpe them.'

Everyone has a more or less definite picture in their mind of the Tudor interior. The great hall is still there, but is rapidly losing its original character, so that by the end of Elizabeth's reign it is no more than an imposing entrance to the house. Conservatively minded people who clung to the old customs might deplore the new-fangled fashion of the family eating in the dining parlour apart from their dependants, but the charms of privacy were now more fully appreciated. The long gallery on the first floor (with the great chamber) had become the focal point of the social life of the household. Here there was music and dancing in the evenings; here the children could play their games and romp on rainy days. From a child's point of view the long gallery was perhaps the most satisfying feature ever introduced into domestic architecture.

It would be out of place in this book to attempt a detailed description of a 16th-century house, of its rich but restrained decoration in early Tudor times, and of the exuberance of its carving and plaster work later in the century which seems to express the robust appetite for life and adventure of the Elizabethan epoch. It is enough to try and visualize these interiors through the eyes of a child of that century.

The author of *The English Interior*, Arthur Stratton, has said that the Tudor room was designed to give the 'sense of being within-doors'.

'God grant me alwaie the key of the fields I will like it better than to be in bondage in the fayrest wainscotted or tapestried chamber' points the contrast.

The fields were all very well in fine weather, but on a cold winter's night when the rain and the wind were beating on the mullioned windows, how cosy those panelled or tapestried rooms must have been, the firelight from the great fireplaces with their sumptuous chimney pieces, flickering on the honey-toned oak panels. The child would feel itself as snug as a kernel in a nut. If the room was panelled in the lovely linen-fold design, popular in the reigns of the Tudor Henrys, the walls, to the very small child, would have the reassuring friendliness of its nurse's pleated ruff. Or the tapestried figures of beasts and birds would spring to mysterious life in the fire-glow. What imaginative child looking at tapestry has not wanted to step into that woven landscape?

There is an old house of this period at Carrick-on-Suir, Co.

Tipperary, that belonged to the Butler family. It has crumbled sadly while awaiting restoration, but the walls and most of the floors are intact, and being shown over it on a chill November day, I was struck by the warm, dry feeling in the rooms that had been unlived in, so the caretaker told me, for over ninety years. The immensely thick walls and deep-set windows were, I supposed, responsible for this, and it occurred to me that our Tudor ancestors probably suffered less from draughts than many of us do.

Room opened into room in the early 16th-century house. Later in the century corridors became more general, but they were still little more than passage ways, not the long, dark, cold stretches along which later generations of children were to creep or scuttle to bed. Bay and oriel windows, with their panes often emblazoned brightly with heraldic devices, were little rooms in themselves, lending themselves to uninterrupted play-times, or to ambushes at hide and seek. The great, oak staircase with its wealth of carving might have heraldic animals surmounting the newel posts, for small hands to fondle.

One must not picture the panelled walls as we would see them now in an old house, dark with smoke and time, but pale as honey in the beautiful natural colour of the oak; the plaster between the ceiling and the panelling would be carved and coloured in brilliant hues.

Some children would be brought up in old manor houses that had been only partly adapted to the new conditions of life, with moats that had not been filled up, others lived in modest country houses half-timbered, or built in warm brick-work, surrounded by the paths and yew hedges of a pleasant formal garden; for the children of the new aristocracy 'home' would mean a great Italianate palace, like Hardwicke Hall 'more glass than wall', that had been built, or was in process of being built on confiscated monastic land. But whatever the type of house, it was no longer a fortress, large or small, but a setting for a family's life.

Sir Thomas More, Erasmus wrote, had built himself a commodious house near London (Chelsea) 'where he converseth affably with his wife, his son and daughter-in-law, his three daughters and their husbands with eleven grandchildren'.

2

It might perhaps be considered that pre-natal and nursery matters were beneath the consideration of male writers, but in former times when few women ventured into print, men were never backward in giving their advice.

We have seen a medieval Franciscan friar giving useful hints to mothers. Now in Tudor times the invaluable Andrew Boorde in his *Fyrst Book of the introduction of Knowledge,* gives advice on such problems as 'Curding of Milk in Women's Breasts' and 'Pregnant Womens Unnatural Appetite' also how to increase the supply of milk. (He recommends for this 'lettyse', adding that 'sawge' i.e. sage is 'good to helpe a woman to conceyve'.)

For the first mentioned complaint he dismisses an old-fashioned remedy 'repercussives' (which sounds tolerably drastic) with, 'I wolde not do so, I do thus: I do take Draganant (Tragacanth—a gum) and gomme Arabycke, and do compounde them with the whyte of rawe egges, and the oyle of violettes and do make a playster. Or else I do take pytch and do lyquifye it in the Oyle of Roses, puttynge a lytle doves dange to it, and dregges of wyne or ale, and make playsters.'

As regards the expectant mother's appetite, Boorde is of the opinion that, 'it is best that women have their desyre if it be gotten'.

He has a good deal to say about 'The Want of Training for Midwives'. Rather surprisingly, to our ideas, he considers that this should be remedied by the Bishops. Every midwife, he says, should be presented to the Bishop by honest women who would testify that she was 'a sadde woman, wyse and discrete, havynge experience and worthy to have the office of midwyfe'. Then the Bishop 'with the counsel of a doctor of physick ought to examine her and to instruct her in that thynge that she is ignoraunt and thus proved and admitted is a laudable thynge; for and this were used in Englande, there sholde not half so many women myscary; nor so many chyldren perish in every place in England as there be'. He ends this excellent advice with a severe: 'The Byshops ought to look on this matter.'

Andrew Boorde was in advance of his time in realizing the

urgent need for better trained midwives and in deploring the
tragic wastage of infant life.

Sir Robert Sidney, whose letters were preserved at Penshurst,
was a devoted husband, who found time, in the press of public
affairs, to write to his wife Barbara, who was expecting a baby:
'I sent you the plasters I spoke of, which I hear wonderfully
praised; you must lay them on your breasts after you are
delivered and let them ly on ten days.' He adds playfully: 'You
see that with a little help I would prove a pretty pothecary for
you.'

The fashions of the time, with the stiff, bell-like skirts, must
have been a considerable help to the expectant mother, and
may explain, in the following anecdote, why no kind friend
enlightened Lady Effingham, who must have been singularly
vague, as to her condition:[1] 'It is said that the Lady Effingham
as she was playing at shuttlecock, upon a sudden felt herself
somewhat, and thereupon retiring herself into a chamber was
brought to bed of a child without a midwife, she never suspect-
ing that she had been with child.'

The baby, newly born into the 16th century, received very
much the same treatment as it would have done in medieval
times. Ambroise Paré, the celebrated French physician and
surgeon, who may be taken as representing the most enlightened opinion of the period, advised that the child should be
washed at birth with a decoction of red roses, to which had
been added myrtle leaves and salt. He also recommended that
the baby's fingers and joints should be worked, and that it
should be rocked gently and sung to sleep. The baby, swathed
in swaddling clothes though with its arms and feet left free, still
resembled a little mummy, for neither in England nor in France
had it occurred to anyone that the new-born infant should be
allowed the unhampered use of its limbs.

Fashionable mothers still delegated their maternal duties to
wet-nurses, to the disapproval of sage and learned men. A
French doctor of this period puts the case for breast-feeding
with a persuasiveness that could hardly be bettered. Why, he
asks bluntly, did Nature give women breasts—for ornament or
for nourishing their children? If only women realized the

[1] Manninghan's Diary, December 24th, 1602.

pleasure that they were missing they would not hand their babies over to wet-nurses. He gives a charming picture of the child at the breast, its little laughs and gestures as it 'flatters' its nurse. Its small joys and griefs are described as '*semblables chosettes*'. The child's love for its nurse is so pleasant and agreeable that it ravishes her heart. How can mothers willingly deny themselves this extreme pleasure? Some women, he continues, excuse themselves on the grounds that their husbands object to the child's crying, and that therefore they would have to occupy separate bed-chambers. In other cases it is the husbands who object, saying that it spoils their wives' figures. But apparently these fastidious husbands are more often than not engaged in making love to the nurses! Moral: Let the wives do their duty and not employ nurses, thereby guarding their husbands from mortal sin.

It was several centuries, however, before the wet-nurse was ousted from her key position in either French or English nurseries. The choice of a wet-nurse was considered of such importance that even the great Ambroise Paré gave detailed advice about it. The nurse, he said, should have two or three children of her own. (Another chirugien recommended that the nurse should have lain in five or six weeks previously of a male child.) She should not be younger than twenty-five or older than thirty-five, healthy, of a good complexion, neither too fat nor too thin, with a well-built chest. '*Une rousse*'—a red-haired woman —was to be avoided; better a brunette than a blonde. The nurse must be diligent, chaste, joyful, singing and laughing to the child, holding it carefully, loving her little charge as well if not better than her own children.

Jacques Guillemeau, chirugien to several French kings (Charles IX, Henri III and Henri IV) gave even more detailed instructions as to the 'points' to be looked for in a wet-nurse. She should have an agreeable face, clear eye, well-made nose, red mouth, white teeth, strong round neck, deep chest. The shape of her breasts was considered of prime importance, and minute particulars were given as to their size and appearance. It was essential that the nurse should not be pregnant; she should have good morals, not desiring the company of her husband (still less the company of her employer's husband!)

She must not be a wine-bibber or a glutton, must not be easily vexed or given to sadness or anger. She must treat her nursling joyfully and gently, never refusing it the breast, and able to guess its needs. She must frequently unswaddle it to tidy and wash it.

When one considers that this paragon had also to have an agreeable singing voice with which to lull the baby to sleep, it is not surprising that the wet-nurse considered herself far superior to the other servants in the household.

That breast-feeding was the right diet for the new-born child, whether it was the mother or a nurse who provided the nourishment, was never questioned, hardly to be wondered at in view of the popular belief that if the baby drank the milk of an animal, it would always to some extent partake of that animal's nature.

A peril more sinister than any natural disease was believed to menace the newly-born infant. Though witchcraft had been condemned since early times by the Church, it was at its height during the 16th and 17th centuries, or perhaps merely appeared to be so because it was then that the witch-persecution was at its fiercest in England and throughout Europe.

Whether witchcraft was a survival of an ancient fertility cult, as Dr. Margaret Murray suggests (and this theory seems to account for many of the otherwise inexplicable facts) or whether it was a strange psychological perversion or a mixture of both, must always remain a mystery. But there is no doubt about the terror with which witches inspired their fellow creatures, a terror that explains though it does not excuse the ferocious cruelty with which they (and also many innocent people) were hunted out and destroyed.

The terrifying part about witchcraft was that any one might be a witch—a man's wife, or familiar friend, the trusted servant or the seemingly pious cleric might be a member of the dreaded fraternity. Or the homely midwife sitting by the fire in the birth-chamber nursing the new-born child in her capacious lap. When the mother's watchful eyes relaxed in sleep, the unholy rite of initiation would be performed in the firelight, the witch-nurse dedicating her innocent charge to the service of the horned god. 'They who have fallen into the service of the Devil,'

43

according to Nicolas Remy, the author of *Demonology*, 'can rarely be rescued except by death.'

To employ a secret witch as a midwife would obviously be a fearful mischance rather than an everyday occurrence, but it was believed to be a possibility—it might happen!

3

In 1595 the birth of 'a goodly fat son' was announced to Sir Robert Sidney by his trusty agent Rowland Whyte (or White).

Whyte not only kept his patron informed on matters of statecraft and Court intrigue, but also sent him an almost daily bulletin of Lady Sidney's condition just before and after the confinement. Lady Sidney had the bad luck to catch measles from her children, but evidently escaped lightly. Rowland Whyte wrote from London on November 29th, 1595: 'Saturday night. This day my lady hath kept her bed and now it appears to be the measles; she is not sick with them but as the children were. The midwife is in the house. I know not what to say for gossips, for sure I am these great ones you name would be unwilling to come . . .' On December 2nd he announced triumphantly: 'My Lady was safely brought to bed yester-night at 9 o'clock of a goodly sonne being Monday the 1st of December 1595, and now I will tell you of the circumstance, he is a goodly fatt boy but as full of the measles in the face as can be. They gave it some of the nurses mylke and safron which he suckt out of a spoone, and they keepe yt very warme; he suckes as wel as any child doth and cries as strongly. . . . Dr. Brown lay here all last night and is a most careful man of his profession. . . .'

The baby safely arrived, the indefatigable Mr. Whyte busied himself in collecting together the gossips, i.e. godparents, which he felt was going to be a difficult task on account of the measles, but when he approached Lady Rich she made light of the risk of infection: 'Lady Rich agrees to be godmother. When I told her that my Lady and the child had measles, she replied that after eight days there was no danger, and it should be no occasion to keep her from doing Sir Robert Sidney and his lady a greater kindness.' The conscientious Whyte 'besought her to take a longer time to think on the danger, which she did til the

afternoon—she told me she was resolved'. Mr. Whyte then went
on to Holborn and tackled 'my Lord Montjoy at his house', no
doubt fortified by Lady Rich's acceptance and her optimistic
eight-day quarantine theory. He seems to have had no difficulty
in getting Lord Montjoy's consent. Not long after this, he was
able to report, 'My Lady hath taken good rest yesterday night,
and this goodly boy is quite rid of the measels, sleeps, suckes,
and cries wel, and God willing, he shall live many yeares to
your comfort'.

After describing the christening, saying that the gossips 'gave
three fair standing bowls all of one fashion that may be worth
20 l. a piece. Here were many gentlewomen and gentlemen', he
added. 'All things were so provided that they had no cause to
fear the measles', which seems to indicate that people were not
as careless about infection in those days as one has been led to
believe. One wonders what precautions were taken. Did the
ladies in their upstanding ruffs and gorgeous, grotesquely
shaped gowns (for this was the end of the century when fashions
had run wild) hold scented pomanders to their noses, were
aromatic herbs strewn around the room, or did the company
just keep as far away from Lady Sidney and her infant as was
consistent with politeness?

Sir Robert scolded his wife gently for not having taken better
care of herself before the baby was born. 'Dec. 9th, Flushing. I
have received the joyful news of your safe delivery and that you
and the little boy are well recovered . . . I never heard that you
had the measels til I heard you were safely brought to bed and
wel againe. I must a little [censure] your venturing yourself
among our other children being in the case you were in. . . .
Sweet Barbara farewell and love stil your assured loving
husband, Sidney.'

Next year it was the same story—'Lord Southampton will
most willingly be godfather . . . Lady Sussex swore that she
longed to be godmother and is most proud that she is chosen'
but without the measels, and with 'a little pretty new born
daughter' Bridget, instead of a 'goodly fatt son' as the centre of
attention.

Though large families were the rule and announcements of
this kind almost annual events, the birth of each child into a

16th-century family was considered an occasion for ceremonial rejoicing. A decade earlier than these Sidney letters, on June 6th, 1586, John Stubbe[1] wrote in a similar strain to his patron, Lord Willoughby, who was also in the Low Countries: 'I woat not whether to begin on this side seas for God's mercie in the increase of your honourable family by one chylde.' In this case 'your hoame joy' was the birth of a daughter. He proceeded to give the absent father an account of the christening which, as would be expected from the rank of the family concerned was a grand affair. As will be seen there seems to have been a lack of organization among the godparents in the matter of the baby's name, and one is left in some doubt as to what she was called in the end. 'My lady being now to take other gossips, the child was baptized on Monday following at your parish church, the name referred wholly to my Lady Huntingdon, who having some notice of my Ladies' intention towards the ambassador [Danish] wold have it Sophia, and indeed at the font the Countesse called it Sophia. But the Lord and th'other lady called it Katherin, after the Countess's name, as so it was named by Mr. Crowly. So you have you a Katherin after my lady's grace your mother's name, and yet to please the Danish Queen, you may rightly say that at the font by the most honourable gossip, it was named Sophia, and if you will instead of Sophia Elizabetha, which is that Queen's name, you may cal yt Sophia Katherin in regard of the honourable grandmother ... my lady told her [Lady Huntingdon] and I was told to tell her that you loved the name of Katherin right well. . . . Mr. Alleyn preached very well at the baptisme, and with honourable mention of your lordship. The banquet was very well performed for the charge and order. It was honoured also with Erles, knights, ladies, esquires, and gentlemen good stour that loved you. . . .'

Poor Mr. Stubbe seems to have shown more tact when dealing with Lady Willoughby than he did with the Queen, for he

---

[1] The writer of this letter, John Stubbe, who was a Puritan gentleman from Norfolk, makes a brief appearance in history as the author of a pamphlet (1579) against Queen Elizabeth's proposed marriage to the Duc d'Anjou in which he was tactless enough to urge the Queen to ask her physicians if it might not be dangerous at her age to bear children. Both he and his publisher lost their right hands in consequence.

adds: 'My lady was right glad to heare your Lordship' good and honourable successes' [how fond he is of the word 'honourable'] 'but imparting to hyr the postscripts of your letter concerning her, I found them grevous and unseasonable for the estate of childbedd, and therfor meself to have faulted in doeing it.'

The Willoughby's little daughter certainly would have received gifts from her godparents, who would not forget her nurse either. An Elizabethan account book has the entry: 'To the nurse of my godchild 1/4. To the mydwff 1/-' and 'In a gylte spoone to my brother vyolets chylde at cersonynge 14/8'.

The historian, A. L. Rowse in *The England of Elizabeth* has said of the Reformed Church that 'the rule of general observance was strictly pressed, and the national Church included the great bulk of the English people in its discipline and rule'. This discipline began at the cradle. The baby had to be brought to its parish church to be baptized before it was a month old; infringement of this rule meant a fine. The baptism took place after the morning service. 'They baptise most commonly at the font in the church, with some ceremonies taken from the Catholic Church, as with the sign of the cross, but that is most odious to the purer sort' as a contemporary writer put it.

It was the custom in those days to sprinkle the back of the baby's head, not its forehead, with water; its heels were dipped in the font and its breast anointed with oil.

New ideas were in the air; the ferment of the Renaissance was making itself felt in every branch of western life. But medicine was still permeated with medieval practices and superstitions. Belief in the curative properties of precious and semi-precious stones was firmly held. A branch of coral was one of the things that mothers were advised to hang round the child's neck—the tooth of a hare or a female dog, the right eye of a bear, and a sachet containing the skin of a donkey were also considered beneficial. Among the many remedies for teething troubles was the tooth of a male viper enclosed in gold or silver and hung round the child's neck. The difficulty of procuring a male viper when required must have been considerable, and one wonders how many mothers attempted to carry out these complicated, and often nauseating, prescriptions.

Another remedy was to rub the gums of the teething baby with a finger moistened with fresh butter and the milk of a bitch mingled with the brains of a pig. It is a relief to come across such an innocuous remedy as the root of the marsh mallow.

When poking fun at vipers' teeth and so on, it is as well to remember how soon the nursery methods of one generation appear old-fashioned to the young mother of the next. There is no doubt that according to the ideas that prevailed at the time, the Tudor baby received every possible care and attention.

John Hake (1574) broke into verse in praise of the conscientiousness of children's nurses:

> '. . . their child they never feed
> With all that comes to hand, but they
> Observe with careful heed
> Both what to give and how to give;
> What quantity to use,
> And eke to feed it leisurely.'

Another writer, Peter Erondell, a Huguenot refugee who lived in England, gives a very detailed account of a lady's morning visit to her nursery. His book, a conversational manual, was published in 1605, two years after Queen Elizabeth's death, but to all intents and purposes it comes within the Elizabethan period.

For 'visit' one might substitute the word 'inspection'. As will be seen the mother, almost pathologically conscientious, puts the long-suffering nurse through a gruelling cross-examination. This is how their conversation goes:

Lady: Good morrow nurse.

Nurse: God give you good morrow, Madame.

Lady: How now, how doth the childe?

Nurse: He is fayre and plumpe, and doth very wel thanks be to God, saving that he hath been somewhat waiward the last night.

Lady: Hath he so? What shold ail him? It may be he hath some tooth a growing, is he in his cradle? See if he sleepeth.

Nurse: He is full awaken, Madame.

Lady: He is not yet made readie is he?

Nurse: No, Madame, I have let him sleepe all this morning.

Lady: Unswaddle him, undoe his swaddling bands, give him his brekefast while I am heere, make his pappe, take away that fier-brand that smoketh for it will taste of the smoke, where is his little spoone? Wash him before me, have you cleane water? O my little hart! God blesse thee. Rub the crowne of his head.

After telling the nurse to wash his ears and face, and to lift up his hair a little in search of some dirt that she fancies she sees on his forehead, the lady goes on: 'What hath he upon his eyelid? Me thinks his eyes are somewhat watrish, make them cleane; how quick is his eyebal, hath he not a pimple upon his nose? His little cheeks are wet, I believe you did leave him alone to crye and weepe; picke his nostrils, wipe his mouth and his lips. How many teethe hath he?' (Astonishing that such an observant mother should not know this!) 'His gummes be sore. Showe me his tongue, let me see the pallet of his mouth, he hathe a prettie chin. What a fair necke he hath! Pull off his shirt, thou art prety and fat my little darling, wash his arme-pits; what ayleth his elboe? O what an arme he hath! His hand wrist is very small; open his right hand; the palme of his left hand is all on water, did he sweat? How he spreadeth his small fingers.'

Then comes a revealing remark: 'His thumbe and little finger are Flea-bitten, for the black spots are there yet, is there any Fleas in your Chamber? . . .' She is soon off on another tack: '. . . he hath rubbed one foot against the other, for his anckle bone is flayed, see how he beateth with his heeles, doe you kicke, sirha? You have not washed the insides nor the soles of his feete; forget not to make cleane his toes, the great toe and all, now swaddle him againe, but first put on his biggin, and his little band with an edge, where is his little petticoat? give him his coate of changeable taffeta, and his sattin sleeves; where is his bibbe? Let him have his gathered aprone with stringes, and hang a muckinder to it; you need not yet to give him his corall with the small golden chayne, for I beleeve it is better to let him sleepe till the afternoone. Give him some sucke. . . .'

A 'maid' is told to fetch the cradle, make his bed, find his pillow. 'Set on the coverlet, now put him in his cradle and rocke him till he sleepe but bring him to me first that I may kisse him; God send thee good rest my little boykin. I pray you Nurse have a care of him.'

'Doubt not of it, madame, with the grace of God,' the nurse replies, no doubt fervently longing for her mistress to leave the nursery, which she does with a final; 'Well, then, God be with you till anon.'

Mention of the baby's fingers and toes, reminds me that it is supposed that the playful names by which each separate one was known in nursery circles may have evolved at this time. The fingers were named: 'Thumb, Toucher, Longman, Lece-Man, Little Man.' (The names varied in different regions. For instance in Essex they were called, 'Tom Thumbkin, Bess Bumpkin, Long Lonken, Bill Wilkin, Little Dick'.) The toes were 'Toe Tipe, Penny Wipe, Tommy Tisle, Bill Whistle, and Tripping-go'.

When the child grew older, it was part of the nurse's duty, according to John Hake, to teach it to speak by 'talking-forth' their words—'dad-dad' for father, and 'din' for dinner, and so on, so that gradually 'the baby speaketh plain'.

Dr. Boorde comes in here again with some solemn and not very helpful comments on late-speaking children. 'Chyldren that can not speake onto the tyme that they do come to a certain age, doth speke these III words: arra, acca, agon. Arra doth signify father; Acca doth signify joye or myrth; agon doth signify dolour or sorow.' (All of which I suspect was pure guess-work on Dr. Boorde's part.) He goes on to say; 'All infants doth speke these wordes if a man do make them, and what *wa* doth signify when they crye I coulde never rede of it; if it do signify anythinge it is displeasure or not contented.' Could it be that 'wa' was the infant's protest against being made the subject of Dr. Boorde's linguistic experiments? I picture him with a stiff ruff, and a beard that scratched the child as he bent owlishly over it.

The modern theory that children should not be taught baby-talk, had its supporters in Tudor times. A distinguished man, Sir Thomas Elyot, who as well as being a member of Parliament and an ambassador was also an affectionate uncle, went so far as to say that nurses should learn Latin so that their charges could imbibe the language effortlessly from their earliest years. Perhaps realizing that this was expecting a good deal, he suggested that at least they should refrain from mutilating the English language with baby-talk.

50

But baby-talk will probably endure as long as there are babies to be addressed in playful and caressing tones. (Something of the same instinct I suppose makes the Irish use a pet name for every conceivable Christian name, though the 'diminutive' may be as long, or even longer, than the actual name.)

Sir David Lyndsay, writing of James V of Scotland's childhood, reminds him:

> 'How as a chapman bears his pack,
> I bore thy grace upon my back
> And sometimes straddling on my neck
> Dancing with many a bend and beck.'

He recalled that his sovereign's first words were, 'Pa Da Lyn' ('Play David Lyndsay') and how for his entertainment he would play jig after jig on his lute.

How vividly these records of trivial domestic happenings bring the past to life! So much that at the time seems incomparably more important and more enduring has been lost in oblivion, sunk in the vast ocean of time, while some sentence like this—'When I was a babie my father would lay me down upon my back and laugh at me because I could not rise I was so fatt', drifts past us like flotsam from a great wreck.

A contemporary drawing in the State Papers Office of James VI of Scotland as a very small child, shows him sitting up in a little, uncurtained and uncanopied four-poster bed, set flat on the floor like a box. He wears a long-sleeved garment gathered at the wrists with a wrist band. This, of course would be his night attire (night clothes had now come into fashion). The clothes worn by a 16th-century baby in the day time are clearly indicated in Peter Erondell's dialogue between the lady and the nurse—the biggin,[1] and the band with an edge, the taffeta coat of shot colours and the satin sleeves, the petticoat, the gathered apron, the bib and the muckinder (or feeder). The baby sounds very much bundled up by modern ideas, but it was a period when everyone was elaborately overclothed, and no attention was paid to the good advice given by Richard Mulcaster,

---

[1] I have seen this variously described as 'a little cap' (from the French *beguine*) and as 'garters or soft boots'.

Master of the Merchant Taylor's school in Queen Elizabeth's reign, to the effect that young children should be warmly but lightly clad. Children were dressed like miniature adults; in an age when men and women displayed their wealth in their persons, to dress a child simply would have seemed a sign of poverty or at any rate of stinginess.

James VI of Scotland is shown as a small boy, in a portrait in the National Portrait Gallery, wearing a high-perched hat with a plume, a stranglingly-tight looking ruff, a pinched-in doublet of quilted white satin, and vast padded green velvet breeches. Lady Arbella Stuart (often called 'Arabella') 'her sweet jewel Arbel'[1] as her grandmother called her—escaped the ruff when she was a little girl of three or four, according to her portrait (her doll wears one instead) but she has the padded and puffed clothes of the period, which seem so grotesquely unsuited to playful young bodies. On the head she wears a kind of coal-scuttle cap ornamented with a wreath of flowers. Poor Lady Arbella's life was a sad and frustrated one; she was the victim of her rank, being too near the throne for comfort or happiness.

An account of the pitiful state of the wardrobe of a future Queen regnant of England when she was three years old, is given in the well-known letter written by Elizabeth Tudor's governess Lady Bryan to Lord Cromwell. It also gives a list of the clothes considered necessary for a little girl of that age. The Princess, whose sex had been so bitter a disappointment to Henry VIII and had undoubtedly contributed to Anne Boleyn's downfall, shared in her dead mother's disgrace, and had been publicly repudiated by her father as illegitimate. In desperation Lady Bryan wrote: 'I beseech you be good my lord to my lady and that she may have some raiment. She has neither gown nor kirtle, nor petticoat, nor no manner of linen, nor foresmocks, nor kerchiefs, nor sleeves, nor rails, nor body stitchets [corsets] nor mufflers, nor biggins.'

At her death the great Queen possessed two thousand (some say three thousand) dresses. How much her inordinate love of fine clothes sprang from her early deprivation in this respect is a matter for the psychologists!

[1] 'Jewel' seems to have been a favourite term of endearment for children. A grandfather calls his little grandson, Rodger, 'my jewel Hodge'.

It may be of interest to give the price of some items of children's clothing from contemporary accounts (bearing in mind the very different value of money at that time). The following entries are from the household accounts of 'Richard Bertie Esquire and the lady Katherine, Duchess of Suffolk, his wife'.

1561. 'For 8 payer of knitt hose for the children 3s. 4d.'

'For 7 yardes of crimson satin at 13s. the yarde for a Dutch gowne for Mistress Suzan. £4 11s.'

'For a varthingell of mocahdo for her 7s.'

'For a thousand and a halfe of pynnes for Mistress Suzan. 16d.' (I imagine the little girl bristling with pins like a hedgehog.)

1562. 'Paid for a cawle of gold worke for Mistress Suzan. 45s.'

Among Sir Henry Sidney's accounts for the years 1566–68 was the entry:

'For children of the said Sir Henry, 2 caps for the 2 young gentlewomen and 9 pairs of children's shoes. 19s. 6d.'

4

The well-to-do Tudor household was still run on patriarchal lines, comprising to our ideas a vast amount of people, not only the members of the family itself, but relatives of all kinds, and attendants of every degree from a chaplain, gentleman usher, waiting gentlewomen, yeoman of the pantry and pages, to the lowly scullions toiling away in the back regions.

The Tudor woman—at any rate in the country—whether she was a great lady or a farmer's wife, was no idler. A town lady might have time to go to the Exchange to shop, but the mistress of a large country house had a hundred and one housewifely duties to attend to in supervising the management of her large and practically self-supporting household.

Early hours were still the rule. By five o'clock in the morning it was 'fie upon all sluggards who are still in bed'. Six o'clock found even the idlest astir. 'The sun at every window calls the sleepers from their beds.' What happened on rainy or overcast days is not recorded, but one suspects that the discipline of the rod, freely applied in those days to children and servants alike, did the sun's work for it.

The author of the *Boke of Nurture; or Schoole of Good Manners* (1577) Sir Hugh Rhodes, Master of the Children of the Chapel Royal, says that the child should rise at six, say his prayers, make his bed, wash his face and hands, button or lace his clothes, and blow his nose before leaving his chamber.

The great Erasmus in *A Little Book of Good Manners for Children* tells the child to make the sign of the cross on his forehead and breast both on waking and before sleeping. Dr. Boorde is also in favour of hands, face, eyes and teeth being washed in the morning. (He shares the general prejudice against night air: 'In the night, let the wyndows of your house, specially of your chamber be closed.')

It may seem suspicious that directions for personal washing are confined almost entirely to the parts that show. Yet soap was bought in large quantities—the Bertie family bought a barrel of soap for 50/- at Stourbridge Fair in 1562—and there are receipts for making soap out of such fragrant ingredients as rose leaves and lavender flowers, as well as recipes for tooth paste and mouth washes. Baths, it seems, were sometimes taken in wooden tubs before the bedroom fire. An old laundry account proves that a country gentleman, staying in London, sent six shirts and six to eight handkerchiefs to the wash every week. All of which indicates a reasonably high standard of personal hygiene. On the other hand there is Erasmus's well-known complaint of the filthy condition of the floors in English houses. Against that, Anthony Munday in *Romayne Life* says that the steps of St. John Lateran, were 'as clean as the fine houses in London where you may see your face in the boards', and domestic accounts show that floor rushes were bought and changed at regular intervals. So it is hard to know what to think, except that standards of cleanliness must have varied considerably in different houses.

The life of the normal family was built—or if one likes to think of it as a piece of tapestry, stretched—upon a framework of religion. The young children joined morning and evening in the household devotions, and from the age of six at the latest would learn their catechism from the chaplain or rector of the parish in preparation for their confirmations at the age of fourteen.

Breakfast was eaten in private in one's own room. Children who were too young to drink home-brewed ale, were given warm milk or hot spiced barley water. Dinner between ten o'clock and noon, was still an important and ceremonial occasion. The food was as rich and abundant as in medieval times, but with the addition of some newly-introduced fruits and vegetables, including 'that sweete roote' the potato. (Though it has nothing to do with children I cannot resist quoting this agreeable culinary item from an Elizabethan letter, 'My Lord Treasurer gives you thanks for your 2 bore pies.')

There is some definite information now of the kind of food eaten by the young, such as the entry quoted at the beginning of this chapter, which gives the breakfast menu of the Percy children. In the *Diary of John Melville*, 1556, is an even more detailed description of children's diet:

'Our breakfast is bread and butter and fruit. To dinner we have greens or porrige. On fish days bread and milk, or if fish be reasonable in price we have it fresh, if not salt fish but well soaked, and beans and pease. Some drink small beer and a few have wine well watered. Afternoon we have bread and raisons, almonds, apples and cherries. For supper salad with salt, roots and herbs, a gallantine of minced meat, marvellous savoury. Sometimes we have roasted meat and sometimes pancakes, cheese and nuts. We have as much bread as we will, and other things sufficient for nourishment but not for the filling of our bellies.'

Except for the 'marvellous savoury' galantine and the roast meat, this sounds not unlike a food reform menu. Sausages, cabbage and porridge are also mentioned elsewhere as being served to children.

Besides this plain, basic fare, there must often have been sweetmeats—almond, butter, marchpane, gingerbread, all made by the ladies of the household—to be begged off indulgent grown-ups.

For country children there would be treats of curds and cream, and frumenty which was made of new wheat, boiled soft, and milk, eggs, and coloured with saffron ('if ye egges be pale') served in bowls with candy sugar or honey.

People were beginning to take an interest in children's diet as such. Juan Luis Vives in his treatise *Of the Upbringing of a Christian Woman* (little guessing that the young princess for whose instruction he wrote it, would be known to later generations by the repellent nickname of 'Bloody Mary') recommended a plain diet for the royal child, without 'potage, sauces or sops', and not richly spiced. Her drink was to be clear water with a little wine in it. ('There is no wyne good for chyldren and maidens'—Dr. Boorde again.)

Richard Mulcaster in the book already mentioned that he wrote for the guidance of parents, gave sensible advice against overloading young stomachs with too much food, particularly with meat.

To continue the outline of the Tudor child's day: Supper a light meal, was at five o'clock, and after that:

> 'In winter at nine and in summer at ten,
> To bed after supper both maidens and men'

was the rule for the servants in the household, so the children would probably have been packed off to bed some hours earlier.

Before going to rest they asked their mother for her blessing, and received her 'God be with you all'. It is easy to imagine the unhappiness of the child who through some misdemeanour had to go to bed without the maternal benediction.

It is almost impossible for modern parents, trained by psychologists to be apologetic, to realize the superb importance of being a mother (and still more a father) in those days. This is brought out very well in one of Peter Erondell's dialogues. The lady, having been addressed by her children as 'Madame', says; 'My children, seeing it hath pleased God (the only giver of all good) who might have made me some base creature and of no dignity to call me to that degree; I am Lady to all, but mother specially to my children, therefore the sweetest and most pleasant name that they can give me is to call me Mother.'

This sense of the impregnable sanctity of their status, must have given dignity and authority to the best type of parents, but led to disastrous results if they were cold-hearted, stupid or bad-tempered.

Lady Jane Grey gave a poignant account of her childhood and girlhood to the great scholar, Roger Ascham, who was

56

Elizabeth Tudor's tutor. When he expressed his surprise that so
young a girl should have such studious tastes, she said: 'One of
the greatest benefits that God ever gave me is that He sent me
with sharp, severe parents, so gentle a schoolmaster. When I
am in the presence of either father or mother, whether I speak,
keep silent, sit, stand or go, eat, drink, be merry or sad, be
sewing, playing, dancing or doing anything else, I must do it,
as it were, in such weight, measure, or number, even so perfectly
as God made the world, or else I am so sharply taunted, so
cruelly threatened, yea presented sometimes with pinches, nips
and bobs and other things (which I will not name for the honour
I bear them) so without measure disordered that I think myself
in Hell till the time comes when I must go to Mr. Alymer, who
teacheth me so gently, so pleasantly and with such pure allure-
ments to learn . . .'

Against that poignant 'I think myself in Hell' should be set
Sir Thomas More's remark to his daughter: 'I have given you
kisses enough, but stripes hardly ever.' Or the endearing picture
of family affection that is given in the letters of Sir Robert
Sidney to his 'sweet wenche', his 'sweet Barbara', Lady Sidney.
Nothing could be more tender and loving than the way he
addresses her, or his allusions to their children. 'Kiss all your
little ones from me, and give them my blessing.' 'There is no
desyre in me so dear as the love I bear you and our children.'
'I desire infinitely to see you and my children.'

His anxiety for her to join him in Flushing was at odds with
his solicitude for the children's health. He writes bidding her
'make you ready to kome over in May; it will be a good time
and by that time you will be strong. . . . But I ame afraid of my
children, especially the bigger ones, the aire being so eceeding
dangerous here for children.'

In another letter from Flushing (April 22nd, 1597) he dis-
cusses further plans for the children: 'Since I speake of your
koming over I will speake a little more of your children. I know
you are unwilling to part with them, and for the girls I will not
much stick with you yet for a yeare or more till they bee bigger,
and therefore will leave it to your own discretion whether you
will bring them or not. But indeed I must begin to take heed
to the boy. For hee is now almost seven years old and lieth still

with his mayde and doth not learn anything. As I wrote in my
other letter I could be content he were at Sir Charles Morison's.
For there I know hee should be wel looked unto and should
loose no time. But in truth I ame afraid of this ayre for the
children.'

By the 9th of May a solution had been found, at any rate for
the educational problem. Sir Robert wrote: 'Sweet hart, I am
sorry to hear Will hath had the meazels, but I trust by this
time hee is recovered of them, and then it will rather have
done him good than hurt. I have found out by great chance a
schoolmaster for him, one whome I like very wel of. He is of a
race of gentlemen of these countries, but poverty constraineth
him to seeke meanes to live. He speaketh both High Dutch and
Low Dutch, French and some English, besides Latin and
Greeke. As soon as you kome over I will place him with him.'

But Lady Sidney was still alarmed about the unsalubrious
climate of Flushing. Rowland Whyte wrote to his patron: 'My
lady fearing the vile [evil?] aire of Flushing is marvailous
willing to obey you in leaving the 3 greater behynd her, if she
could tell where. She was with my Lady Huntingdon, and
offered the three daughters and Mr. William with allowance,
but because of her debt she gave her no contented answer. She
knowe not where to leave them, unless yt were at Penshurst,
with a schoolmaster, a gentlewoman and a mayd and some
necessary servants to attend them till they grow greater; truly
she is much troubled lest any of them shold fall sicke in
Flushing.'

One hopes that the '3 daughters and Mr. William' were
allowed to stay at their own lovely home Penshurst with its
'dreamy house and green-hedged garden',[1] and not pushed on
to the unwilling Lady Huntingdon.

Sir Robert seems to have had a particularly soft spot in his
heart for his little daughter, Mary, or Mall or Malkin as he
sometimes called her. He bade his wife 'make much of little
Mall'.

'I thank Malkin for her letter,' he wrote, 'and am exceeding
glad to see shee write so wel, tel her from me I wil give her a
new gown for her letter.'

[1] *English Country Houses*, V. Sackville West.

Whether 'Mrs. Mary Sidney', as Whyte called her, got that new gown she was promised will never be known, but it can hardly be doubted that Sir Robert responded to this plea from his agent: 'I wold to God your lordship wold bestow a letter upon Mrs. Mary, yt wold greatly encourage her to do well, for once you said you wold write, she by her speeches showed a longing for yt.'

From his allusions to the Sidney children one feels that Mr. Whyte was genuinely fond of the young. 'Your lady and all your sweet creatures are in very good health at Penshurst', he wrote, and, on another occasion: 'All your children are well and this little pretty new-born daughter is as faire as the rest.' 'My lady and all yours are well; they are kept at their bookes, they dance, they sing, they play on the lute, and are carefully kept unto yt.'

The upbringing of the Sidney children carried out one of Lord Burleigh's precepts: 'Bring up children in learning and obedience; yet without austerity; the foolish cockering of some parents and the overstern carriage of others causeth more men and women to take ill courses than their own inclinations.'

'Everything while it is pretie and yonge draws liking', as Richard Mulcaster observed in his book, from which he concluded that the very young child would be more in danger of being spoilt by 'dalying and cockering' than by too much severity. No doubt many parents, yielding to their natural instincts made a pet of the child while it was very small, tightening up their discipline, in conformity with the ideas of the age, when it lost its playful baby ways and became, as they thought, in need of constant correction. For to the 16th-century mind precocity was the ideal. It was still the custom to send both boys and girls, once they had emerged from the nursery, to families of rather higher rank than their own to be educated. The aim of the average conscientious parent or teacher was by training the child in 'virtue, good manners and godly learning' to bring them to maturity as soon as possible, a point of view symbolized by the elaborate and unsuitable garments in which their little bodies were encased. No wonder that the portraits of so many 16th-century children give them the appearance of miniature grown-ups, their joyless little faces already pinched by the apprehension of troubles ahead.

5

The indifference, and even scorn, for clerkly accomplishments which was one of the characteristics of the medieval ruling classes, had long since been replaced, under the influence of the Renaissance, by a passionate regard for learning. What would formerly have been regarded as the chief knightly accomplishments, riding, tilting, hawking, and hunting, were still part of the education of the well-born young man, but he was also expected to be cultured, to be able to speak French and Italian, as well as Latin, and to be able to appreciate poetry and music. How this enthusiasm for learning affected the Tudor child must be discussed later. Before handing over the little creatures in their ruffs and doublets or stiff-bodiced gowns to their tutors with their Latin grammar books and their birches, let us watch them for a few moments at their play. Too soon they will be taken away from the uninterrupted enjoyment of their toys and games and set to study.

These toys and games had hardly altered since the Middle Ages. The old pastimes were still in favour—children (and also adults) bowled hoops, flew kites, played at marbles, whipped tops, rode hobby horses, skipped, ran around with paper windmills, walked on stilts, played at blind-man's-buff and leapfrog, and at being soldiers, and of course played at horses, for though it was no longer derogatory to travel in a wheeled vehicle (though exceedingly uncomfortable, as the cumbersome coaches which now lumbered along the highways had no springs) the horse was still very much in the ascendant, and riding the usual way of getting about. In fine weather the child traveller would ride pillion behind one of its elders.

Comparatively few specimens of 16th-century toys survive, but I have read an account of a 16th-century doll in the possession of a private collector in France.[1] The doll is described as wearing a falling ruffle, a dress of green satin richly embroidered in gold and silver thread in a design of crowns. Another doll, belonging to the Valois period, was dressed in embroidered white silk quilted in lozenges and ornamented with guipure and

[1] *Toys of Other Days*, Mrs. Jackson.

passementerie. She, too wore a ruffle, edged with lace at her neck, and a high satin cap. She carried a tiny baby doll, elaborately dressed, on her arm.

Other dolls of this century are described as having their heads and shoulders made of 'beautifully modelled composition'. All their finery was for show; their underclothes consisted of cambric petticoats. They hardly conformed to the standards of a Victorian dressmaker who (according to a family legend) stressed the importance to her customer of being 'a lady underneath'. One of these dolls wore a blue silk dress trimmed with hand-made lace, and embroidered with gold thread, her tiny shoes were also embroidered, and had red heels.

These exquisite doll-ladies must have been the exception rather than the rule, but it shows to what heights the art of doll-dressing (in France at any rate) had attained.

The doll in the portrait of the three-year-old Lady Arbella Stuart was made of wax; or possibly of wood with a composition face, and wore a red dress with modish puffed and slashed sleeves, a ruff and a head-dress.

One of the earliest doll's houses of which there is record dates from 1558. The inventory of its furniture was made forty years later. It had a ground floor, and a first and second floor, four outside doors and sixteen windows.

In 1576 the daughter of Henri IV of France ordered a tiny set of silver buffet pots, plates, bowls and other utensils to be made as a present for the newly born child of the Duchess of Bavaria, but again this belonged to the higher levels of toy making.

To include a lute among a child's playthings is perhaps stretching a point. In the musical England of those days, when barber's shops provided lutes for their waiting customers, and a host expected a guest to be able to pick up a piece of music and read his part in an elaborate part song at sight, music was considered an essential part of a child's education, and children were given lessons in playing the lute when they were still of nursery age. Yet nothing gives a child greater satisfaction than its first acquisition of a 'grown-up' object: the first wrist-watch, pen-knife or fountain pen, these are cherished by their young owners as much as any toy. One hopes that 'Mr. Peregrine and Mistress Suzan', children of 'Richard Bertie, Esq. and of the

Lady Katherine, Duchess of Suffolk his wife' felt pleasure as well as pride in the new lute that was bought for them, at a cost of 46/8 in January, 1562, when they were only seven and six years old.

Other entries in the family account books give a glimpse of their amusements at this age, and leave the impression of a pair of friendly, happy children. In August 1561, 12d. were paid 'To certayne women of Spilesbury which bestowed wyne and cakes upon Mr. Peregrine and Mistress Suzan'. 'To Mr. Peregrine, Mistress Susan and the rest by her Grace to buy them fayringes of a pedlar at the gate 2s.'—brings back not only a carefree moment of their childhood, but an England that has vanished long ago.

6

'Better unborn than untaught' was a favourite Elizabethan saying, and it is sad that the genuine love of learning that inspired it should have been responsible for so much unhappiness and even suffering among the young.

Christina Hole in her book, *Haunted England* tells of the ghost of Bisham Abbey. According to tradition its mistress in Elizabethan times was a certain Lady Hoby, a woman of scholarly tastes who, intolerant of stupidity or slowness in the young, beat her little son William so cruelly that he died. Her ghost could be seen emerging from a bedroom washing her hands, Lady Macbeth-fashion, in a basin (an apparition made all the more terrifying by the fact that, according to some accounts, she appeared like a photographic negative with black face and hands and a white dress). As Miss Hole points out, the strange part about the story is that though Lady Hoby was a real person, there is no record of her having had a son called William by either of her two marriages. Yet there is some confirmation of this terrible tale in the story that (to quote Miss Hole) 'when some alterations were made to the house, some very old and badly blotted copybooks were found hidden away behind a skirting board as though someone had hastily pushed them there. They bore the name of William Hoby written in a childish hand.'

Even if the maltreatment and death of poor young William is only a legend, it is one, unfortunately that was grounded on fact. It was the age of the rod; children who lacked ability, had a cony's memory,[1] or, as must often have been the case, appeared stupid through ill-health or nervousness, were beaten as severely as though they were deliberately idle.

> 'My child and scholar, take good heed,
> Unto the words which here are set;
> And see you do accordingly,
> Or else be sure you shall be beat.'
> (Cootes, *English Schoolmaster*.)

Standards were high. The revival of classical learning had brought with it a stern devotion to grammar and to the study of Latin and Greek. Princess Elizabeth Tudor by the age of six, had been taught Latin and Greek, could speak and write French fluently, play the lute and virginals, and was already a skilful needlewoman. Her half-sister, Mary Tudor was expected by her tutor to be able to write and speak Latin from her early years. A little boy, only five years old, is mentioned in the *School Colloquies of Corderius* as speaking fluent Latin though he was still too young to attend school. A child, hardly able to speak plainly, would learn to recite some of the Psalms, the Gloria in Excelsis, the Nicene Creed and the Paternoster in Latin. No wonder that the little creatures were made to learn their letters at the tender age of two.

Fortunately there were some educationalists like Sir Thomas Elyot, Richard Mulcaster and Dr. Colet, who enlightened by their sincere love for children, realized that harsh discipline was not the only or even the best way of training the young.

'Teach that thou hast learn lovingly' was kind Dean Colet's advice to teachers. His juvenile readers—'all lytle bebys, all lytle chyldrene'—he exhorted to 'lerne gladlie this lytel treatise' and to 'lift up their lytel white hands for him who prayed to God for them.' His advice to children was sound; it would be hard in any age to better it. He told them 'To fear God and to love Him . . . Thrust down pride; refrain thy wrath, forget trespasses, wash clean; be no sluggard; learn diligently.'

[1] Cony—rabbit.

Richard Mulcaster certainly held the theory that the young child should learn to read Latin as soon as it could speak and before learning to read its mother tongue, but the reason he gave for this showed consideration for the little pupil, as he held the view that Latin was easier to spell and pronounce than English. (Considering the superb and carefree catholicity of Tudor spelling, one would have thought it next to impossible to be a bad speller, in those days.) After reading, Mulcaster said, should come writing, drawing, 'cozen germaine to faire writing'. The child should be allowed to amuse itself by colouring the drawings. He approved of music, both instrumental and vocal, and of dancing being taught early. William Bathe in his *Brief Introduction to the Skill of Song* (1587) claimed that he had taught a child of eight, in a month, to 'sing a number of songs, difficult crabbed songs, at the first sight, to be so indifferent to all parts, alterations, staves, flats and sharps that he could sing a part ofthat kind, of which he never learned any song'. Richard Mulcaster was particularly in favour of singing for children, for did not Nature itself teach them to shout and cry so as to exercise their lungs? Ball games too, he considered beneficial. When whipping tops, children should be encouraged to use both hands. In wet weather children should use the long gallery, and be allowed to make as much noise as they liked. This last piece of advice has an unexpectedly modern flavour about it. But social and domestic history is full of these surprises. For instance alphabetical bricks were invented by an Elizabethan, Sir Hugh Platt.

The horn book, however, was the usual method of teaching the alphabet, and to think of a child of this period is to imagine it with its horn book in its hand, or hanging by a chain from its waist. In fact, though horn books are known to date from the end of the 15th century, they probably existed before the invention of printing.

The horn book was popularly called the 'Christ cross row' from the sign of the cross before the top row of letters. Some early specimens of horn books have the rhyme:

'Christes Cross be my speede
In all virtue to proceede.'

5a. An English Doll in the costume of about 1690

5b. The Interior of an English Doll's House of the time of Queen Anne

6. Prince James Francis Edward Stuart (The Old Pretender) born 1688, with his sister Princess Louise Maria Theresa Stuart, born 1692. From a painting of 1695 by Nicholas de Largilliere

The early types had the old black or gothic lettering, but this was gradually replaced by the new Roman letters.

These horn books could be very decorative, their wooden backs (so useful for battledore and shuttlecock) covered with embossed or gilded leather. Some horn books were even made of silver, and these became family heirlooms.

After mastering the alphabet, the Tudor child would learn to put vowels and consonants together. Paper was so expensive that slates and tablets were still used for writing lessons.

A wooden frame with coloured beads strung across it on a wire is said to date back to remote times, so it is very likely that this was one of the ways in which the 16th-century child learnt to count. An elementary grammar for children by Holt, called *Mylke for Chyldrene* showed a print of the human hand with the five principal cases printed on the five fingers and the sixth case on the ball of the thumb.

The little girls were set to work at an early age on a sampler or 'exampler' which at this time consisted of drawn-thread work, 'cut work', quilting and fine, close stitching in geometrical patterns.

Perhaps riddles and nursery rhymes should come under the heading of amusement rather than instruction, yet the very small child would learn to speak by hearing its mother or nurse repeat some nursery jingle, or when it grew older, might be allowed to sharpen its wits on Wynken de Worde's collection of riddles, *Demaundes Joyeuses* (a very early black letter book published in 1511). Riddles such as 'A house full, a yard full and ye cannot catch a bowl full', or 'There was a little green house and inside it a little brown house, and inside that a little yellow house, and inside that a little white house' would fascinate and mystify generations of children.[1]

It is impossible at this distance in time to guess with any exactitude the origin or date of most of these nursery rhymes and jingles, many of them mysterious in their meanings or apparent lack of meanings, but 'Ding Dong Dell, Pussy's in the well' goes back to Elizabethan times at least, as it is quoted in *The Tempest* and in *The Merchant of Venice*, and the 'Song of

---

[1] For those readers who are as abjectly stupid at guessing riddles as I am, the answers are 'smoke' and 'a walnut'.

Sixpence' also has the distinction of a Shakespearian mention, being alluded to in *Twelfth Night*, also in a Beaumont and Fletcher play. Old tales would be repeated from one generation to another. A Saxon or even earlier origin has been attributed to 'Beauty and the Beast' and 'Jack the Giant Killer'. 'Tom Thumb' too, is believed to have come from a very ancient legend.

Children's books in our sense of the word were non-existent, but the child who had acquired the art of reading would be richly rewarded for its diligence by being allowed to read one of the remarkable books of natural history or of traveller's tales (such as the inimitable *Travels of Sir John Mandeville*) which appealed so much to the taste of that wonder-loving age.

'Dragons there are in Ethiopia ten fathoms long' might not be a useful piece of information, but no one could deny its interest, and it was encouraging for a child to learn on Pliny's authority that the lion, an animal 'full of nobleness and clemency', had a nice sense of chivalry and would 'sooner assail men than women and never young children unless it be for great famine'. This charming picture of the dolphin is, as we know, at least partly founded on fact, as far as its friendliness towards human beings goes: 'Above the nature of other fishes they love young children, and the sound of instruments, they live 300 years. They rejoice when one calleth them Simon, and they love human voice.'

Edward Topsell's *History of Serpents*, a book upon which the author boldly claims the reader might 'look on the Holiest days . . . and pass away the Sabbaths in heavenly meditation upon earthly creatures', was a mine of information upon dragons. In Macedonia the dragon, it seemed, was to be seen at its most amiable; the children there made pets of them, 'riding upon them and pinching them as they would dogs' (poor Tudor dogs!) 'without any harm and sleeping with them in their bed'.

One imagines the 16th-century child, wide-eyed, reading Mr. Topsell's hints on the correct diet for dragons, just in case (and in that age of marvels everything was possible) some seafaring uncle or elder brother brought back a tame dragon as a present. Eggs were excellent for them, but not so apples, unless

66

the dragon also ate wild lettuce which 'greatly preserves his health'. And in the end the child would have to be content with a more conventional pet, a dog or a cat. Cats by now had to some extent lived down their sinister reputation of the Middle Ages (though they were still associated with witches) and were more popular as pets, in spite of warnings about them carrying infection, and the dangers of taking them to bed. (Preferable though to a dragon, one would think.) As for dogs, one writer, evidently not a dog-lover, wrote of them: 'The Dog is an uncleanly beast that is lightly angry, and gladly biteth strange dogges. He barketh much, but he knoweth his name, loveth his master and learneth many games.' This last accomplishment would more than atone in juvenile eyes for his alleged short-comings. Harrison in his *Description of England* has a delightful expression—'except it were a *dog in a doublet*' (my italics) 'you shall not see any so disguised as are my countrymen of England'.

Finally—in the natural history books—there was the croco-dile who cried and sobbed 'like a Christian body'.

The horizons of the known world were rapidly expanding as the gallant little ships with their tough, valiant crews set off from London docks or Plymouth in search of gold and adven-ture, but it was still a world whose outer edges were peopled with strange and fantastic shapes, with monsters and savages, mermaids and dragons, unicorns and sorcerers.

I have already mentioned witches in connection with newly born children, earlier in this chapter. One of the most repulsive features of the witch persecution were the cases where children obviously suffering from hysteria, accused so-called witches (most of them probably quite innocent of any malignant intentions) of having bewitched them.

Here are some typical cases of this kind:

On April 7th, 1593, Alice Samuel and her husband and daughter were executed at Huntingdon for having bewitched to death the Lady Cromwell and the daughters of Robert Throck-morton, Esq., The children had suffered from strange fits and had accused Mother Samuel of bewitching them.

Three years later, a boy called Thomas Darling who had fits, complained of being troubled by a green cat, and stated that he had met in a coppice 'a little old woman; she had on a grey gown with a black fringe about the cape, a broad thrummed hat and three warts on her face', who bewitched him. A woman called Alse Goodridge was accused of witchcraft in consequence.

A male witch called Hartley was accused of bewitching the children of a Mr. Starkie, 'he would kiss them if he could and therewith breathe the Devil into their bodies'. As they continued to have fits, Hartley was hanged, but this does not appear to have improved their condition, for when two preachers called for a Bible, the children, who no doubt were thoroughly enjoying all the excitement, burst into unseemly laughter and said, 'Reach them the bibble babble, bibble babble', and 'continued with many other scornings and filthy speeches'.

This brings one to what, in a favourite term of today, is called the 'climate' in which the Tudor child existed, and which after all was more important to its happiness and wellbeing than what it wore or ate, or what lessons or toys it had. It must seem presumptuous to try and sum up such an elusive thing as the spirit of an age, for that is what it amounts to, in a few paragraphs, but in this case the task is simplified by the fact that it is only the child's narrow but intense point of view that need be considered.

An effort must be made to forget our present-day standards and outlook, and to remember that things that would seem intolerable to us were part of the everyday experience of our 16th-century predecessors (and the other way round for that matter). To be beaten by parents or teachers for quite trivial faults would not seem the brutal cruelty, nor would the deaths of several young brothers and sisters seem the terrifying tragedy to children of that age that it would to our children.

Much of our information about nursery matters at that period naturally comes from accounts of the careers of children of royal or semi-royal birth—Elizabeth and Mary Tudor, Lady Jane Grey, Lady Arbella Stuart and so on. Too often and too soon their lives were affected by the political tensions and intrigues around them, and so one is left with the impression of young lives led under the shadow of almost unendurable strain and suspense. But of course there were many children whose normal unrecorded lives were only chequered by the natural troubles and griefs of childhood. There were even children who managed to slip through the close meshes of the educational net, like the little Sidney boy who at seven 'doth learn nothing'. 'About my fifth year the Great Buk (Bible) was put into my handes' one of these happy-go-lucky souls recorded in later life, adding that at seven he knew so little that he had to be sent away to a kinsman at Minster so that he could go to school.

Though the Tudor countryside swarmed with the hordes of beggars that were one of the major social problems of the age, it was still a countryside untouched by industrialism, and its delights which children would enjoy all unconsciously, are described in Breton's *The Court and the Country*. He writes of 'The May painting of the earth with divers flowers of dainty colours and delicate sweets . . . the bird singing . . . the foal neighing. . . . Again we have young rabbits that in a sunny morning sit washing of their faces.' The picture hardly seems complete without a little boy in a bonnet-like cap with a plume and a jerkin, and a little girl wearing a ruff and farthingale like a tiny woman, picking the flowers and watching the rabbits at their play.

Though social life was becoming increasingly sophisticated, people still enjoyed their pastimes with a boisterous zest that must have narrowed the gulf between adults and children. Children, kept indoors by inclement weather, would have no difficulty in finding some grown-up ready to play games with them in the long gallery—hot cockles, nine-pins or leapfrog, or some kind of forfeit or guessing game. They would join in the popular festivities that enlivened the year. Everyone went a-maying on May Day, country people and town folk, old men and matrons, young men and girls, and of course, children. The Puritans disapproved violently of this ancient pagan survival, alleging that it was merely an excuse for bawdy behaviour. Stow gave a more favourable account of it: 'On May morning every man would walk into the street, meadows and green woods, there to rejoice their spirits with the beauty and savour of sweet flowers, praising God in their kind.'

To the children it would just be tremendous fun—the teams of oxen, each beast 'having a sweet nosegay of flowers placed on the tip of his horns' dragging the Maypole, bedecked with garlands of flowers to the appointed spot, the Maypole being reared into position, its coloured streamers fluttering in the breeze, everyone cheering and laughing and dancing round it.

With what excitement and delight the children must have watched the Lord of Misrule and his mob of followers in their fantastic, gaudy clothes hung with ribbons and trinkets and bells, come rollicking on their way to the church, a wildly revelling horde with 'hobby horses, dragons and other antics', 'their pipers piping, their drummers thundering, their stumps dancing, their bells jingling, their handkerchiefs swinging about their heads like madmen, their hobby horses and other monsters skirmishing amongst the rout'.

The noise and shouting and the capering antics of the hobby horse and 'other monsters' must sometimes have frightened the smaller and more timid children, who would hide their faces against their mothers' or nurses' skirts, and have to be picked up and comforted till the crazy procession had swept by.

There was revelling in every household, and 'much mirth and good cheer' from Christmas to Twelfth Night—dancing, and banquets and masques and mummings. However strictly the children were kept in order during the rest of the year, they were allowed to join in these gaieties, and even in the gaming. Peregrine Bertie and his sister Susan were given 5/- for 'play' (at cards) when they were only seven and six years old. Their father gave them a New Year's gift of 10/- each in 1561. Next year the present had gone up to 20/-.

One would like to leave the Tudor child in this gay, noisy, brilliantly coloured setting, where the leaping flames from the great fireplace are reflected in the wainscoted walls of the long gallery of the great hall, or lend a fleeting, fantastic semblance of life to the figures and the beasts and birds of the tapestries. The revelry goes on for hour after hour, till at last the child, so sleepy that he can hardly keep his eyes open, is picked up by his nurse and carried away to his little truckle bed.

III

❖❖

Stuart

I

IT is not easy to define the exact boundaries of any particular historical era. As one looks closely at it, it seems to melt and alter shape like the contents of the mysterious shop, kept by the old sheep, in *Alice Through the Looking Glass*.

Though the first two decades of the 17th century, from the accession of James I to his death, belong to the Stuart period dynastically and politically, I cannot help regarding them as a kind of interim time between the Elizabethan and the Stuart eras. I imagined that this was the result of an undue preoccupation on my part with the clothes of the period. The stiff, bolster-like skirts, farthingales and bombasted breeches, the ruffs and heavily embroidered and decorated materials, were a 'hang-over' from the fashions of Elizabeth's reign, in the same way as the lush Jacobean architecture was an overblown development of the Tudor style. However, I have found that other people regard James I's reign in the same light, though for different reasons. ('After all there were a lot of Elizabethans left over from the previous reign' as someone put it). Elizabeth Jenkins in her book *Six Criminal Women* brilliantly sums up the Jacobean age with its 'aspect of gloomy richness, morbid elaboration, intellectual greatness that was enigmatic and passion whose loveliness had turned to horror'.

Yet Lord David Cecil can write of the years that immediately succeeded James' death in 1625, that the society of the 17th

71

century 'reached its most delicate flowering in the early years of Charles I's reign'.

Considering the epoch from a nursery angle, the reign of James I was not favourable to family life, at any rate as regards the example set by the Court, which, after the death of James' overdressed and extravagant Queen, Anne of Denmark, became notorious for drinking, indecent buffoonery and vice.

Whatever his defects as a monarch, Charles I's personal life had a dignity that was singularly lacking in that of his father. He was sedate, cultured, and a devoted husband and father. His French bride, Henrietta Maria, had a taste for elegant simplicity; her influence on society soon found expression in the graceful new fashions.

If one ignores the threatening political aspect, a mellow golden light like the sunshine of a morning in early summer, seems to bathe the landscape of the years between 1625 and 1642. In the country houses, great and small, which were so lovely a feature of 17th-century England, life was gracious and seemly, imbued with a deep religious sense, yet with a strong feeling for the beauties and pleasures of existence.

The manor house was still, as in the Middle Ages and Tudor times, a largely self-supporting and self-contained unit, with its bake- and brew-houses, its still-room and cheese-press house, its dairy, laundry, dove-cot and stew-pond, its carpenter's shop, saw-pit and riding house. Its hospitable roof still sheltered a considerable number of relations and servants (sixty people would not be regarded as an extraordinarily large household); the latter were regarded almost as members of the family, and looked after and chastised accordingly.

But the standard of comfort was steadily improving. Wainscoting and tapestries still gave an air of snugness to the great or the little parlour on winter nights when the wind cried down the wide chimneys, but furniture was now more plentiful and better designed. Chairs were covered with gilded leather, velvet, or the beautiful, intricate embroideries worked by the ladies of the family. Carpets were sometimes used for floors as well as for the tops of tables. The best beds were sumptuous with their high cornices and valences, topped by ostrich feathers, and hung with curtains of damask and velvet in exquisite combinations of colours, silver and green or silver and blue, crimson and olive, carnation or rose on a cream ground.

Fine silver, glass and china were in daily use, while the more sophisticated or wealthy collected classical sculpture from Italy, porcelain from the Far East, and Venetian mirrors and glass. The gardens of the period with their topiary work, sundials, formal paths and flower beds, were as pleasant and decorous as the houses they enshrined.

Though marriages were still a matter of family policy, the wishes of the young people concerned often being ignored, or only consulted in a perfunctory way, the atmosphere of the time seems to have been particularly favourable to happy marriages. Among the various reasons that may account for this, two occur to me—the sincere personal piety and concern for serious matters that was the mainspring of the best contemporary thought, and the way in which married women of the upper classes were encouraged to take an active part in the management not only of their households but of their husbands' estates. Foreigners considered England 'the paradise of married women'. (While on the subject of marriages, child-marriages were unusual by now, though Lady Mary Villiers was a widow before she was nine, and early betrothals were common. The Earl of Cork, in the first half of the century, recorded a treaty he had made with the Lord Moor, 'touching an unripe matche between his son and heir and my youngest daughter the Lady Margaret' who was then only a year old.)

Certainly it is easy to think of examples of outstandingly happy marriages at this time—marriages that prospered not only in the good days, but stood up to the separations and hardships of the Civil War. 'That looks on tempests and is never shaken.' There was Charles I and Henrietta Maria themselves (after an unpropitious start); Ralph and Mary Verney ('Oh— my deare, deare' was the poignant entry in Sir Ralph's diary after Mary's death at the age of 34); young Lord and Lady Sunderland whose idyllic happiness was cut short when he was killed at Newbury—in his last letter to her before the battle, he signs himself 'most passionately and perfectly yours'—the Puritan Colonel and Mrs. Hutchinson, and, in the opposite camp, Sir Richard and Lady Fanshaw, whose courtship during the Civil War, and subsequent adventures together read like a romance.

These were particularly successful marriages. It is not to be supposed that all married couples were so fortunate, but in spite of the entirely prosaic and often mercenary spirit in which matches were arranged, happiness in marriage was now established as an ideal to be hoped for, and in many cases was at least partly attained. The women who signed themselves 'your faithful affectionate wife' were conditioned to make the best of their husbands. Those who had not the high-spirited devotion of an Anne Fanshawe might have the submissive dutifulness of a Brilliana Harvey. The husband's position as undisputed head of the family and household must have developed not only his possessive but also his protective instinct. One way and another the children could be sure, more often than not, of one of the most important ingredients of a happy childhood—parents who lived together in amicable accord.

The morning sunshine of those early Carolean years was brief. The storm clouds gathered and burst in the tempest of the Civil War. One has only to read the Verney memoirs and other contemporary papers to realize its disruptive effect on family life—particularly on the family life of the country gentry. With rents unpaid and produce unsold, their menfolk away fighting, the women had a hard struggle to keep their homes together. Houses were besieged, plundered or burnt down, estates sequestered, their owners going into exile abroad. Hasty flights necessitated children being left with relations, or in forsaken houses in the care of servants. Families were separated, or more tragically divided by opposing loyalties. The loss of life was considerable, taking into account the comparatively small number of people taking part in the fighting (according to modern standards). There are accounts of pathetic young widows in their 'teens, left desolate with new-born children. A cousin of the Verneys laments that everyone connected with her who was fighting in the Civil War had been killed. Elsewhere she writes: 'These are miserable times we live in and sartainly those are happiest that goes first. My sister's children will be sudenly in a condition to starve, and most of my friends.'

With the end of the war and the triumph of the Parliamentarians, things gradually settled down. It appears that in spite of the repressive discipline of the extreme Puritans life jogged on very much as usual, in the country at any rate. (It is comforting to know that even clothes were quite gay. I have always felt sad for those girls whose youth was passed in the years between 1645 and 1660). Like John Evelyn, many who hoped for the restoration of the monarchy, endeavoured to 'lead a settl'd life . . . there being now so little appearance of any change for the better, all things being entirely in the Rebell's hands'.

When the Restoration came at last, a new spirit came with it—cynical and worldly. The corrupting effect of war had tainted the ideals which had inspired both parties in their internecine struggle. Something decorous and comely had gone out of life that would never quite be replaced.

This (very roughly sketched in) was the background against which the young children of the 17th century lived their lives.

2

Dr. Boorde had passed away, but he had a worthy successor in Henry Claderton, who, writing to his cousin John Cotton at Warblington, gave him the following notable and Boorde-like piece of advice: 'My daughter, Maria, tells me that you and my cousin have had three children all daughters. You would be glad, I doubt not the rest God send should be sons. You will say this is as God send them. True, but human observances may be used.' (A believer evidently in the axiom, 'God helps those that help themselves'.) 'My grandmother held and taught many (with whom it never failed) that if the mother lieth on her right side, her child will be a boy, and if on her left side a girl. Now it is the common custom of most to lie and take their rest towards the bed's board, and as I remember your chambers at Warblington, both your wives lay at the left side of the bed towards the chamber doors, wherefore according to the above observation, both had all daughters (save only your one son by your first wife).'

This theory at any rate had the merit of simplicity. One wonders if as a result of it, the second Mrs. Cotton was told to move over to the other side of the bed, and whether she made her husband 'a glad Father of many goodly and godly boys and some wenches among them'.[1]

Though daughters were often deeply loved, and from a family point of view were valuable as matrimonial counters, boys were in great demand, especially where a title was involved. The Reverend Mr. Garrard, writing to the Lord Deputy (The Earl of Strafford) reports that 'the Earl of Northumberland's lady is in daily expectation to be brought to Bed. If God send them a son you shall hear of it from me, God willing; if otherwise some body else shall send the news.' However he did later write facetiously that the Countess of Northumberland 'was brought to Bed of a daughter; he hath now four. He is but a Bungler at getting of Boys, but I hope they will come.'

Families were still very large, but for the first time—during the distresses of the Civil War—one comes across a note of complaint, disguised as resignation, when a forthcoming birth is announced. 'Sweet Nan' is expecting a child, 'An unseasonable blessing' her husband, Sir Nathaniel Hobart, writes plaintively, 'but God's will be done'.

In the ordinary way of course, a baby's birth was still a matter for the warmest congratulations. Lady Sussex wrote to Ralph Verney after his wife Mary had given birth to a daughter, Margaret: 'Non was more glader than myselfe to heare of your wife's safe delivery and that you have so brave a swite baby, which pray God may live long to bee a comfort to you both.'

This last wish was by no means a formality. Infancy and childhood were surrounded with dangers, and many babies only left their cradles for the grave. The Ralph Verneys lost at least six children. One would like to believe that these frequent, almost inevitable losses, blunted the parents' feelings, but the pathetic letters about the deaths of these young children and babies, and the epitaphs that survive hardly bear out this comforting theory.

[1] Denzell Hollis to his brother-in-law Thomas Wentworth (Earl of Strafford).

Here are two such epitaphs from the Verney MSS.

On an Infant

'Here lies a blossom of the world's great tree,
Which was as faire as Buds of Roses bee,
She died an infant, Heaven was made for suche,
Live thou as infants doe shall have as muche.'

The other one reads:

'Tread softly passengers, for heere dothe lie
A tender parsell of sweet Infancie,
A Harmelesse Babe that only came and criede
Through Baptisme to be washte from sin. So died.'

Beneath the conventional piety of the sentiments, the human grief is unmistakable.

Even more moving because of its simple tenderness and resignation, based on a sincere religious belief, is Sir Edmund Verney's letter to his son Ralph (written at one o'clock in the morning on May 19th, 1638) warning him that his little daughter Anne Maria was dying: 'Raphe, your sweete child is going apace to a better world; she has but a short time to staye with us.'[1]

The 17th century was a mixture of awakening interest in scientific matters, and credulity. The witch persecution for instance, continued unabated throughout the century. In 1619 two supposed witches, Margaret and Philippa Flower, who were servants of the Earl and Countess of Rutland at Belvoir Castle, were accused of causing the death of their heir, and of another son and daughter, also of having cast a spell to prevent the Rutlands having any more children. Both women were executed.

Astrology was still almost universally believed in as a science. Considering how frail a hold on life so many new-born babies had, it is not surprising that anxious parents and grandparents made a careful note of the position of the stars at the natal hour. Here is a typical entry from the Lismore papers made by

---

[1] There were other hazards besides illness for the 17th-century infant. A baby daughter of Lady Strange died soon after birth—suffocated in the nurse's bed.

Richard Boyle, the 'Great' Earl of Cork, a shrewd, hard-headed business man, if ever there was one:

'My wife, god be thanked, was safely delivered of her fixt son at Lismore about x of the clock in the evening of Wednesday, being the XXV day of June 1632, the signe being on Libia.'[1]

Less than ten years later he recorded with satisfaction that his fourth daughter, 'the Lady Joan Boyle, Countess of Kildare was ('thalmighty god be ever thanked and praised) in my house in Dublin, safely delivered of her firste son, whom I beseech God to make the beste and happiest man that ever was barron of Orphalye and Earl of Kildare'. Family pride and piety are nicely blended here.

Christenings in the earlier part of the century followed the usual pattern, with a stately ceremony, influential godparents, eagerly sought after by the baby's parents, expressing their extreme delight at being invited to be 'gossips', and duly presenting their godchildren with handsome 'guylt' bowls.

The Earl of Strafford, writing to a cousin Christopher Wandesworth in 1623, says:

'The good news of the Birth of your young Boy, I may say truly, was the best welcome that ever you writ me. . . . So soon as I come to London, one of my first Visits, God willing, shall be to see the young Gentleman and his Virtuous Mother, to whom I wish in the mean Time the Increase of perfect, constant, good Health; and in the Interim you will do me the Favour to present the Service of her gladsome Gossip, and let her know in Assurance never any man was more willing or proud of being Godfather . . .'

But after the Civil War, with its disintegrating effect on old traditions and customs, a problem arose for parents of royalist (or even of moderately Puritan views like the Verneys)[2] whether to christen the baby in the new manner, or whether to risk getting into trouble with the authorities by adhering to the old forms.

[1] I am reading this on another June day, three hundred and twenty-three years later, sitting in my car very near the beautiful river Blackwater, and the Castle, situated finely on its deeply wooded banks, where the little Boyle boy was born.

[2] Ralph Verney, unlike his father Sir Edmund, took the Parliamentarian side in the Civil War, but his conscience did not allow him to sign the 'Solemn League and Covenant' and he went into exile.

Mary Verney, who was over in England, trying to get the sequestration removed from her husband's estates, wrote to him about the christening of their unborn child (neither pregnancy nor ill health discouraged this brave and charming woman from working untiringly in her husband's interests). After telling him that she is determined to call the baby after him if it is a boy, she said: 'And as for the suddaine crisning, I will obey thee and get a minester in the house that will do itt the old way, for t'is not the fashion here to have godfathers or god-mothers, butt for the father to bring the child to church and answer for it. Truly one lives like a heathen in this place.'

In his reply, Ralph told Mary that if it were a daughter he would like it to be called after her. If it should prove to be a son, he said despondently: 'in earnest you must not deny mee, let it bee Richard or what you please, except my owne name. Really I shall take it ill if you contradict me in this. If it be a sonne, I trust God will make him a better and happier man than his father.' He went on more briskly: 'Now for the christen-ing, I pray give noe offence to the State; should it be donn in the old ways perhapps it may bring more trouble upon you than you can immagen, and all to noe purpose, for soe it bee done with common ordinaire water, and that these words, 'I baptise thee in the name of the Father, and of the Sonne, and of the Holy Ghost bee used with the water, I know the child is well baptised. All the rest is but a matter of forme and ceremony which differs almost in every country . . .'

On June 3rd, 1647, Mary was able to write triumphantly at the end of her doctor's letter: 'I have borne you a lusty boy.'

With loving obstinacy she insisted on calling the baby after her husband. The little boy had what his mother called 'a troublesome beginning'. On June 24th she wrote: 'Our poore child was so extreme sick that everybody thought it would have died, butt now I prayse God t'is beyond everybodyes expec-tation.'

The worried father, who had been left in charge of the older children at Blois, begged his wife not to give the new-born baby any 'physick, but such as midwives and old women with the doctor's approbation doe prescribe, but assure yourself they by experience know better than any phisition how to treat such infants'. He adds with playful severity: 'I will not now dispute with you about his name, but assure yourself you shall heare of it at large heerafter.'

Anxious correspondence also passed between husband and wife about seven-year-old Jack, who had been left in the care of doting young aunts at Claydon, the family place, when his parents went to France, and who though he looked 'a brave lusty boy' when his mother first saw him by candlelight, was found next day to have 'the most miserable leggs, crooked as ever I saw any child's', though fortunately he went 'very strongly' upon them, and otherwise was well-grown. He had also been allowed to eat anything 'he had a minde toe' by his too-fond aunts; he had an imperfection in his speech, 'and of all things he hates his books', but in spite of these defects he was 'a very gallant boy', ready-witted and affectionate, follow-ing his mother round everywhere, singing prettily, and express-ing a wish to go into France to see his father.

'I long to see poor Jack,' wrote his father, 'truly the crooked-ness of his Leggs grieves my very Hart, aske some advice about it at London, but doe not Tamper with him.'

To get back to the baby—though he had shown early signs of delicacy, or perhaps because of this, taking into consideration the insanitary state of 17th-century London, Mary decided to send him at three weeks old down with his nurse to Claydon. She wrote careful instructions to the steward about the journey. 'I intend to send my child to St. Albans . . . the nurse sayeth her husband hath a very easy-going horse, and she thinks it will be best for him to carry the child before him upon pillows, because she cannot ride between two panniers and hold the child. When you come there, you will quickly find which will the best way to carry it; pray provide for both wayes, and bring a footman to goe by itt. If her husband doth carry the child, she cannott ride behind him, so you must provide a horse for her. . . . Pray do you see that they take great care of the child, and that they goe very softly, for the weather is very hott; if he carries the child before him, itt must be tied about him with a garter, and truly I think itt will be a very good way, for the child will not endure to be long out of ones armes.'

7. A Late Eighteenth-Century Mother and her Children, by an unidentified artist. Initials G.B.

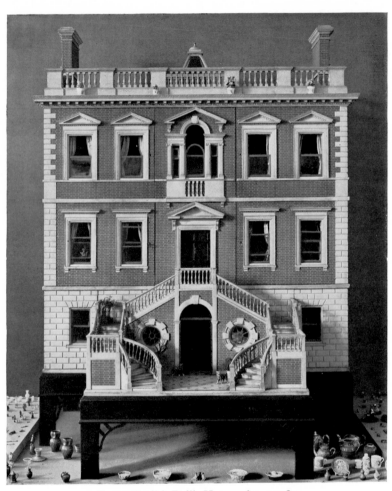

8. An English Doll's House, about 1761

In the end the baby was sent by coach to St. Albans, and there met by the steward with horses.

The wet-nurse was still firmly entrenched in the nursery. Mary Verney tells her husband that she has had to change little Ralph's wet-nurse. It seems strange to us to find so devoted and careful a mother admitting that the only fit person she can find, 'Ralph Rodes' wife' is, 'I feare but poore and looks like a slatterne'. She tries to reassure herself and him by adding, 'but she sayeth if she takes the child she will have a mighty care of it, and truly she hathe two as fine children of her owne as ever I sawe'.

Here is one of the curious contrasts of the age. One visualizes Sir Ralph and Lady Verney's baby, almost certainly clad in an exquisitely stitched shirt, dress and bib, with a lace cap, and perhaps miniature lace mittens (such as Charles I wore at his christening) held in the arms of the well-meaning but slatternly Mrs. Rodes (who was to have 4/- a week for her services, and two loads of wood—'truly 'tis as little as we can offer her being she hath not ye christening, for nurses are much dearer than ever they were'). Yet Mary Verney was making the best arrangement that she could in the circumstances—for it would never have occurred to her to feed the baby herself, (and perhaps as she was consumptive it would have been inadvisable for her to do so) and the only alternative would have been to hand him over to a dry-nurse who would have fed him on milk, bread and pap out of a silver pap boat.

All went well with the baby for a while. When he was nearly three months old, Mary Verney wrote to her husband: 'I meane to coate him this week. I have much adoe to keep the nurse quiett so long without coates.' And before leaving Claydon, she reported proudly that 'my little Raphe is a very fine boy and thrives very well'. But alas! soon afterwards the baby died of 'convulsive fits', and shortly before this the poor Verneys lost their beloved young daughter Peg, who died of dysentery at Blois during her mother's absence.

Mary, though almost distracted with grief at this double blow, had the faith and courage to write to Ralph: 'My trust is in my good God, for he gave them to me and he took them from me, and I hope and trust he will in his good time deliver me out of all my troubles, and give my mind some quiett, and bring me to thee, for untill I am with thee I cannot take any comfort in anything in this world.'

It is satisfactory to know that this devoted and hard-tried couple were safely reunited later.

As it was believed that any agitation might affect the wet-nurse's milk, it does seem, from the following incident, that Sir John Tunstone and his colleagues chose an untimely moment to show their Anglican zeal, and that Henrietta Maria had some excuse for her anger. Lord Cottington, writing to the Lord Deputy, tells how 'Our joy for the Birth of a young Duke of York is much water'd by the Sickness of the Babe, yet at this Instant he is better. The Nurse is a Roman Catholic, to whom Sir John Tunstone offer'd the Oath of Allegiance, and she refus'd it, whereupon there grew a great Noise both in the Town and Court, and the Queen afflicted herself with extreem Passion upon Knowledge of a Resolution to change the Woman, yet after much tampering with the Nurse to convert her, she was let alone to quiet the Queen. Nevertheless this Trouble put the Nurse into so great a Distemper, as the Physicians attribute the Child's sickness, and now again they are resolved to change her.'

Another royal infant, earlier in the century, who seems to have suffered from some mishandling of the wet-nurse situation was the young Dauphin of France (afterwards Louis XIII) who had no less than four wet-nurses in succession.

A very detailed account of his upbringing survives, which, allowing for some difference in French and English methods, gives a good idea of nursery life during the first decade of the century.

Besides the inevitable pap, broth was much recommended for the young baby. The Dauphin was not weaned till he was two years old. However, by the time he was eleven (an age outside the scope of this book, but one may suppose that a seven-year-old would have a modified version of this meal) he was making up for this early abstinence. This is a menu of what he had for supper: egg soup with lemon juice and broth, cock's comb, boiled chicken, boiled veal, a marrow bone, chicken fried in bread crumbs, jelly, apricots, half a sugared chestnut in rose water, preserved cherries, a little bread and some fennel comfits for the digestion (he would need these, I should say).

Spoons had been used for eating *potage* since the 15th century in England, but were only just coming into fashion in France, the usual way of supping broth being to drink it out of the bowl, lifting the sopped bread out with the fingers. A book of manners advises using a sippet of bread for eating a boiled egg, adding the recommendation that the inside of the egg was not to be licked out with the tongue! The young Dauphin almost certainly drank barley water, toast water, and tisanes made with flowers and herbs.

To return to England—the North children were brought up on a Spartan diet, 'plain and rather short than plentiful', and were never indulged with 'bits and curiosities'. They were however allowed as much small beer as they could drink; in fact a stone bottle of it was kept in the nursery quarters so that they could help themselves as they liked. This plain diet forestalled, to some extent, Locke's advice in his celebrated treatise on education, but more of him later.

Swaddling clothes were still the rule in France for the first nine months. (By 1707, Madame de Maintenon was writing about the English system of releasing babies from their swaddling bands at the age of three months, so presumably this was in force for some years previously.) One French doctor, François Mauriceau, even made the alarming suggestion that unless a child was swaddled it might walk on all fours like an animal.

In the best nurseries, swaddling clothes were frequently changed. A little shirt and embroidered jacket were worn over them. Later the baby, regardless of sex, wore a silk petticoat and a frock (one of the Dauphin's frocks was of white satin striped with silver). Babies also wore coral necklaces, and little lace or lawn caps, for to expose even a hardened adult head to the fresh air, was considered rash.

The French-born Countess of Derby, Charlotte de la Tremoille, throws some light on the clothes worn by Stuart babies when she wrote to France for frocks for her small son. 'In this country,' she said, 'children are short-coated at a month or six weeks old. I am considered out of my senses that he is not yet short-coated.'

Lady Derby, and her royal mistress Henrietta Maria, set the attractive fashion of dressing babies in white, rather than in colours.

According to modern ideas, small children were far too much bundled up. John Evelyn's little boy, a prodigy of learning, died at the age of five from an enlarged liver, and his father attributed this to his having been kept too warm as a baby, or as he put it: 'This incomparable hopefull blossom. . . . In my opinion he was suffocated by the women and maids that tended him, and cover'd him too hot with blankets as he lay in a cradle, near an excessive hot fire in a close room.' Whether this treatment would really affect a child's liver, I don't know, but it must have helped to weaken his constitution.

Stuart fathers, on the whole, seem to have taken a keen interest in their children's upbringing, and it would have been as well if their advice, being often based on common sense, had been taken, but the baby was hemmed in by tradition-ridden 'women and maids', many of them profoundly ignorant and superstitious. When the master of the house, dignified in his lace collar, had had his say and left the nursery, one can imagine the nurse, with a pitying smile for masculine presumption, drawing the richly carved, heavily draped cradle, filled with feather pillows and blankets, even nearer to the fire, replacing the discarded coverlet, and rocking her parboiled charge to sleep with a croon of 'Bye Baby Bunting, Father's gone a-hunting'.

Nurses (in the sense of a 'Nanny'—some of them were actually called 'Nan' or 'Nanna',) make their appearance on the Stuart scene. Such a one was Nan Fudd who nursed two generations of the Verney family. Betty Verney's nurse was expected to 'dress hur and to heare her hur booke, and teche her hur worke'—thus almost fulfilling the role of a nursery governess. Anne, Lady North writes about her young grand-daughter's attendant, Betty Harbert, 'It seems that she was promised to be Miss's maid and to have all her clothes and £4 a year wages'.

The true Nanny spirit can be felt in these extracts from letters written by Luce Shepherd, a retainer of the Verneys, about the two little girls, daughters of a Mrs. Eure, who had been placed in her charge at Blois: 'They are very well and love French *potage*, especially Miss Margreat.' 'Little Miss Mary' was reported to be always merry and in good humour. 'As for Miss Margreat she is, thank be to God, a very healthy and wholesum child, and in my opinion will make a hansum woman. . . . Mr. John and Miss Margreat never have chilblains, neither do they ware fur gloves, but Miss Mary wareth furr gloves, not that shee hath any chilblains this yeare on her hands at all, but shee hath chilblains on her feet but no great matter.'

Over three hundred years have passed since this letter was written. Yet in spite of the immense progress in medical science, chilblains are still the winter bane of many adults and children less fortunate than 'Mr. John and Miss Margreat'.

To be 'a very healthy and wholesum child' at that time was no small achievement. Though the 17th century was described as a golden age for European science, and was marked by a great advance as regards research in chemistry and physics,[1] the art of medicine was based mainly on the theory of humours. Good health it was believed depended on a state of harmony existing between the four humours in a person's body—blood, phlegm, choler and melancholy. A doctor's diagnosis was mostly guess-work. In *John Evelyn and His Family Circle* by H. G. Hiscock, a letter is quoted from Evelyn's brother, George about the death of the latter's two-year-old daughter, Elizabeth. He says, 'She never was sick, all her complaint was difficulty of breathing . . . I had the advice of a very able physician, Dr. Hailey . . . let her blood four ounces and gave her other things inwardly . . . His judgement was that her iron bodice was her pain, and had hindered the lungs to grow, and truly the surgeon that surclothed her body found her breast bone pressed very deeply inwardly, and he said two of her ribs were broken, and the straightness of the bodice upon the vitals caused this difficulty of breathing and her death. . . . Both the Doctor and Surgeon did conclude that going into the bodice so young,

[1] The clinical thermometer was invented, and micro-organism discovered in this century.

before her lungs had their growth, and the depression of those joints hastened her death.'

A popular remedy for measles was to place a live sheep in the patient's bed, 'because these creatures are easily infected and draw the venom to themselves by which means some ease may happen to the sick person'. Blood-letting was in great favour, and though some of the current remedies were harmless and possibly beneficial enough like the rhubarb lozenges prescribed for the young Dauphin, or the rhubarb drink that was given to little Edmund Verney, other ingredients in contemporary prescriptions ranged from the fabulous such as the horn of a unicorn or the ineffectual like the much-prized bezoar stone, to the revolting—woodlice, live spiders rolled in butter, human blood and urine, the excrement of animals, the brains of dead thieves, powdered mummies—nothing was too repellent to feature in the 17th-century pharmacopoeia, though, it should be mentioned that Nicholas Culpepper, the eminent herbalist, strongly disapproved of all this. One would like to imagine that the tender stomachs of the young children were spared these horrors, but I think this would be over-optimistic.[1]

As against this, one must remember that the children were eating 'honest' unadulterated food, free from synthetic ingredients, and cooked with interest and care, for 'good housekeeping and all economical virtues were then in reputation' as John Evelyn said. As well as a great variety of meat (which was now only eaten salt after Martinmas) game and poultry, salads were much eaten by this time, as well as numerous kinds of vegetables. Locke considered strawberries, cherries, gooseberries, currants, apples and pears wholesome for children but, for some reason which I cannot explain, not so peaches, melons or plums. The still-room was a hive of activity, out of which was produced the fruit syrups, and home-made wines such as

---

[1] An extract from *An exact enquiry into and Cure of the Acute Diseases of Infants*, 1694, by Walter Harris, M.D. gives as suitable 'anodynes' for 'Tender Infants and Children' the following, '. . . Crabs eyes and claws, Oyster shells, wilks-shell, Cuttle-bone, Egg-shells, chalk, coral, Coraline, Pearls, the Mother of Pearls, both the Bezoars, burn'd Harts' horn, burn'd ivory, the Bone of a Hart's heart, the shavings of Hart-horn and of the Unicorn's horn etc.'—a diet that would seem more suitable to hens in need of grit than to new-born babies.

cowslip, currant and elder which, with tea, coffee and chocolate still expensive luxuries, were in great demand, also infusions of herbs and simples for medicinal use.

There are accounts of childish disorders and the means taken to cure them in the North Letters, written in the 1670's. Lady North suspects 'some kind of aguish distemper' in her little grandson Frank who is 'out of order and not so lively nor so good a stomach' sometimes in the afternoons, but is 'as brisk againe as may be' by the evening. 'Little Misse' is treated for 'a feverish distemper' with an 'opening julep' given by the doctor's direction, which 'wrought very well without the least disturbance to her'. A more drastic remedy is mentioned in Roger North's letter to his sister. His little son had 'a violent access of a cold' so 'for fear of something worse, we resorted to his sheet anchor, bleeding in the jugular, which once saved his life, and perhaps has done the game, for he is much better after it, though weak, having lost at least eight ounces'.

Smallpox and plague were still the twin scourges of western humanity. Sanitation was sketchy and in the towns positively bad. Careful parents who had houses in the country naturally inclined to send their children down to them, away from the foetid air and noise of London. But it should not be supposed that the children of even well-to-do parents were kept out of London altogether. Sir Dudley North as a small child had an alarming adventure when he was living at his parents' house in King's Street, Westminster. 'The chief airing this child had was with his attendant at the door where, by his foreward familiarities, he had made himself known to most people that had to do thereabouts. . . . This overforewardness was like to cost him dear.' His biographer then told how the little boy was swept away by a beggar-woman who later was found stripping him of his clothes. Seventeenth-century London comes to life in this little episode, the close proximity of wealth and abject poverty, of luxury and filth, the passers-by jostling each other in the narrow cobbled streets shadowed by the houses with their overhanging eaves. It was also told of Dudley North's childhood that his father's house was shut up during the Plague, for he and his little sister Mary were both stricken with it in the forsaken house. But their 'excellent mother stayed, and with her own hands nursed her two tender children'. Her devotion was rewarded, 'Neither she nor anyone else in her house had the plague'.

3

I have mentioned the clothes worn by small babies, and it might be as well, before going on to the activities of the older children, to give a brief account of the kind of clothes they wore.

In the early part of the century children, dressed according to the notions of the times like miniature grown-ups, had their poor little bodies squeezed into the grotesque and ungainly fashions of the period. The boys wore padded doublets and breeches and starched ruffs; the girls were laced into stays as stiff as boards, ruffs were fastened round their soft throats, their frizzed hair was dressed high on their foreheads.

One has to remember of course, that children were undoubtedly dressed up in their best clothes when their portraits were being painted. An entry in the accounts of the Porter family for six holland coats for the little Porter boys, with 'fustian and tape to them' gives a glimpse of the more informal and comfortable clothes that children in the first half of the century wore in the nursery.

A boy of seven or eight in King James I's reign is described as wearing a best suit of ash-coloured satin, with doublet, hose, stockings with garters and roses, all to match. He had an embroidered girdle and cloak of the same colour, trimmed with squirrel fur. He went through five pairs of shoes in the year.

The Earl of Cork in 1633 gave an order to a Youghal merchant 'to bring for me out of England crimson shagg and spangled lace for winter clothes for my children'. On another occasion he bought fifteen yards of 'choice white damask from the great ship that was putt in at Kinsale' to send to Lady Clayton who was looking after his motherless daughters Mary and Margaret Boyle, to make 'two summer gounes' for them (which gives one an exact idea of the amount of material required for a little girl's dress in those days).

By now (1634) the charming fashions that one associates with Charles I's reign and Vandyck's portraits were coming into use. The padding and stuffing of breeches which had made the

Jacobean gallants look like animated bolsters had disappeared. A small boy would now wear loosely hanging breeches, tied at the knee with a garter, and a doublet with a falling lace collar. Like their elders, they wore their hair long enough to fall on to their shoulders. Mary and Margaret Boyle would wear the graceful style of dress introduced by Henrietta Maria, with lace edged collars and cuffs and pinafores, and aprons also edged with lace. (To leave off a bib and apron was the girl's equivalent of being breeched.) Their curls were tied back with bunches of ribbons, and they wore lace caps (which their brothers discarded at the age of four or five) till they were eight or even ten years old. Henrietta Maria dressed her babies in long clothes of fine white linen or satin, and then in three-quarter length robes.

The Earl of Cork, an affectionate father, sent his daughter, Mary, aged eight, 'the ffether of diamonds and Rubies that was my wives'. One of those completely unsuitable but memorable presents that can give such pleasure to the young.

By the close of the century, fashions had changed considerably, belonging in spirit more to the 18th than to the 17th century, and children's clothes altered accordingly. The boys, when they emerged from the petticoat stage, were now put into long coats and waistcoats, and sometimes were made to wear stays to improve the set of the coat. Locke inveighs against 'ignorant Nurses and Bodice-makers' who were responsible for the child being put into 'hard bodices'.

Small boys remained in 'coats', i.e. petticoats, till they were six or seven years old. There is an attractive description in *The Lives of the Norths* of the breeching of a little boy called Frank.

His grandmother wrote: 'You cannot beleeve the great concurse that was in the whole family here last Wednesday, it being the day that the taylor was to helpe dress little Frank in his breeches, in order to the making a everyday suit by it. Never had any bride that was to be drest upon her wedding night more hands about her, some the legs and some the arms, the taylor buttoning, and others putting on the sword, and so many lookers on, that had I not a ffinger amongst them I could not have seen him. . . . They are very fitt, everything, and he looks taller and prettyer than in his coats. Little Charles rejoyced as much as he did, for he jumpt all the while about him, and took notice of everything. I went to Bury and bo't everything for another suit which will be finisht upon Saturday. So the coats are to be quite left off on Sunday . . .' Then comes a delicious touch: 'When he was drest he asked Buckle whether muffs were out of fashion because they had not sent him one . . .'

It would be hard to find a more charming and evocative little scene of family life—the grown-ups almost as excited and proud as the little boy himself, the younger brother in his petticoats jumping round and getting in everyone's way, the tailor (I fancy him as elderly rather like the old man in *The Tailor of Gloucester*) benevolent, but absorbed professionally in his task of trying on the new suit, and Frank himself, flushed with youthful masculine vanity which in those days he would be able to indulge to the uttermost. As mothers of sons know, most small boys are just as interested in clothes as girls, till they reach the preparatory school age and are led to believe that such matters are beneath their dignity.

4

It may be apparent by now from some of the quotations in this chapter, that the attitude of adults towards children had undergone a change during this century. Though children were still regarded as appendages to their parents, hope being expressed in letters of congratulation that the new-born baby would grow up to be a comfort to his parents, though children hardly more than infants were (literally) obliged to 'kiss the rod' after a beating, in token of repentance, again and again one comes across evidence not only of a delight in children for their quality of childishness, but of a new awareness of their particular problems and needs.

Under the intimidating title of *The Child Microcosmography*, Bishop Earle wrote:

'Here is Nature's fresh picture newly drawne in oyle which Time and much handling dimmes and defaces. His soule is yet a white paper, not yet scribbled upon with the Observations of the World, wherewith at length it becomes a blurred Note-Book. . . . He kisses and loves all, and when the smart of the

Rod is past, smiles on his Beater. . . . . Nature and his parents alike dandle him and 'tice him on with a bait of sugar to a draught of wormwood. . . . His hardest labour is his tongue, as if he were loth to use so deceitful an organ, and he is best company with it when he can but prattle. Wee laugh at his foolish sports, but his game is our earnest; and his drummes, rattles and hobby-horses but the emblems and mockings of men's business. . . . The elder he growes, hee is a stayre lower from God; and like his first father much worse in his breeches. . . . Could hee put off his body with his little coate, he had got Eternitie without a burthen, and exchanged but one Heaven for another.'

There is a significant change here from the earlier 'child of wrath' attitude, (though, as will be seen later, this still flourished). Of course being a 17th-century divine, and a Bishop at that, his description of the child is used to point a moral. All the same there is a sympathetic attempt to understand the workings of the immature mind.

There is a decidedly Wordsworthian note in this description of infancy by the Poet Traherne: 'I was a little stranger, which at my entrance into the world was saluted and surrounded with innumerable joys. My knowledge was Divine.'

There were unhappily 17th-century fathers and mothers (particularly mothers, I am sorry to say) whose harshness and cruelty remind one of Lady Jane Grey's odious parents, for instance, Elizabeth Tanfield's mother, early in the century, who insisted on her child addressing her on bended knee (luckily Elizabeth had an indulgent father). The following terrible story of a brutal mother was told by Lady Wentworth:

'Hear is a strange unnatural reporte of Lady Abergane that she had in a pation killed her own child about seven years old, she having been a great while whiping it, my Lord being grieved to hear it crye soe terryably, went into the roome to beg for it, and she threw it with such forse to the ground she break the scul; the girl lived but fower howers after it.'

But for one atrocity like this, there are dozens of instances of the tenderness and indulgence of Stuart parents towards their children. In fact, it seems that English parents had the reputation abroad of being extraordinarily fond of their offspring.

A French writer, Misson, commented on this trait in his travel book published in 1698: 'On a une extraordinaire complaisance en Angleterre pour les jeunes Enfants, toujours caresser, toujours applaudie, a ce qu'ils fait.' (There is a distinct suggestion of spoiling, or of what was called 'cockering' here, reminding one that the Restoration had brought about a general laxity in manners and personal discipline.)

The letters of the time are full of touching and agreeable allusions to children. Endymion Porter often mentioned his little boys when he was writing to his wife, Olivia, his 'sweet Love'. When his son George was born he wrote: 'God bless thy child and make him a Saint George' and 'The Lord bless little George and give him grace to be good and virtuous.'

Endymion Porter was in attendance on the Prince of Wales, (afterwards Charles I) when he went to Spain on his rather farcical courtship of the Infanta. His wife had borne him a second son, and where a modern father would demand snapshots, Endymion had to rely on descriptions:

'Send me word,' he wrote, 'how the children do, and whether Charles be black or fair; and who he is like, but I am sure the nurse will swear that he hath my eyes or nose, and you may perchance be angry and say that you never saw anything so like some brother of yours as he is.' (The hot-tempered Olivia had been hearing gossip about her lively husband and the daughter of an innkeeper at Boulogne.) He sent 'six little glass bottles with silver chaines for little George, and I make no doubt he will keep a terrible stir with them.' He enquired solicitously after the children's teeth: 'I pray you send me word whether he hath a great tooth yet or not, and how many teeth little Charles hath', and gave some fatherly advice about bringing up George: 'I would have you cut George his hair somewhat short, and not to beat him overmuch.' Another time he expresses his love for his children in a simple, 'God bless my babies'.

Young Lord Sunderland in his last letter to his wife before he was mortally wounded at the battle of Newbury, had a message for his small daughter: 'Pray bless Popet for me, and tell her I would have writ to her, but that upon mature deliberation I have found it to be uncivile to returne an answer to a Lady in another character than her owne which I am not yet learned enough to do.'

Even after this long lapse of time, one feels a pang of regret that the little girl was deprived of so gay and kind a father.

Lord Strafford, the formidable and much-hated Lord Deputy, was another loving father. 'Wherever they go my prayers shall attend them', he wrote of his daughters, 'those little harmless infants' as he called them, though they were considerably past the age of infancy. 'Nan, they tell me dances prettily,' he said, 'and Arabella is a small practitioner too that way.'

'Nan'—Lady Anne Wentworth, as she would certainly have expected to be called—was eight years old when she wrote in this easy, confidential style to her father:

'Dear Pappa, I told Lady Hariote' (a younger sister), 'that you said as soon as she could speak you would send her a Compliment, and she said "Thank you Pappa". I also told Lady Lucy, and she desires me to give her duty to you, and says she would have writ, but her nurse would not let her. Lady Hariote desires you to bring her a Baby.[1] Please give my duty to Mamma and tell her that Lady Lucy's head is much better ... I am your most affectionate and dutiful daughter,

Anne Wentworth.'

The contrast between the informality of 'Pappa' and 'Mamma', and the formality of 'Lady Hariote' and 'Lady Lucy' when alluding to her small sisters is rather curious. She was evidently a firm-minded but kind elder sister.

There is a pleasing letter written by Charles Stuart (Charles I) to his elder brother Henry, 'Sweet, sweet brother, I will give you everything I have, both my toys and my books and my crossbow. Good brother, love me and I shall ever love and serve you.'

While on the subject of children's letters, here is an engaging one written by a Wentworth boy:

'My cousin Lee has sent me the Dor-mous. But it is dead. The old Dor-mous is very well and in perfect good health.'

Other fond relations, besides parents, come into the picture, giving the impression of a background of staunch family affection.

[1] A doll.

The elder Mrs. Porter, Endymion's mother, was evidently a doting grandmother. She wrote to her son: 'I wish you could see me sitting at the table with my little children, one on either side; in all my life I have not had such an occupation to my content to see them in bed at night and get them up in the morning; the little one is exactly what you were of that age.'

Another loving grandmother—or to be exact, great-grandmother—was Lady Denton. Little Edmund Verney had been living with her. She wrote to his grandfather, Sir Edmund Verney, about him in this tender way: 'My sweet child Mun and your grandson is very wel, and I pray that he may prove as onest and true harted a man to his friends as you have been to your friends.' Later the little boy left her and returned to his father and mother in London. What devoted parents Ralph and Mary Verney were has already been shown. Yet such were the stern educational methods of the day, that Lady Denton, whose years had made her wise and understanding, had to send this impassioned appeal to the three years old 'Mun's' father:

'I hear he is disliked, he is so strange. . . . Son, you did see he was not so, nor is not so to any where he is acquainted, and he must be won by fair means. Let me beg of you and his mother that nobody whip him but Mr. Parry; if you go a violent way with him you will be the first that will rue it, for I verily believe he will receive injury by it . . . indeed Raphe he is to young to be strudgeled in any forcing way. I had intelligence your father was troubled to see him so strange. I pray tell him from me I thought he had more wit to think a child of his age would be acquainted presently. He knows the child was fellow-good enough at my home. I pray show him what I have written about him, and be sure that he is not frightened by no means; he is of a gentle sweet nature, soon corrected.'

Grandparents, aunts and uncles, being less hag-ridden than conscientious parents by an acute sense of responsibility, were probably more agreeable to be with from a child's point of view.

Here is a young, unmarried Verney aunt on her three-year-old nephew:

'I have noe good nuse to send you, but that your boy Jack is growne a sossy child, God be thanked . . . I should be loth to part with Jack's good company, for he is now very fond of mee, and I have a very great love for ye child . . .' Unluckily, as was seen earlier on, her love for her saucy nephew, seems to have made her overlook the fact that he was growing up with crooked legs.

A Verney uncle who was equally affectionate but apparently more observant, reported about his nephew Edward aged two: 'The baby is forward with his teeth; he is very like his mother. He imparts his affection to me, which I am not a little ambitious of. His gummes are so sore that he will suffer none to look into his mouth, but this morning he presented his duty to you as well as hee could do it.'

Godparents were also attentive. 'I entended a cote to my godson this Easter,' Lady Sussex wrote about a Verney child, 'and now I know he is in mourning therefore have sent him a poringer to ete his breakfast in.' Those were the days, of course, when a death in the family meant the most profound mourning for every member of it, old and young, including the servants; beds and rooms were draped in sable, and even the soles of the mourners' shoes blackened.

Another godparent sends: 'My blessing and service to Miss Anne Maria', and a godfather addresses his young god-daughter as 'good sweet hart'.

Apart from these instances of natural affection on the part of adults towards the children closely related to them, or connected to them by baptismal ties, one gets the impression, reading through 17th-century letters, of a greater tenderness generally towards children. The Lord Keeper (Lord Coventry) writing to Lord Strafford, the Lord Deputy, takes it for granted that this great personage will be grieved to hear of the death of his little daughter, all too often as these bereavements occurred in 17th-century families. He says:

'Since I had the Happiness to see your Lordship, I have had a great Loss, in which you have a Part, it having pleased God to take from me at Copthall your little Kinswoman, Mary Savile, which, though it troubles us much, yet in respect of her Mother's great Belly, we have yet found Means to conceal her Death fro her Mother, lest Weakness and Grief meeting together might oppress her. But I bless God, my Daughter hath since been delivered here at Durham-House of a fine Boy, and is now growing well into Strength, so as the Comfort of the one may, I hope, the better digest the grief of the other.'

What an epitome of Stuart family life this is, with its pathetic wastage of child life, and its fecundity.

Children were considered suitable now as subjects for poems. The poet Herrick wrote an epitaph 'Upon a Child that died':

'Here she lies a pretty bud,
Lately made of flesh and blood,
Who as soon fell fast asleep,
As her little eyes did peep,
Give her strewings, but not stir
The earth that lightly covers her.'

He also wrote a grace for a little child:

'Here a little child I stand,
Heaving up my either hand;
Cold as paddocks though they be,
Here I lift them up to thee,
For a benison to fall
On our meat and on us all.'

(It has always puzzled me why the child was apologizing to its Maker for having cold hands.)

Another poet, Matthew Prior, wrote a rhyming letter to a little friend with a long name, Lady Margaret Cavendish-Holles-Harley, which gives an idea of the behaviour expected from a well-brought-up child:

'My noble, lovely little Peggy,
Let this my First Epistle beg ye,
At dawn of morn, and close of eve,
To lift your hands and heart to Heaven,
In double duty say your prayer,
Our Father first, then Notre Père,
And dearest child, along the day,
In everything you do and say,
Obey and please my lord and lady,
So God shall love and angels aid ye,
If to these precepts you attend
No second letter need I send,
And so I rest your constant friend.'

Yet another poet Traherne, wrote of the children's 'angel faces'.

It is puzzling to know what to make of all this—how to draw a just picture of Stuart family life from the caresses and endearments ('my little partridges' a father calls his children) and the severe discipline, and the beatings of children who were still only toddlers. Probably a good idea of life in the average, sober-living upper-class English home of that time is given in an account of his childhood written by one of Lord and Lady Dudley's sons. He says:

'Our childhood past as usual under the Mother's government. We were taught to reverence our father whose care of us consisted chiefly in the gravity and Decorum of his Comportment, Order and Sobriety of Life, whereby no Indecent or Mischievous Impression took place with us from his Example, and when he deposed his temper and condescended to entertain the little credulous Impertinents, it was with an agreeable as well as moral Effect, tending either to instruct or encourage what was good, and to defie the contrary; which is not onely a care but a skill in Parents to doe without Relucting the tender minds of children by the Austeritie of Commands and Threats. The constant reward of Blessing, which was observed as sacred, was a petite Regale in his closet, and allwais came as a Reward of what was encouraged and denied when demerited; whereby it appears that great use may be made of the fondness which disposeth Parents to gratfie Children's little craving appetites by doing it with an adjunct of precept, as a reward of obedience and vertue, such as they are capable of, and at the same time being kind and tender in gratifying them.'

It will be seen from this long-winded account that Lord Dudley's role as a father was mostly confined to looking stately and setting a Good Example, with an occasional 'regale' in his closet when the children were deemed worthy of a reward. This naturally threw most of the responsibility of their upbringing on to Lady Dudley who was a strict but loving mother. She certainly made her children feel her authority (when reproving them she was 'fluent and pungent'), but she was not above amusing them, and at such moments was 'debonair and familiar'. A woman of wit and culture, she guided their reading and instructed them in religious knowledge. The tone of the household in manners and morals was distinctly Puritan. Sunday stories were told on Sunday afternoons, and of course Lady Dudley was a believer in the 'good rail' or rod. But the fact was that children expected to be whipped in those days, and provided that their parents were fundamentally kind and loving, took it quite as a matter of course.

5

What kind of toys did those children play with in their nurseries and in the long galleries—the little Verneys and Norths and Boyles, 'noble, lovely little Peggy', and all the other children who are shown in the portraits of the time, charmingly if deceptively demure in their satin doublets and long skirts and lace collars?

There is nothing much to report about dolls. The great age of the doll had yet to come. An elegant English doll of painted wood is dressed in the fashions of about 1690, and is seated in a walnut chair. There is an allusion in the Lismore letters of a present, sent to England, of 'two little Yrish boys', i.e. dolls dressed in the native costume.

English doll-houses, or Baby-houses, as they were called, need not be considered till the very early 18th century, but Germany, already leading the way in toy making, had produced a beautiful and fully equipped doll's house as early as 1639, and Nuremberg Kitchens, furnished with all the paraphernalia in miniature of a 17th-century kitchen—saucepans of copper and brass, kettles, coffee pots, brooms, mops, warming pans, jelly moulds and so on—were also being made in the 17th century.

Silver toys, exquisite lilliputian models of everyday objects such as tea services, mirrors and fire-dogs were fashionable in Stuart England, but there seems to be a good deal of doubt as to whether these silver toys were really children's toys at all, or were primarily intended for adult collectors.

The old toys that had been popular for countless generations still held pride of place in 17th-century nurseries—tops and drums, battledores and shuttlecock, and balls (not yet made of indiarubber). Locke was in favour of children making their own toys in preference to 'chargeable and curious Toys from the shops', but he conceded that Tops, Gigs and Battledores, etc., which they could not be expected to make could be bought. There is mention of clay monkeys, a little cart with a dog harnessed to it, and toy soldiers of lead, pewter, cardboard and earthenware (these toys all belonged to the Dauphin of France). Charles II, as a small boy had a wooden toy which he took to bed with him; when he reached the age of eight and was given a governor and a tutor, the cherished toy was taken away from him.

That splendid animal the rocking horse, had made its appearance in English nurseries. One archaic looking steed, dating from the middle of the century, had no hind legs; it consisted merely of a head and neck mounted on rockers. But to its young owner it was probably equal in beauty and value to the Godolphin Arabian. Moreover it was provided, in a very practical way, with a pillion seat and pistol holsters.

The old, mysterious games continued. According to an expert on these matters, children's games often reflected the atmosphere or the events of the adult world around them. The refrain of 'London Bridge' gained a new topicality when the bridge was burnt down in the Great Fire.

> 'Queen Anne, Queen Anne, she sits in the sun,
> As fair as the lily, as white as the swan'

is said to allude to James I's blonde Queen. During the Commonwealth a favourite nursery game was 'Questions and Commands' with its oblique ridiculing of monarchy—one child pretending to be a king, the other his servitor. Another game alluded in disrespectful terms to the clergy—'The Parson hath lost his fuddling cap'. In the gay and lax 'climate' of the Restoration, love games—'I love my love with an A', and 'A Flower and a Lady'—became the Nursery vogue. The nursery classic, 'Hide and Seek', touches history during this epoch. It was during a game of 'Hide and Seek', that Charles I's young son, James, Duke of York, who with his brother and sister was in the custody of the Earl of Northumberland at St. James's Palace, was spirited away to his elder sister at The Hague.

As the Stuart nurse rocked the baby's cradle, she crooned to it the traditional lullabies. The older children standing by the waiting gentlewoman's knee as she sat by the fire, listened as though hypnotized to her store of rhymes and jingles, some of which can definitely be traced to this period. The curious tale of the lady who loved a swine appears in an unpublished play of Charles I's time, in this version:

> 'There was a lady lov'd a hogge,
> Ugh, quoth hee!
> Woo't thou lie with me to-night?
> Ugh, quoth hee!'

The following melancholy, and rather sinister rhyme speaks for itself:

> 'As I was going by Charing Cross,
> I saw a black man upon a black horse,
> They told me it was King Charles The First,
> Oh dear, my heart was ready to burst.'

That persistent old favourite, 'Three Blind Mice' appears in a music book dating from 1609 called *Deuteromelia, or the Second Part of Musicke's Melody*. A memory jingle that has helped generations of children to the present day to fix in their minds the erratic numbering of the months, 'Thirty Days hath September', also dates from the first few years of the century if not earlier—as it occurs in a play printed in 1609. The venomous little warning to nursery informers,

> 'Tell tale tit,
> Thy tongue shall be slit,
> And every dog in the town,
> Shall have a little bit'

was extant in 1632. Howell's collection of Proverbs, made in 1659, contains 'Jack Spratt would eat no fat', also 'Rain, Rain go to Spain', so one may imagine a child in a lace cap, its face pressed against the rain-dashed window chanting this strangely reassuring incantation. It would be interesting to know why some jingles like these are still part of nursery lore, while others have fallen into disuse.

Among the spate of 17th-century books written for the

edification of the young, the *Stories of Mother Goose* stand out as a pleasing landmark. This was a translation of a French book by Charles Perrault which was published in Paris in 1696 called *Histoires ou Contes de temps Passé; avec des Moralitez*. For the first time, the ancient nursery tales, Red Riding Hood, Cinderella, The Sleeping Beauty, Blue Beard and Puss in Boots (many of them of very ancient origin) were collected together in book form.

Blessedly free as they were from moral implications, (unless indeed 'Blue Beard' may be taken as a warning against curiosity) it is a pity that they were not translated earlier in the century[1] to act as an antidote to books like the works of James Janeway, an eminent Puritan divine, whose *A Looking Glass for Children* and *A Token for Children* were highly thought of during the later part of the 17th century. Janeway's attitude towards children can best be summed up in his exhortation to parents: 'Your child is never too little to go to hell'. Ruthlessly he catechized the 'pretty dear child' on the lines of 'How dost thou spend thy time—is it in play and idleness with wicked children?' (Yet oddly enough, while breathing out threats of hell fire for juvenile delinquents, Janeway was capable of composing a gentle little prayer for the use of a very young child.) The subject matter of his stories was in the same tone—'Of a Child that was admirably affected with the things of God when he was between two and three years old', 'Of a little Girl that was wrought upon when she was between four and five years old'. 'Of a Notorious Wicked Child that was taken up for Begging and admirably converted.' 'His Holy Life and Joyful Death when he was 9 years old.'

Another writer of 'juveniles' was Thomas White who though evidently a child-lover (he had some comforting remarks to make about guardian angels) also had these unpleasant warnings to deliver to his young readers: 'Sleep not in church, for the Devil rocks the cradle. Be not proud of thy clothes nor curious in putting them on, for the Devil holds the glass. Fight not with thy playfellows for the Devil will be thy second. Play not on the Lord's day, for the Devil will be thy playfellow. Play

---

[1] Some of the tales had appeared in a book published at the Hague 1696–7 bearing the inscription *Contes de ma mère L'Oie*. It may be that their English translation really belongs to the next chapter.

not at cards for they are the Devil's books. They that go to bed
without praying have the Devil for their bed-fellow.'

He also gave some sombre advice about their reading matter: 'When you can read, read no ballads nor foolish books, but
let your reading be the Bible, "The Plain Man's Pathway to
Heaven", and get your father to buy you *The Practice of Piety*,
Mr. Baxter's *Call to the Unconverted*, Allen's *Allarum to the Unconverted* and Fox's *Book of Martyrs*.'

All the same his book was popular; it was in its 3rd edition
by 1703, and embellished by a portrait of Queen Anne. As well
as religious and moral exhortation, it had a pictorial alphabet,
and some easy little riddles and puzzles.

Bunyan also wrote a book for children which combined
religious and elementary educational instruction. In it 'An
Awakened Child' lamented:

> 'When Adam was deceived,
> I was of life bereaved,
> Of late too I perceived
> I was in sin conceived'

and so on for 29 verses. Other verses pointed out gratuitously
that

> 'This bee was an emblem of sin
> Whose sweet unto a many death hath been'

(calculated to alarm those children whose fathers were
apiarists!).

6

Piety was inculcated very early into children in serious
minded families; as soon as they could speak, indeed before they
could speak plain, they took part in the religious exercises of
the household, morning and evening prayers, besides personal
devotions and Bible reading. Locke advised parents to teach
their children to say the Lord's Prayer and the Ten Command-
ments before they were able to read them. The infant, Lettice
Morrison (as related by her chaplain in after years in *The Holy
Life and Death of Lettice Vi-Countess Falkland*) 'came not from her
nurse's arms without some knowledge of the principles of the
Christian religion'. Little Mrs. Lucy Apsley (afterwards Mrs.

Hutchinson) was taken to sermons at the age of four (and sermons were sermons in those days) and was able to give an account of them, for which she was 'caressed' by her elders, with the regrettable result that she took to preaching to her mother's maids. The Apsleys were Puritans, but here is an account (as related by one of her 'rockers') of the death of Charles I's little daughter, Princess Anne: '. . . being minded by those about her to call upon God when the pangs of death were upon her, "I am not able," saith she, "to say my long prayer (meaning the Lord's Prayer), but I will say my short one, 'Lighten mine eyes, O Lord, lest I sleep the sleep of death'. " This done the little lamb gave up the ghost.' These were instances of normal infant piety. It can be imagined the deplorable effect that books of the Janeway type (which were to haunt the nursery bookshelves till the early 19th century) must have had on nervous and over-sensitive children, with their exhortations to 'all ye wicked children who are of the seed of the evil-doers', their emphasis on the Devil rather than on the Good Shepherd.

One reads of a child of six called Nicholas Ferrar who 'in extreme grief rose at midnight cold and frosty', and going down to the garden threw himself upon the ground with a cry of, 'Yes there is, there must be a God, and He no question if I duly and earnestly seek it of him, will teach me not only how to know but how to serve him acceptably'.

One hopes that he was pursued down to the garden by a sensible nurse, who tucked him up in bed with a hot posset, and told him that all God required of children of his age at that hour of night was to go to sleep.

Even more pathetic is the account of that infant prodigy, Richard Evelyn who, when he was dying, aged five, was anxious to know if God would be offended with him if he folded his hands under his bedclothes when he prayed, as he had been told not to throw his bedclothes off, also if he 'should offend God by using his holy name so often calling for ease'. Fortunately he had a devoted father, John Evelyn, to soothe these pitiful fears. But something should certainly have been done to calm down this precocious and morbidly pious child. Not only 'would he of himself select the most pathetic psalms and chapters out of Job to read to his mayde during his sicknesse . . .'

but 'a yeare before he fell sicke, he would desire those who came to see him to pray with him alone in some corner'. As though pathetically anxious to reassure himself that such behaviour in a small child was normal, his proud but disconsolate father added, 'He was all life, all prettiness . . .'

Then there were examples of youthful prigs like 'Mr. John Langham' aged five and a half, who was word perfect in the Assembly's Shorter Catechism and was in the habit of cross-examining his younger sister as to whether she put her trust in God. Another little horror, John Hervey, reproved a relation for insobriety, read Baxter's works with 'much satisfaction', rebuked his younger brothers and sisters for their folly when they showed pleasure in their new clothes, and at the age of two and a half went off to school at his own wish and 'presented himself to his master with a request to be taught'.

Against these extreme cases of infant religiosity, one may set a summary of the simple religious teaching that Lady Falkland gave her eleven children; she told them 'when they loved any-thing that they were to love God more than it, that they must love and honour Him more than their father. He gave them their father, He sent them every good thing, and made it for them; the King was His servant, and He made all kings, and gave them their kingdoms. If they would be good He would give them better things than any they had or saw here.'

Yet even this fond mother who took 'great pleasure' in her children's clothes and recreations, was quick to use the rod, and one at least of her children had what we would consider a mor-bidly sensitive conscience. Lady Falkland was quick-tempered and, being annoyed with the child, declared with an oath that she would whip him. She then relented and 'would have let him off', but he on his knees and with tears in his eyes, begged her not to forswear herself, so she was obliged to whip him. (But one suspects not very hard.)

More in tune with modern ideas is the imaginary dialogue written by Bishop Ken for his little friends the daughters of Lord Weymouth. This reads:

> FAN: 'Dear Molly say, what shall we teach
>   Our Brother when he aims at speech?'

MOLLY:	'Dear Fan, it must be our first task
	To teach him blessing how to ask.'
FAN:	'No, Molly, we our Parents dear
	Next to great God must still revere,
	God ought to tincture first his thoughts,
	As we you know, at first were taught.'
MOLLY:	'We'll make it, Fanny, then our care,
	To teach him first our Saviour's prayer.'
FAN:	'No, Molly, that's too long as yet,
	We'll teach him well by heart to get,
	'Glory to God' and soon he'll try,
	Blessing to ask like you and I.'

If some of the religious and moral teaching given to children at this time seems unduly rigorous, one must remember that the aim of children's upbringing in general was to fit them to take their place worthily either in the adult world, or in the next world as the case might be, rather than to spare them a premature contact with the darker side of life. Before Lord Russell's execution for his part in the Rye House Plot, his wife Rachel took their three children to Newgate to say farewell to him. The girls were nine and seven years old, the boy, fortunately for him too young to realize what was happening, only three. One cannot imagine a modern mother, with even a smattering of child psychology, willingly imposing such an ordeal on her children, far less sharing Lady Russell's melancholy regret later that only the eldest girl seemed 'so insensible' to the tragedy in their family life.

In the Stuart as in the Tudor age, children fell into the hands of the educationalist when they were hardly out of leading reins.

John Evelyn, it is true, recorded in his diary that 'I was not instructed in any rudiments till I was four years of age', but from the way he writes, it is evident that he considers this rather late to begin lessons. (He did not learn any Latin till he was eight.)

'As soon as I was weaned,' Mrs. Lucy Apsley recalled, 'a Frenchwoman was taken to be my dry-nurse, and I was taught to speak French and English together.' By the time she was about seven years old, she was receiving instruction from no less than eight tutors for languages, music, needlework, dancing and writing. But Lucy was a bit of a prodigy (as well as being a considerable prig—'Play among other children I despised' she said). However her mental attainments fell far short of those of Richard Evelyn. At the age of two and a half he was able to 'read perfectly any of the English, Latin, French or Gothic letters, pronouncing the first three languages perfectly, while by the time he had reached the end of his brief span of five and a half years he could read Latin, was making congrous syntax and had a strong passion for Greek'. His father recorded, after his death, that 'the number of verses he could recite was prodigious, he had a wonderful disposition to mathematics, having by heart diverse propositions of Euclid that were read to him in play'.

The average child, however, was not weighed down either with an undue sense of sin or with too much learning. When it was quite small it was given a horn book (Miss Campion aged two years and two months is shown holding one in her portrait in Andrew Tuer's *History of the Horn Book*) and then progressed to reading 'A was an Archer who shot at a Frog' (which was the successor to 'A for Apple')[1] in one of the pictorial alphabets that featured in contemporary primers.

There is a copy in the British Museum of a primer by Edward Coote, Master of the Free School at Bury St. Edmunds, published in 1639, in which he gives rhyming sentences of one syllable, such as 'Ah it is so, he is my foe' (I wonder when the Cat that sat on the Mat of my childhood came into use). In the next chapter, single letters are combined to form words like 'Bat', 'Bad', and 'Bag', and then comes a simple tale which, like most three-letter tales, is a model of ingenuity if not of coherence. After this there were rules of pronunciation, little dialogues about grammar, some elementary arithmetic, writing to be copied, and a catechism of religion. The margin of this well-worn book has the names of some of the children who learnt from it scribbled in it—'Frank ... Elizabeth ... Anne ... Richard'.

---

[1] One authority (Harvey Darton) says that this celebrated line did not appear in print till after 1702—but probably it was in current use before that.

The Stuart child was spared one bugbear of many modern children—spelling. Edward Coote admitted in this book that some variation of spelling was permissible as even learned men were not agreed on the subject. With this state of uncertainty prevailing at 'top level', even the spelling of adults, particularly of women, was wildly individualistic.[1]

The educationalist, Locke, considered that a child should be 'cozened' into learning to read as soon as he could talk, by means of Sir Hugh Platt's alphabetical bricks and some simple little picture book.

The education of little girls was particularly the mother's province, in spite of the number of girls' schools which started up round London during the first half of the century, and which anyhow come outside the scope of this book.

It was the high noon of the art of embroidery in England, and naturally the little girl as soon as she could hold a needle would be set to work to learn the elementary principles of an accomplishment that would occupy so many of her adult hours. Seventeenth-century samplers are rare—many must have been destroyed or lost when houses were burnt down or deserted during the Civil War—but the small girl would certainly start off with the simpler stitches such as cross-stitch, feather stitch and long and short stitch. Mary Boyle as a child made night-caps and laced handkerchiefs as Christmas and New Year presents for her father the Earl of Cork.

Needlework, with French, dancing and the virginals, would be the mainstay of most little girls' educations. In fact, some parents positively discouraged scholarly tastes in their daughters. Lady Tanfield, an unsympathetic mother, whipped her daughter Elizabeth when she considered she was becoming too bookish, though she had allowed her to learn to read at the age of four. (This was in James I's reign.)

Though, as will be seen, the old methods of education persisted, the ice was cracking. Below the surface, new ideas were flowing.

A Moravian bishop called John Komensky, who came to England as a refugee from the Thirty Years War, and who

[1] Lady Sussex, in a letter, wrote: 'Amazes me' as 'a maisis me' and spelt 'Yorkshire'—'Oyskeschei'.

became a friend of Milton's and John Evelyn's, evolved an educational system for small children that in some ways anticipated the methods used by the Froebel Kindergarten. He suggested that young children should be taught to make mats and baskets with strips of coloured paper, also models in clay. His main idea was to follow the light of Nature in training infants. They were, he pointed out, quick to observe and full of curiosity, with a retentive memory for words, but reasoning power or sustained effort could not be expected from them. Therefore the teacher was merely wasting his time trying to force grammar into the infant mind. The best way to teach a child Latin or French, was to allow it to absorb these languages naturally, as it would its mother tongue. His books, published in Germany, soon became extremely popular in England. One of them, *Arbis Pictus or the Visible World in Pictures* had Latin sentences illustrated by a little picture. The book was designed for the child from his first attempts to read up to the age of six or seven, and showed all kinds of natural objects, flowers, birds and animals, as well as some entertaining monsters and fabulous beasts, objects in common use, musical and astronomical instruments, besides children's games and compendiums of the principal religions of the world.

7

I have more than once mentioned John Locke, philosopher, author and physician, whose book, *Some Thoughts Concerning Education* was to revolutionize the whole system of children's upbringing and education. Published as it was, in 1692, it is obvious that its influence on the parents of the 17th century (if one rather arbitrarily ignores the 'Stuart' heading of this chapter which would carry one on to 1714) was negligible compared to its effect on parents throughout the 18th century. Yet to conclude this chapter without some account of it, would be to ignore the profound changes that had taken place in this sphere, as in so many others, during the span of years between the accession of James I to the throne, and (to take a convenient date, and an appropriate one for a book about children) the death of Queen Anne's young son, the Duke of Gloucester in

1700, which diverted the crown of England to the Hanoverian line.

The average Jacobean parent, bolster-stiff in ruff and padded clothes, might have read with approval Locke's dictum: 'Children should be used to submit their Desires and go without their Longings, even from their Cradles.' His wife, encased in her farthingale, would have found nothing surprising or reprehensible in his account of 'a prudent and kind mother of my acquaintance' who 'was forc'd to whip her little Daughter, at her first coming home from Nurse, eight times successively the same morning, before she could master her Stubbornness'.

But what would they have made of this remark: 'Children are to be treated as rational creatures' (there is the authentic note of the coming century there)—the very core of his educational system—or of his insistence, in spite of the story of that 'prudent and kind mother' that whipping should be kept as a last resort, and only used for incorrigible stubbornness.

It is hardly possible for us nowadays to realize what a revolutionary doctrine this was, reversing the established customs not of centuries but of immemorial ages. Solomon's 'Spare the rod, spoil the child' had given generations of parents a notion that child-beating was divinely sanctioned. Anyhow it was the usual punishment for disobedient or culpable inferiors. Wife-beating was a privilege of the medieval husband; daughters who resisted their parent's matrimonial plans, negligent or impertinent servants, idle schoolboys and apprentices were all chastised with the rod, and so of course were small children who transgressed the adult code of behaviour and annoyed their elders. Yet here was Locke, not indeed forbidding beating altogether (even he had not the boldness to advocate such a drastic break with time-hallowed tradition) but stating: 'The usual lazy and short way by chastisement and the Rod is the most unfit of any to be us'd in Education, because it tends to both these Mischiefs', i.e. it makes the child unable to 'resist the Importunity of present Pleasure or Pain' on the one hand, and is liable to 'curb and abase' the child's natural high spirits, which Locke insisted should be kept 'easy, active and free', though disciplined. To reconcile 'these seeming contradictions' lies, in his opinion 'the true secret of Education'.

Locke's ideal was that of a 'sound mind in a sound body', and all his advice to parents and tutors (for he seems to have taken little or no interest in the education of girls) led in that direction. Many of his remarks are in line with modern ideas on child-welfare and upbringing.

'The little, or almost insensible impression on our tender Infancies have very important and lasting consequences.' Children's lives should, he held, be made as 'pleasant and agreeable to them as may be'. 'Innocent Folly, Playing, and Childish Actions are to be left perfectly free and unrestrained.' 'Inadvertancy, Carelessness and Gaiety is the Character of that age.' 'If these Faults of their Age,' he says elsewhere, 'rather than of the Children themselves, were as they should be left only to Time and Imitation and riper years to cure, Children would escape a great deal of misapply'd and useless Correction.' Curiosity in the young should not be suppressed. Children should be trained, not by a number of rules but by practice and example. Nor should they be 'much tormented about Punctilios or Niceties of Breeding'. 'Children love Liberty and therefore they should be brought to do the things that are for them, without any feeling of Restraint laid upon them', for instance they should be 'taught to read without perceiving it to be anything but a Sport'.

Though the idea of God as the Supreme Being, loving but inscrutable, should be early implanted in the child's mind, Locke advised that the Bible stories that were read to them should be chosen with discrimination, and that the child's 'tender mind' should be guarded against 'all Impressions and Notions of Spirits and Goblins, or any fearful Apprehensions of the Dark' (or of Dr. Janeway's warnings of hell, one presumes!) for the effect of a fright on a young child could leave an indelible impression.

Locke believed in as little physic as possible for young children and plenty of sleep. There is common sense as well as a real tenderness for the young in his injunction to adults to wake the child gently: 'They being forc'd from their Sleep, how gently so ever you do it, is Pain enough to them and care should be taken not to add any other Uneasiness to it, especially such as may terrify them.'

He was firmly of the opinion that 'most Children's Constitutions are either spoil'd or at least harm'd by Cockering and Tenderness', and remembering how poor little Richard Evelyn was almost stifled by his female attendants, he was probably right. But in his zeal to inculcate into the child a Spartan indifference to discomfort and fear, the bachelor philosopher went rather far. He realized that his advice that children's shoes should be purposely made so thin that they would leak, would not appeal to mothers and nurses; (even if, as he declared it would, among other benefits, prevent corns) 'Here I fear I shall have the Mother and Maid too against me', he said uneasily and 'How fond Mothers are like to receive this Doctrine is not hard to foresee. "What can it be less than to murder their tender Babes, to use them thus? What! put their Feet in Cold Water in Frost and Snow, when all one can do is little enough to keep them warm." '

I must admit that this would be my own reaction, and that I would prefer bare feet to leaky shoes.

As a proof of the benefits of cold water baths in all weather, Locke quoted the example of Seneca, adding, 'There are at this Day, Ladies in the Highlands of Scotland who use this Discipline to the Children in the midst of Winter, and find that cold water does them no Harm even when there is Ice in it'. One wonders how many shivering little Southerners were plunged into icy water by their enthusiastic mothers in imitation of those hardy Highland families.

Because so many of his views seem to us to be based on a wise and loving understanding of child nature, it is a shock to find Locke advocating the establishment of 'working schools for pauper children of from three years upwards, where they would be fed on a diet of bread to which may be added without any trouble in cold weather a little warm water', a regimen which suggests some horrible Dickensian workhouse.

In fairness to Locke, it should be added that, as he rightly remarked, bread and water in more meagre quantities, was all that they would be getting at home. All the same that an obviously benevolent man could make such a proposal does reveal a lack of social conscience that grates on modern sensibilities.

There are a number of glimpses of life in the 17th-century home here and there in his book. He condemns feather or 'down beds', with the fearful warning that 'being bury'd every night in Feathers melts and dissolves the Body, is often the cause of Weakness and Forerunner of an early Grave'.

He urged parents to have their children with them as much as possible, and not to leave them to the care of servants who may be 'clownish or vicious', frighten them with tales of 'Rawhead' and 'Bloody Bones', and counteract the parental discipline by indulging them with 'strong drinks, Wine, Fruit, Playthings and other such matters'. (One recalls that those were the days when a man such as John Evelyn's father kept 116 servants in livery.) At the same time civility to servants, 'a gentle, courteous, affable Carriage towards the lower ranks of Men' was to be insisted on from children.

This was several hundreds of years before the word 'snobbishness' had come into being. Locke's ingenious plan for instilling a desire to learn into a small child, is typical of the age (as will be seen, one of its disadvantages was that it would not work with an elder son). He recalls a case where the adults said in the hearing of a 'younger son, a child in coats', 'that it was the Privilege and advantage of Heirs and elder Brothers to be scholars; and that this made them fine Gentlemen, and beloved by everybody; and that for younger Brothers, 'twas a Favour to admit them to Breeding; to be taught to read and write was more than came to their share; they might be ignorant Bumpkins and Clowns if they pleased'. After which awful pronouncement, the little boy, who evidently had a well developed social sense though still in petticoats, came to his mother to learn 'and would not let his Maid be quiet till she heard him his lesson'. (One wonders what would have happened if some child had called his elders' bluff and elected to remain an 'ignorant Bumpkin and Clown'.)

Locke gives an example of how to cure a child of timidity. 'Your child shrieks and runs away at the sight of a Frog; let another catch it and lay it down at a good Distance from him; at first accustom him to look upon it . . . then to come nearer to it, and see it leap without Emotion; then to touch it lightly, when it is held fast in another's Hand; and so on till he can

come to handle it as confidently as a Butterfly or a Sparrow.'
This conjures up for me a picture of a 17th-century knot garden
—its beds marked out in fantastic patterns with low hedges
of sweet briar, thrift and marjoram—there are clipped yew
hedges, antique statues and a lily pond. I have a feeling of
compassion for the frog that was made the object of this well-
intentioned experiment, if it is true, as I have been told (or read
somewhere) that a frog, being a cold-blooded creature, feels as
though it were scorched when held by a human being. Alas! for
that frog being 'handled as confidently as a Butterfly' (alas, for
the fragile butterfly too!) in that hot little 17th-century hand.

Kindness to animals was part of Locke's educational system.
Children should be taught, he said, 'an abhorrence of killing or
tormenting any living creature; and be taught not to spoil or
destroy anything, unless it be for the Preservation or Advantage
of some other that is nobler', which, in practice might pose
some tricky problems when one comes to think of it.

Locke, as I have said, seldom mentioned little girls. He lost
his own mother when he was young, and had no sister or wife.
His courage seems to have faltered when it came to advising on
the upbringing of the female young. Yet he had observed them
thoughtfully: 'I have seen little girls exercise whole Hours together and take abundance of Pains to be expert at Dibstones,
as they call them', noting, with perhaps a twinge of apprehension, the single-mindedness of the sex in pursuit of its objective.

He ventures however into feminine preserves when he rebukes
mothers for encouraging vanity and a love of clothes in their
children. 'When the little girl is trick'd up in her new gown and
commode, how can her mother do less than teach her to admire
herself, by calling her, *her little Queen* and *her Princess.*'

This little description has exactly the opposite effect on me
that Mr. Locke intended. I should like to be able to gaze into
a very old mirror, and see reflected in its misty surface, that
proud mother bending over her little daughter, starry-eyed
with feminine vanity in her new finery!

IV

Eighteenth Century

I

HE French have a useful expression, *'embarras de richesse'* which came into my mind when I was planning this part. I must admit that I have been embarrassed at the richness that confronted me—not only at the wealth of material available in contemporary diaries, letters and memoirs, (there seemed a danger that one might browse away on these for the rest of one's life) but by the vast panorama that the words '18th century' suggest.

Here was a century that began as the age of reason and ended as the age of sensibility; that witnessed the proverbial death of Queen Anne, and the rise to power of Napoleon Bonaparte; it was mirrored in the paintings of Hogarth and in the early novels of Jane Austen, produced Lord Chesterfield and John Wesley, the monumental buildings of Vanburgh and the fantasies of Strawberry Hill. As in a whirling kaleidoscope one sees a lady with a high lace cap on her head sipping chocolate from a porcelain cup against a background of Chinese wallpaper; the tumbril carries Marie Antoinette to the guillotine; chairmen amble with a sedan chair along the narrow, badly-lit streets; Blanchard and Jeffries make the first aerial crossing of the English Channel in a balloon; one sees the 'rural neatness and elegance' of the countryside so much admired by foreigners, and the ominous shadows of Blake's 'dark, satanic mills'. Ladies fall into 'strong hysterics' at the slightest alarm; they bear the unrelieved pangs of childbirth with spartan fortitude. A witch dies at the stake, the last victim of an age-long delusion; Hargreaves, inventor of the 'Spinning Jenny', flees from the infuriated spinners who, fearful of unemployment, break up his machines.

But fortunately it is not our concern to try and disentangle this cat's cradle of events, beliefs, ideas, tastes and tendencies, or only in so much as they affect the lives of the young children who were born into the century. Like the muted crash and thunder of great ocean waves, these things echoed in the nursery cave where the children lived a self-contained existence that altered perhaps as little as any other aspect of the 18th century.

The children's outward appearance certainly changed considerably. The little boy of the early 1700's in a full-skirted coat, his young sister with her buckram bodice, flowered petticoat and high pleated cap, were still miniature adults in appearance —for by no stretch of the imagination could that style of costume be considered suitable for children—with all that this implied of mental and physical restriction. At the other end of the scale, the children of the 1790's were dressed with a graceful simplicity that must have given them almost as much freedom of movement as the modern child. The small boys in their short nankeen trousers, buttoned on to a blouse that was open at the neck with a frilled collar, were as sensibly and comfortably dressed as a modern child in jeans. The basic fashion for little girls were as simple; a short-sleeved dress, usually of white muslin, cut low at the neck and tied round the waist with a coloured sash. The chief disadvantage of this style from the wearer's point of view, was the ankle length skirt, which must have led to many mishaps of the kind immortalized by Beatrix Potter, when Tom Kitten's sisters, dressed up in clean white frocks for their mother's tea party, tripped and fell on their noses on the garden path.[1]

[1] With regard to the materials worn by children, as early as 1719 in the 'Just complaint of the poor Weavers' etc., the woollen weavers were lamenting that those who would formerly have worn 'their women's stuffs made at Norwich and London or in Cantaloons and crepes etc., are now clothed in Callicoe and printed Linnen; moved to it as well, for the cheapness as the

These fashions for children, surely the most attractive ever devised, merely copied those of the grown-ups; it was just fortunate for the children that they happened to emancipate them from the stiff corsets that had held young bodies in thrall for centuries.[1] The beneficial results of this freedom can be seen, I think, in the contrasting expressions of children in portraits or 'conversation pieces' of the first half of the century, and of the children portrayed by Gainsborough, Romney and Hoppner and Reynolds (though perhaps this is allowing too much credit to the clothes and not enough to these painters).

Yet in spite of these sartorial changes, which may have gone deeper than mere appearance, nursery life in many respects gives the impression of having remained static during the century, or of having altered so little that I abandoned my first idea of dividing this chapter into two parts as impractical. I need hardly say, though, that changes were taking place all the time. It was though the tide was rising and the rippling veil of water, forerunner of the great waves outside, was flowing into the cave. Apart from the inevitable effect on childhood of the social and economic changes that were taking place in the outside world, at least two events of far-reaching significance in the limited sphere of the nursery, took place during this century. In 1744, John Newbery published, *A Little Pretty Pocket Book intended for the Instruction and Amusement of Little Master Tommy and Pretty Miss Polly*—the first trickle in the huge spate of juvenile literature produced as a commercial proposition—while in 1762, Jean Jacques Rousseau brought out a book called *Emile*, which has been called 'The Child's Charter'.

Lightness of the cloth and gaiety of the colours'. This applied not only to 'all the mean People' such as servant maids, but to 'the children universally, whose Frocks and Coats were all either made of Tannies work'd at Coventry or of strip'd thin stuffs made in Spittlefields', but who now appear in 'Printed Callicoes and Printed Linnens,' and not only the poorer children, but also 'the better sort'. This information was kindly supplied to me by Mrs. Leask. (A. R. Longfield.)

[1] It might be argued that it was the other way round, as according to James Laver, in *English Costume in the 18th Century*, there was already a tendency to simplicity in children's clothes as early as 1760.

2

One of the ways in which, as a child, I alleviated my boredom in church during the sermon, was by reading the service for the churching of women. The words, 'the great pain and peril of childbirth' never failed to give me a feeling of fascinated horror, hinting as they did at a frightful ordeal which, in the normal course of nature awaited me and other girl-children. This description of childbirth is now happily obsolete, thanks to the immense advances made by medical science in this sphere. Nowadays, though some agitation is permissible and becoming in an expectant father awaiting the birth of his first child, modern husbands have no need for serious alarm. Indeed they may even feel that some of the sympathy that would formerly have gone to their wives might be diverted to their plight, left, in a servantless age to 'do' for themselves (unless they have been able to take refuge with mother or mother-in-law). But even in the 18th century when domestic help was plentiful and cheap, husbands whose wives were 'in the straw' (in the elegant phrase of the time) had their difficulties. These are plainly set forth in a rather harassed letter written by Ralph Palmer, a connection of the Verney family, to his namesake Ralph Verney in August 1716: 'I need your kind congratulations on the birth of my son. . . . I bless God we are here in a very Hopeful way, this being my wife's ninth day, and I hope she will be able to mistress it in the family [i.e. household] in a little time which needs it pretty much. I think there never was such servants. . . .' He goes on to complain that he cannot 'meet with a footman that can keep himself sober above an hour in the morning', while the rest of his domestics would not 'doe every individual thing they know it their duty to do' unless he spoke to them personally about it.

Incidentally these complaints about servants, which occur frequently in 18th-century letters and diaries, are a sign of the new age, and of a new, less stable relationship between employers and their domestic servants. One correspondent in the Verney letters, complains that $2\frac{3}{4}$ years is 'an age to keep a servant in these parts'. The feudal spirit was wearing thin.

(Poor Ralph Palmer, there is pathos in that, 'We are here in a very Hopeful way' when one knows that he and his wife had already lost four little girls in infancy. Eight years previously when his wife was expecting a child, he had expressed the very natural hope that 'we may add a little to peopling this world as well as increasing the Kingdom of Heaven with little Angels'. But though the daughter, Cornelia, who had been born subsequently was a 'lusty, brown-haired girl big enough to have been born a boy', alas! she, too, was destined to become a little angel, and died of convulsions during teething when she was hardly more than a year old.)

A confinement was indeed an anxious time for all concerned. Ignorance of the importance of pre- and ante-natal care, and the rudimentary obstetrical methods of the time often made childbirth a deadly business for both mother and child. This sad little story was all too common: 'Pray tell your father that prety Lady Boucher dyed this day senight . . . her boy live to be Xtined but they are both buried together' (January 1700). On another occasion a nurse's carelessness was blamed for a disaster. 'I hear Sir Richard Hoare's son's wife is died in her Lyeing-inn, by her nurse's raping [wrapping] a quilt about her that was not aired, at her first getting up, which killed her in half an hour' (Lady Cave to Lord Fermanagh—1705). One suspects that something more lethal than a damp quilt caused the unfortunate lady's death.

At other times, though the mother survived, the long months of hopeful waiting ended in disappointment. Sometimes the doctor's incompetence was blamed: 'Lady Cardigan is brought to bed of a dead child. Dr. Shadwell gave her a vomit six weeks before her time . . . my lord threatens to stab him when he meets him' (Catherine Verney to her husband, 1709). But more often a spirit of melancholy resignation prevails. A sister-in-law is 'truly concerned for your loss and is heartily sorry for the poor little baby', when her brother's wife, Catherine Verney is delivered of a dead child. An aunt reports to Catherine's father-in-law, Lord Fermanagh, that she has had a good night, 'all the people about her think she will live and I hope will bring you many grandsons'. 'If at first you don't succeed, try,

try, again' was certainly the motto of these poor young mothers.[1]

It was in no mood of bravado or self-pity but real fortitude and faith that made Mary Lovett (another Verney by birth) write before the birth of her first child in 1704: 'I rely wholly on God to bring me through what he has appointed for me which I heartily pray I may submit to as I ought.' She was one of the fortunate ones. Her husband was able to write triumphantly to Lord Fermanagh: 'I thank God this afternoon about four o'clock your Daughter made you a grandfather, but itt is a girl . . . we are all very happy.'

To go for a moment to the end of the century, the same story of dangerous and difficult confinements occurs. Lord Sheffield in the 90's writes to his daughter Maria-Josepha about her step-mother: 'The most Precious woman is said to be safe. . . . The Doctor and all the Women declare they never observed such an Instance of fortitude and Patience in all their experience or a more painful one. . . . The mother and son could not both be saved. I am perfectly satisfied that the dear Woman is safe.' An aunt comments approvingly: 'That the good aimable woman is safe seems completely to comfort my Brother for the Death of the Babe, and he thinks of nothing but her Patience and her not being disappointed. I love him for it, as it is often the contrary in Men.'

It cannot often have been 'the contrary' in the men folk of the Verney clan, who seem to have made the most exemplary husbands and fathers. It is quite a pleasure to meet the Verney family and their connections again in this century. Like their 17th-century predecessors they are full of domestic affection and gossip. Not only the women but also the men write to one another exchanging news of their 'little fry' or 'olive branches'. Here is Ralph Palmer again, writing to Ralph Verney whose wife has given birth to a daughter. He hopes that 'your Deare Precious is past all danger by this time and all her Little Rogues well about her.'

Sir Thomas Cave, who married another of Lord Fermanagh's

[1] Dr. Buchan (*Domestic Medicine*, 1783) says: 'The methods taken to impress the minds of women with the apprehensions of the great *pain* and *peril* of childbirth are very hurtful'—thus anticipating the modern exponents of 'Natural Childbirth'.

daughters, Margaret, was jocular about his trials as an expectant father. His nights were disturbed, he told his father-in-law, 'in the night the Little Bratt kicks, my wife coughs and I leave it to you to guess how I am put to it to quiett both ... and my Lord amidst other sufferings comes the loss of many of my hounds.'

Lord Fermanagh warns this daughter Lady Cave, not to get up too soon as she did after the birth of her first child, 'therefore do not do so now, I intreate you, lest you take cold, which may bring a cough and then to Asses milk againe'.

For some reason that I am unable to explain, Lady Mary Wortley Montagu, whose husband was Ambassador to Turkey in the early 18th century, found that childbirth was 'not half so mortifying here as in England, there being as much difference as there is between a little cold in the head and the consumptive cough so common London'. No Turkish lady, she said, kept to their houses for a month after lying-in (which was evidently the usual convalescence time in England).

Lady Mary herself only had two children, a very small family for those days, and in later years regarded with some concern her daughter Lady Bute's rapidly increasing brood. 'I have already wished you joy of your new daughter,' she wrote to her in 1749. 'I don't know whether I shall make my court to you in saying it, but I cannot help thinking that your family is numerous enough and that the education and disposal of four girls is employment for a whole life.' (Lady Bute in spite of this maternal advice continued to breed.) In this, as in other ways, Lady Mary was decidedly modern in her outlook. In general, throughout the greater part of the 18th century, the birth of every child, in spite of the dangers attendant on the actual confinement, and the terribly precarious hold on life of young children (Gibbon estimated that one third of English babies would probably die before the age of five[1]) was a matter for unqualified rejoicing. Relations sent presents—cradles, Indian quilts, silk pillows and baskets, as well as blessings and wishes for 'a good houre'.

[1] Buchan in *Domestic Medicine* stated that 'almost one half of the human race perished in infancy by improper management or neglect'. Rousseau in *Emile* was equally pessimistic. 'Of all the children who are born scarcely one half reach adolescence, and it is very likely your pupil will not live to be a man.'

Captain Verney Lloyd wishes Ralph Verney 'with all my harte all joy of my new She-Relation, and that you may increase both male and female'. When a Mrs. Breton was delivered of a son and heir, not only did her family rejoice, but 'all the Bells in that country were rung'.

It is only towards the end of the century that one detects a different attitude. It is reported in the Wynne Diaries that Lady Westmoreland 'is again breeding which greatly vexes her for she hates children and is every instant pretending to be in hysterics'. (This entry is actually dated from 1801, a year after the close of this century.) How this would have shocked the Verneys!

The greater the social consequence of the family, the more a boy was valued. 'I am never in pain for any of that sex', as Lady Mary Wortley Montague put it when writing to congratulate her daughter on the birth of a son. 'God bless Franscis, and give him sonnes and no daughters,' was the Duchess of Buccleuch's bluntly expressed wish in 1720. There was an economic as well as dynastic reason for this. Married daughters were a financial loss, for when they left the family, their marriage portions left with them, while daughters who remained unwed had to be supported permanently by their relations, or found a job in the family circle as a waiting gentlewoman. Parents of daughters had to endure tiresome letters of this kind: 'Many thanks for the good news . . . and the little stranger's name, and I hope it will not be long before I wish you joy of another little stranger of another sort. Your poore old aunt and humble servant.'

All the same, new 'She-Relations' were made welcome too, with certain qualifications, certainly in the warm-hearted Verney family. 'I hope you'll have a boy but if a girl it's welcome,' Lord Fermanagh told his daughter Mrs. Lovett. Jovial Sir Thomas Cave, invited to be godfather to Ralph Verney's child, was facetious. He was 'glad to find my Sister safely delivered, tho' of a sort less esteemed in this vain world, and there's no good to be done without 'Em. I am proud of the favour you doe me in asking my care and tuition for the pretty lady.'

It must have been a great blow to Lord Fermanagh when his son's young widow gave birth to a daughter instead of the

longed-for heir, but he did not allow any sign of disappointment to escape him; 'Yesterday my daughter Verney was
brought to bed of a sweet, pretty girl,' he announced, adding
sadly, 'I wish the dear Father had been alive to see it.'

Little girls were cherished for their 'prettiness', potential
if not actual. 'I wish you joy of the pretty little one in Southampton Street tho' I had rather it had been the other sex'
alluded to Lady Fermanagh's newly born daughter. 'Miss
Penn' (less than a month old) is rather touchingly described as
having 'Promises of Beauty'.

The Reverend Potts Davies in a gossiping letter says: 'I suppose, my Lord, you have heard of the joy in Mr. Lovett's
family on the addition of a very pretty little lady, very like the
smiling Father; the Lady Mother is in a Brave way, and tho'
there are many rooms in Liscombe House, it is very promising
that they will be every one well filled.' Girl children thus, at
the worst, were evidence of that fecundity that was so much
esteemed.

Intimate glimpses into the routine of childbirth and nursery
life are to be found in the letters written by Mrs. Boscawen in
the 1740's and 50's, to her distinguished naval husband. Their
married life was one continual 'hail and farewell', and Mrs.
Boscawen, a fervently devoted wife and mother, consoled herself and her husband for their long separations, by projecting
on to paper, a magic lantern picture as it were, of the family life
of which he was deprived. She judged, no doubt rightly, that
no detail about herself and the children, would be too trivial
to interest him. The result is that one gets an extraordinary
vivid picture of the Boscawen nursery.

Mrs. Boscawen is waiting to 'increase the number' of the
Admiral's children. A false alarm made her summon Mr. Chap-
man, the doctor, but his assistance was not required after all,
and Mrs. Boscawen remained in a state of uncomfortable
suspense 'much as I was with the boy, when (if you recollect) I
sent for both the nurses in a vast hurry and went three weeks'.
For some reason or other, for she was a woman of considerable
courage and spirit, and seems to have been very healthy herself
and to have produced healthy children (all of whom she
successfully reared), she was 'miserably terrified with the

thoughts of it—such horrors and tremblings as were indeed dreadful'. (One compares this with the modern methods of relaxation and controlled breathing.) Probably it was anxiety on her husband's behalf, not her own, that was the trouble, for when she heard that the Admiral had distinguished himself and been wounded at the battle of Finnesterre[1] 'I think nothing of it [her own fears]. I think of you and you only.'

Another time Mrs. Boscawen contemplated springing a little surprise on her husband. 'I believe it is pretty certain I am not with child. When I thought I was, I longed to refrain from telling you, both because 'twould have been an agreeable surprise to you to have found a little Willy-boy sucking at the breast, with blue eyes and a fair face.'

Betsy Fremantle was another naval wife who was seldom able to count on the support of her husband's presence during her numerous confinements. These events were not made any easier by the lack of the various swift means of communication that we take for granted. A telephone for instance would have been handy for Betsy when to her surprise and alarm, she was taken ill in the middle of the night 'as I did not expect to be brought to bed till the end of the month, and my nurse was not to come till the twentieth'. The doctor was hurriedly summoned; meanwhile the Cook acted as head nurse. One can almost see the scene in the house at Swanbourne—the running up and down stairs and lighting of candles, the heating of water in the big kettle that hung from a chain over the kitchen fire, Cook in her print dress and mob cap bending over the bed with its chintz curtains, the man servant pulling on his clothes and hastening down to the village for the doctor. The result was 'a nice little girl but owing to her being born before her time is very delicate and small'.

On another occasion the midwife 'arrived just in time'; later Betsy Fremantle recorded in her diary, 'The Nurse is a dreadful bore, I only got up to tea on Saturday. I am however as well as possible and the baby thrives nicely.' Except for the use of the word 'thrives' this might have been written today[2].

[1] He was promoted Rear Admiral of the Blue before the battle.
[2] Incidentally any woman could become a midwife by buying a licence from the Ordinary for 18/4d.

Ladies who travelled when they were near their 'good hour' did so at their own risk in a period when journeys were slow and there was no quick way of summoning medical aid. 'Nov. 7th, 1791, Dover. Mrs. Maynard was brought to bed last night of a fine girl at 9 o'clock in the Packet Boat.' More deplorable still was the plight of poor Lady Ongley who, through some miscalculation or mischance, was taken ill on the road 'went a stage in the gig, all the time in labour pains, and was brought to bed at a miserable Inn at Farringdon of a dead child. She had nothing with her and it must have been a wretched business.' (So Betsy Fremantle relates.)

The first thing that a Highland nurse did when the baby was born was to give it a spoonful of gin, a substitute for the traditional mixed spoonful of earth and whisky. The baby was then dipped in cold water, whatever the time of year, as though to remind it that it was a member of a hardy and vigorous race, and wrapped in a woman's shift if it was a male, or in a man's shirt if it was a female.[1] Some propitiatory rite seems to be indicated here.

'It is strange,' Dr. Buchan commented, 'how people came to think that the first thing given to a child should be drugs.' He went on to condemn the practice of cramming the new-born infant with syrups and oils, etc. Nor did it need wine or cordials.

Innumerable superstitions still clustered round the new-born infant, but as the century, which prided itself on being the age of reason, wore on, these must have become 'exploded' among the more educated and sophisticated people, lingering on among nurses and servants, and in remote country districts. To give only a few—when the baby left its mother's room for the first time, it must be taken upstairs or it would never rise in the world. If there was no upper storey, fate could be cheated by climbing on a chair with the baby in one's arms. A cradle made from ash or elder wood was lucky. It was unlucky to mention the baby's name, or to take it out of the house before the christening. This last precaution was, in its turn, bad luck on the baby who was probably being kept in an overheated room with tightly closed windows. 'When the air comes through a hole, Take care of your soul' was a favourite saying.

[1] *The Domestic Life of Scotland in the 18th Century*, Marjorie Plant.

The christening usually took place about a month after the child's birth. An early Georgian print shows the ceremony being held in the mother's bedroom. She is sitting up in an armchair. A table covered with a cloth has a bowl for the baptismal water on it. Before the christening, the mother received visits of congratulation from her friends and entertained them with caudle, a drink made of oatmeal, sugar, and white wine or ale which was thought to be very beneficial after a confinement. Sir Thomas Cave told his father-in-law, Lord Fermanagh, that he was 'provided for caudle better than expected, for his Grace the Duke of Mountague has sent his gentn. with nine doz of fine French White wine, as a present against my wife's lying in'. A handsome gift which must have been quite a support to Sir Thomas.

After the actual christening there were social junketings; family and friends gathered together in their best clothes (imagine the flowered and corded silks, and taffetas, the paduasoys and satins, and the lovely 18th-century colours— cherry and scarlet, golden-olive and lilac!) to drink the 'new-made Christian's' health. It is on record that one christening party did this so thoroughly that the male guests were 'all very merry' while the ladies (this was in Scotland) were charmingly described as being 'very blythe'! The usual number of god-parents were three, two of the same sex as the baby and one of the opposite sex, but the modern custom of having more than three is found not to be modern at all, as this extract from a late 18th-century letter shows: 'My lady has expressed her wish that I should be one of the Sponsers for her Babe be it male or Female, as it is no uncommon thing to have four.' Families being the size they were, one would have expected a more sparing use of godparents.

The 'gossips', or as they were called later in the century, 'the sponsors' gave the baby presents of apostle spoons, bowls and mugs, and in the earlier part of the century at any rate, the nurse also expected a present. Archbishop Tillotson in a sermon deplored the habit of giving expensive gifts to nurses at christenings.

Sir Thomas Cave, invited to be godfather to a baby daughter of the Ralph Verneys wrote, jocular as usual, to Ralph, 'Pray

kiss the gossips my Partners as much as if I was present to do
it . . . and dont otherwise omit my respects to the Lady in the
Straw'.

Jean Jacques Rousseau in *Emile*, the book in which he
expounded with revolutionary fervour his beliefs on education
(taking the word in its widest sense) was strongly in favour of
breast-feeding, and predicted that the reluctance of women to
suckle their children would lead to a revulsion against motherhood itself and eventually to a Europe reduced to the condition
of a desert and a 'home of wild beasts'. (Incidentally his own
children were consigned to the Foundlings.) He conceded that
it might be better for the child to 'suck the breast of a healthy
nurse rather that of a petted mother', adding, however, that
'there is no substitute for mother's love'. The influence of *Emile*
undoubtedly made itself felt in England as well as in France
(where we are told fashionable young women took enthusi-
astically to feeding their young without leading the regular life
necessary to a nursing mother, often with disastrous results to
the babies), but breast-feeding had its English advocates before
Rousseau. Dr. William Cadogan, a pioneer in child welfare, in
his 'Essay on Nursing' 1747, urged the importance of breast-
feeding—in fact he considered that the children of the poor had
a better chance of survival than those from well-to-do families
because their mothers suckled them—but advised that babies
should only be fed two to three times in twenty-four hours.

By the end of the century, whether as a result of the admonitions of Rousseau, or of Dr. Cadogan and others it seems to
have been taken quite as a matter of course that a mother
should feed her infant.[1] Betsy Fremantle went to a ball but
'could not dance being a nurse'. It was five o'clock and just
daylight when she got home. 'Charles [the baby] had been
good.' A month later came the entry: 'I weaned Charles and
took some physic that made me miserably sick. I hope the poor
child will not mind.'

[1] 'The mother's milk, or that of a healthy nurse is unquestionably the
best food for an infant' was Dr. Buchan's opinion, 'children may seem to
thrive without the breast,' he said, but 'when teething, the small-pox and
other diseases incident to childhood, come on, they generally perish'. He

If the mother was unable or unwilling to nurse her child, a wet-nurse was often procured, but this was admitted to be a risk, partly because the idea that the child might imbibe the nurse's vices still prevailed (Archbishop Tillotson in a sermon warned mothers against the dangers of 'strange milk') and also for the more practical reason that these wet-nurses were sometimes gin addicts, and might even give the baby sips of gin to keep it quiet. The difficulty of finding a suitable nurse was described plaintively by a Mrs. Scott who was the wife of the British Envoy in Hanover. 'I am more perplexed than ever about a nurse' she wrote, 'I found, as I thought, by good chance, a young woman whose child died at three months old. She was recommended here by a physician, a very honest man . . . no sooner was it known, than I am told twenty frightful things of her . . . as that her child died of convulsions occasionned by her wicked temper; that her husband and she beat one another; and that she is of so devilish a nature that when alone she takes fainting fits upon remembering past things, and to crown all, they say she is with child! What think you of this for a nurse?' The answer in a modern phrase is 'Not much!'

The babies who were fed naturally were the lucky ones. The alternative was pap—a mixture of bread and milk or rice flour and arrowroot mixed with milk (asses milk which was very highly esteemed, was considered more digestible than cow's milk). This was given to the baby through a 'bubbly pot' made of horn or earthenware, and often fitted inside with a piece of sponge to regulate the flow of milk. A fine repository for germs. No wonder that thrush was a common complaint among babies.

Dr. Cadogan recommended—if breast-feeding was impossible—a diet for infants of manna and the pulp of coffee dissolved in a thin broth, also fruit and vegetables. He added the

was not prepared however to lay down any hard and fast rule on the subject. 'Women of delicate constitutions subject to hysteric fits or other nervous affections make very bad nurses,' he said, also (rather alarmingly!) '. . . children who are suckled by delicate women either die young or continue weak and sickly all their lives'. In fact he was against 'a delicate female, brought up within doors, an utter stranger to exercise and open air who lives on tea and other slops' venturing into motherhood at all. Her child 'will hardly be fit to live'.

discouraging statement that ninety out of a hundred babies fed by hand died miserably. This pessimistic statistic seems more credible when one reads another physician, Sir William Fordyce's indictment of contemporary methods of infant-feeding; He wrote in 1773, 'They are fed on meat before they have got their teeth, and what is, if possible still worse, on biscuits not fermented, or buttered rolls, or tough muffins floated in oiled butter ...'

Dr. Buchan was in favour of milk for the first three or four months, and then a supplementary diet of 'water-pap, milk-pottage, weak broth with bread in it'.

In 1707, Madame de Maintenon expressed approval of the English system of releasing babies after three months from their swaddling bands, which she commended both for comfort and cleanliness. Nearly fifty years later Rousseau was lashing out at the pernicious swaddling habit, exposing the fallacy of the argument that unswaddled infants would assume faulty positions and make movements that would injure the proper development of their limbs '. . . we have not yet decided to swaddle our kittens and puppies' he went on sarcastically, 'are they any the worse for it?' The custom died hard in France—a French baby's layette at the end of the century included a dozen swaddling bands—and it is evident that English babies were released or partially released from their bonds long before their fellow-babies across the Channel. They were still wrapped in linen or cotton bandages, but the extreme mummified type of swaddling was no longer the fashion. The evidence on this point is somewhat contradictory. Mrs. Boscawen in 1756 tells of a dream in which she tried to dress 'a small but very fine bantling in swaddling clothes', but J. J. Rousseau writes in *Emile* (published in 1762) of 'the example of England, where the senseless and barbarous swaddling clothes have become almost obsolete'. Though Dr. Buchan, writing towards the end of the century, states that in most parts of Britain, 'the practice of rolling children with so many bandages is now, in some measure laid aside', elsewhere he says that 'In many parts of Britain at this day, a roller, eight or ten feet in length is applied tightly round the child's body as soon as it is born'. He recalled

9a. Late Eighteenth-Century Mahogany Cradle

9b. An English Doll, 1820-25

10. Two Little Boys and their Sister, 1853

a case where he had 'known a child seized with convulsion-fits soon after the midwife had done swaddling it who, upon taking off the rollers and bandages, was immediately relieved'. To dress the new-born infant in its complicated wrappings was, as Dr. Buchan pointed out, part of the midwife's technique, and an opportunity to show off her skill which no doubt she abandoned very reluctantly.

Needlework in the grand style was no longer the chief indoor occupation of women of leisure. A variety of 'accomplishments', knotting silk purses, making wax flowers and shell pictures, cutting out silhouettes in black paper and so on, challenged its supremacy. But exquisite care and skill still went into the making and embellishment of wearing apparel, as for instance an embroidered waistcoat for a husband or brother, and into baby clothes of cambric and lawn. Christening robes were often of white satin worn with a frilled lace cap. Woollen clothes were seldom worn by babies and never next to the skin. A Scotch baby, a young Lowlander, was described as wearing 'wee little mutches with lace borders and side knots of blue three-halfpenny ribbon . . . long muslin frockies vandyked across the breast, welsh flannel petticoaties and a coral gun-stick'. I find those 'side knots of blue three-halfpenny ribbon' very tasty—to use an Irish expression.

Among many other items listed in the French layette I have mentioned, were 24 round caps of muslin or lace, 6 woollen bonnets and 24 nightcaps. It would have been unheard of for either an English or French baby to have its head exposed to the dangers of fresh air. Babies were certainly overdressed according to modern ideas, or even for that matter, to enlight-ened contemporary opinions. Here is Dr. Buchan on the sub-ject. 'It is amazing how children escape suffocation, considering the manner in which they are often rolled up in flannels etc. I lately attended an infant, whom I found muffled up over head and ears in many folds of flannel, though it was the middle of June. I begged for a little free air to the poor babe, but though this indulgence was granted during my stay, I found it always on my return in the same situation. Death, as might be expected, freed the infant from all its miseries.'

As early as 1701 an 'Employment Agency' in Edinburgh was claiming to be able to provide 'all sorts of Nurses who either come to gentlemen's houses or nurse children in their own'. As will be seen from this, in the early part of the century anyhow, the infants of well-to-do parents were still sometimes sent to foster-mothers in the country and remained with them till they were five or six years old.[1] No doubt this often worked out for the best, for instance when the real parents were of the worthless type depicted in Hogarth's 'Marriage à la Mode', and the foster parents were kindly, decent folk. But it is with the child that was brought up in its parents' home, and these surroundings that we are considering.

The words '18th-century interior' convey an impression of elegance and of a greatly improved standard of comfort—sash windows and polished floors, walls decorated with wall-paper or painted in pastel colours, graceful furniture of walnut, mahogany and satin wood, Adam chimney pieces and stucco ceilings, cabinets filled with oriental porcelain. Even the more modest houses had the air of dignity that comes from good proportion and honest workmanship.

In the children's quarters however, a spartan simplicity still prevailed; it had not yet occurred to even the most fond parents that nurseries could be anything but functional, or might be decorated and furnished to suit the tastes and size of their small inmates. In the earlier part of the century many houses would still bear the impress of the 17th century and the Yellow Nursery at Southampton House in 1711 was hung with three pieces of landscape tapestry—but even at a later date when the lady of the house was doing up her bedroom or boudoir with 'white paper with a border of pink silk with white and gold flowers stuck upon it . . .' and '. . . window curtains, pink linen with white silk fringes', the nursery would be austere, with low, curtainless beds and bare floors. The nursery at Southampton House, already mentioned, was more luxurious than most with its yellow damask furniture with yellow serge curtains, its feather bed, white striped dimity

[1] Dr. Buchan pointed out the danger of sending a child whose infancy had been spent in over-heated rooms into the country to be nursed in a cold house.

window curtains, its cane elbow chairs, nursing chair and walnut-tree table. An early 18th-century Scotch nursery was equipped with beds, chairs and stools, a cradle and hanging cradle, wooden cups and pewter dishes, collop-tongs, a dry rubber and a wet rubber and an ironing blanket. An 18th-century writer, Smith, mentions cots being used instead of cradles with rockers as though it was quite an innovation. But an odd nursery device also described, called 'a black pudding', was evidently well established; it was a round, thickly padded cap of black velvet which the toddler wore to save it hurting its head when it fell.

When the parsonage at Epworth went on fire, John Wesley, then a child of six, was sleeping with his infant brother Charles, three sisters and a nurse. But even in more opulent households, the sleeping accommodation for the children of the family was not much superior to that provided for the upper servants, and little notice was taken of Dr. Buchan's pronouncement that 'The Nursery ought always to be the largest and best aired room in the house'. Horace Walpole told of the shocking fire that destroyed Lady Molesworth's London house, and in which she herself and two of her six daughters, also a French governess, lost their lives (two other daughters being badly injured). The youngest girl Charlotte who slept in a garret with the governess, managed to clamber on to the roof, but finding her way barred by chimneys and spikes, jumped out of the window and landed safely on a mattress.

A little boy, not yet seven, who appears in the Verney letters, was too tenderly cherished to be consigned to a garret. 'He lyes in a little Room hung with Paper, which is a sort of alcove within ours.' Of this charming little boy it was said: 'The sweetness of his Temper and Vivacity of Spirit, joyn'd with the Innocence of his Age, renders him the delight of all about him.'

Though the Faithful Old Nurse was well established by now in literature and fable, the true Nanny type—a power in the household, devoted heart and soul to her charges and to the family—was slow in emerging. It is significant that in J. J. Hecht's comprehensive work, *The Domestic Class in England in the 18th Century*, children's nurses are not even mentioned.

During the first part of the century, the lady's waiting woman or 'own woman' as she was called, often looked after the children as well as attending to her mistress. She might be assisted in this task by underlings. Mention is made in the Verney letters of 'Mrs. Baker's Nursery Maid, a sickly creature'. Mrs. Boscawen after complaining of a drunken cook says, 'I have likewise had three nursery maids since Bab went'. In the late 40's she had a nurse and nurserymaid in a domestic staff of nine. In 1742 a nurse's wages were £5 6s. a year. Betsy Fremantle has a complaint to make about her nurse: 'On Nurse Smith wishing to leave me and having for some time perceived her increase of size, I had some suspicious and now find she is with child, has neither friend or money and must remain upon this parish. It is a most awkward circumstance and I must part with her immediately.' A great gulf yawns between this unfortunate and the majestic Nanny of the Victorian nursery.

The 18th-century baby was, like its predecessor, at the mercy of all kinds of well-meaning people with pet theories about infant management. A grandfather, Sir Roger Newdigate, prescribed for his daughter's baby, 'cold water to roll in every morning and best milk and a good deal of it'. Also that he should be 'tossed about by a stout nimble nurse from morning to evening'.

Tossing babies about was apparently a common practice, and must have been bad for their nerves and digestions, especially if they had been fed beforehand on 'tough muffins floated in oiled butter'.

Dr. Buchan, on the whole, had a rather poor opinion of nurses. There were those who allowed their charges to cry too long and vehemently, causing ruptures, and others who 'dealt much' on Godfrey's cordial, Daffy's Elixir and carminative and other medicines instead of relying on good food, air, exercise and cleanliness.

3

To look at the enchanting child portraits by Reynolds, Gainsborough, Romney, Hoppner and other 18th-century painters, one might imagine that these children with their sturdy limbs and faces like full-blown roses could never know a moment's illness. Yet contemporary letters and diaries show that the parents whose children had emerged successfully from infancy were still beset by many anxieties. Medical knowledge was pitifully inadequate to deal with serious illness, and small-pox, typhus fever or putrid fever, and scarlet fever were still rife. There was also a great deal of consumption and malaria. (Fortunately there was no serious outbreak of plague in England after the terrible one of 1665.)

On April 1st, 1717, Lady Mary Wortley Montagu wrote an epoch-making letter from Constantinople to her friend Miss Sarah Chiswell. In it she told her of the Turkish habit of engrafting for smallpox, adding that there was 'no example of anyone that died of it; and you may believe I am very well satisfied of the safety of these experiments, since I intend to try it on my deare little son'. This she had the courage to do, and was able to report that 'the boy was engrafted last Tuesday, and is at this time singing and playing, and very impatient for his supper. I pray God my next may give as good an account of him. I cannot engraft the girl; her nurse has not had the smallpox.' The last sentence indicates the chief disadvantage of engrafting—that the patient was infectious during the slight attack of smallpox that it produced. Nevertheless it remained the only preventative of smallpox till vaccination was dis-covered by Jenner in 1797, and when Lady Mary introduced 'this useful invention', as she called inoculation, into England in 1720, many parents availed themselves of it for their children.

In the middle of the century, Mrs. Boscawen wrote to her husband: 'I must beg you not to be uneasy about the child. He is in the most desirable state for innoculation that can be. Mr. Hawkins felt his pulse and said he wanted no bleeding, no purging but a little rhubarb, and he assures me that in all his practice he never observed a more favourable run of innocu-lated patients. . . . I have been summoned upstairs to assist at the solemnity of poor Billy's rhubarb, for the pretty cur was asleep when Burges sent it.' She was only able however to get him to take half the dose, and had to keep the rest for the morning. '. . . the sweet soul was sleepy and tired, and tried so honestly to do his best to oblige "May", the little stomach heaving all the while, that I must have had a heart of flint to torment him any more.' Then she described the inoculation itself.

'April 20th. Pray Papa! Pray God to bless us, for we are innoculated. This day exactly at noon it was done; no fuss, no rout, no assistance. Nobody but me and the servants. I held the child myself and so effectually employed his eyes and attention (by a bit of gold lace which I was putting into forms to lace his waistcoat) that he never was sensible of the first aim. For the second, he pretended to wince a little, but I had a sugar plum ready, which stopped the whimper before it was well formed, and he is now (Mr. Hawkins gone) tattling here by my bureau with some cards and papers, etc., for the weather is so very hot that I reckon the chief service I can do him is to provide him such amusements as will keep him still and quiet. So that instead of waggons, carts and post-chaises, we shall deal together in mills, pictures, dolls, London cries, and such sedentary amusements. The nurse-maids are both innoculated, too.'

This account of a small domestic happening (one nevertheless that seemed very important to Mrs. Boscawen) is in its very simple way so vivid that one has the sensation of standing outside in the garden of Mrs. Boscawen's house on that hot April day two hundred years ago, looking through the window at the little group within—the fond, anxious mother in her full-skirted morning dress of patterned dimity or lawn and her neat cap, holding on her knee the 'sweet cur' Billy, aged three and a half, distracting his attention with the piece of gold lace, while Mr. Hawkins in his black suit and ruffles prepares his implements. I have read somewhere that sound waves never die, rippling on as it were through space and eternity. I should like to be able to catch the sound of those London Cries with which Mrs. Boscawen amused her little son.

Many years later in 1789, Betsy Fremantle is 'afraid Tommy must be it [inoculated] too, as there is so much danger of his catching smallpox'.

The following year there was an epidemic of smallpox in the village—'two babies are dead of the smallpox'—and Betsy was worried as to whether she should have her baby daughter inoculated. The doctor was away, but on his return it was decided that 'he will innoculate poor little Emma tomorrow'.

An extract from the letters in 'The Girlhood of Maria Josepha Holroyd' (also at the end of the century) reads, 'The Gardener's Baby just turned the month was innoculated at the same time'. Firm-minded and benevolent employers would see to it that their dependants were also rendered immune.

It has been stated that smallpox, though widespread throughout the 18th century, was no longer the deadly disease that it had been, and in fact that (as is the case with measles, chickenpox and so-called 'childish' diseases nowadays) it was considered, on the whole, quite a good thing to get it over early in life. The following rather startling comment (on the illness of some children) bears this out: 'I had hopes that it would have been the smallpox.' Lady Mary Wortley Montagu told her daughter, 'I sincerely wish you joy of your infant having gone happily through the smallpox'.

Certainly people were amazingly careless about infection. Betsy Fremantle during the smallpox epidemic in the village went to see a woman who had it—'a horrid sight'. Lord Lovat writing to his agent in Edinburgh, excused himself for his delay in answering a business letter thus: 'My house has been all this week full of company as well as the last, and my child's lying in the smallpox makes me unfit to answer such a letter of business as yours.'

Mrs. Papiendieck and her children spent Christmas in the house of her brother who had just died of smallpox. The only precautions taken were to keep the doors open to cause a draught, and to place pans of vinegar that had been boiled with spices on the landings.

Even Mrs. Boscawen, most conscientious of mothers, when she was assuring her husband that she would devote herself to the care of their children during his absence, wrote: 'I do not ask you for any direction, as to whether, if one has the smallpox, I shall put away the others etc., for I reckon that in all these cases ones conduct must chiefly depend *sur le conjecture*, and therefore 'tis impossible to take any resolution beforehand!'

Yet this apparent disregard of infection went side by side with an acute fear of catching the dangerous and often disfiguring disease. Mrs. Boscawen's alarm was intense when her footman fell ill and was found to have the smallpox, although 'the poor fellow was assured by his parents that he had had it'. (It was usual to enquire of servants whether they had had the disease or not before engaging them.) His parents too were convinced that he had had it. But the doctor pronounced otherwise, and the alarming news was brought to Mrs. Boscawen privately by her lady's maid. 'I shall never forget that hour nor the terror it threw me into. My three children and my cousin!' The sick footman was hastily smuggled out of the house in a closed post-chaise, with the apothecary's man in attendance. 'When I heard the chaise roll away, I began to breathe, but from ten in the morning to seven at night I was in an agony not to be described.' The footman who had been sent to a woman, who 'was used to nurse people with the smallpox', died on the 14th day, to Mrs. Boscawen's distress. Meanwhile she was in agony in case her children had caught the disease, but luckily they escaped.

Contrast this with the happy-go-lucky attitude of Mrs. Boscawen's brother-in-law. Mrs. Boscawen writes to her husband: 'I hear the Colonel George [Boscawen] is immensely angry with me for telling him he should wash his hands after nursing his boy with smallpox.' She adds very reasonably: 'Now 'tis certain that if my fears are ridiculous (and I don't pretend to defend 'em) the folly is mine and reflects upon me not him.'

No self-respecting nursery in the 18th century was without Daffy's Elixir, compounded of senna, jalop, aniseed, carraway seeds and juniper berries steeped in alcohol and water and mixed with treacle and water, a venerable remedy, considered good for colic, 'much recommended to the public by Dr. King, physician to King Charles II, and the late learned and ingenious Dr. Rod. Cliffe'. Dalby's Carminative and Godfrey's Cordial were also standbys of the nursery medicine cupboard. Another, rather sinister, remedy was Dr. James's Powder for ailing infants, the chief principle of which was antimony.

As might be expected in this age of transition, remedies ranged from the beneficial or harmless to the nauseous, and the entirely superstitious. Here is a remedy for coughs recommended by Mrs. Delany: 'Two or three snails boiled in her barley water or tea water might be of great service to her.' Snails and earthworms, boiled and strained, were one of the ordeals to which consumptives might have to submit. A broth made of 'old stewed owl and two puppies' for coughs and bronchitis reads like a ghastly parody of an Edward Lear poem, and is as horrible as a similar French prescription which begins: 'Take two small newly born dogs' [earth worms came into it too] and which was alleged to be good for fortifying the nerves. (Another French remedy, 'La Poudre de Madame de Carrignan' contained gold leaf, and was, it was claimed, 'sovereign against children's convulsions'.)

In country districts particularly, belief in the efficacy of purely superstitious remedies still flourished. For instance it was believed that to pass a child through the cleft trunk of an ash or hazel tree would cure it of rickets.[1]

Even more sophisticated mothers pinned their faith on Dr. Anodyne's necklaces which were said to have a marvellous effect on children who were 'about their teeth'. 'After wearing them for one night, children have immediately cut their teeth with safety who, but just before, were on the brink of the grave with their teeth, fits, fevers, convulsions, gripes, looseness etc., all proceeding from the teeth, and have miraculously recovered.'

Perhaps the belief in 'touching' for the 'Evil'—that is to say scrofula, a common complaint in the 18th century—should come under the heading of 'faith healing', as it was believed to be a gift divinely bestowed on the sovereign. Queen Anne was the last monarch to be credited with this healing power; it was not thought to have been handed on to the Hanoverians.

After a service in the chapel of St. James's Palace, the Queen, seated in state with her courtiers and chaplains in attendance, touched the patients. Dr. Johnson suffered from scrofula as a child, and when he was two and a half years old, his mother was advised by a prominent Lichfield doctor to take him to be

---

[1] When I was living in the North of Ireland in the 30's, I was assured by my young maid that to pass a child under a donkey would be beneficial treatment for whooping cough. One would presumably choose for this experiment what I saw described in an advertisement in an Irish newspaper as 'a kind and quiet donkey'.

touched by Queen Anne. Mary Lovett (who appears in the
Verney letters) was advised by a well-known surgeon to have
her daughter Betty, who was suffering from a painfully swollen
neck, 'toucht' for the 'Evil' (she was also to leave off Physick,
which must have been a relief to the poor child, and to drink
malt and wine). Everyone assured Mrs. Lovett that, as the
child was to be touched, no other remedies must be applied
meanwhile. Betty duly received the royal touch, and was given
a piece of gold known as an 'angel' to wear round her neck.
Every morning she was to rub the affected part with it.

One is struck with the violence of the remedies that were
applied with the most loving intentions in the world to those
poor little bodies and stomachs. Purging, blistering and bleeding, that trio of old favourites, were still an important part of
the medical routine at the end of the century and beyond. In
1787 a small boy who was ill had a blister applied to him and
was given a little Florence wine in his rice water. Quinine or
Jesuit's Bark had been brought to England in the previous
century and was soon found to be a valuable medicine for the
malaria and other fevers that were so prevalent. But three
quarts of Bark seems an unbelievably drastic dose for a child.

A very harmless remedy, asses milk, was in enormous demand
and favour at this period, for delicate people and ailing children.
In the Verney letters a sick child is reported to be drinking
'Asses milk twice a day and it is his best support'. One suspects
that a good many children of even well-to-do families suffered
from rickets or other similar complaints, due to faulty diet and
lack of sufficient fresh air[1]; Ralph Palmer reports to Ralph
Verney that his cherished little son 'is all life but very weak in
his legs and thighs and very poor in his flesh which makes us
long till he gets more strength and substance'. Lady Mary
Wortley Montagu was worried because her young son had 'a
Bigness in his joints, but not much; his ankles seem chiefly to
have a weakness'. She is anxious to have Dr. Garth's advice and
'whether he approves rubbing them with spirits'.

The Fremantle children were always ailing. Their mother's

---

[1] Dr. Buchan blamed lack of exercise, the use of leading reins for toddlers,
and 'cramped clothes' in infancy for the 'high shoulders, crooked spines and
flat breasts' to be seen among adults.

diary was full of entries like this. 'Poor little Harry's humour is breaking out again violently. Mr. Nagle calls it an inveterate species of the tetters, and will try something to cure them, he dont approve of bathing him in salt and water, which would throw the child in agonies. He really suffers very much and is a miserable little creature.' Or, 'Mr. Cowley called to see Emma and rather alarmed me for he said her Bile must be attended as some tumour might grow there and being immediately on the backbone might prove dangerous, the poor child was in great pain and quite an object'.

It is quite a relief to come across the Boscawen children, earlier in the century, who seem from their mother's letters to her husband to have been unusually robust. They are 'I thank God, in perfect health . . . your children are perfectly well, the boy vastly grown'. Elizabeth is 'the finest child in the world . . . your children are all charming, in health as well as in beauty'. When she walks in Englefield Green with them and enquires the age of other children, she always has 'the pleasure to find that my boy and Bess are taller by the head than anything of their age and stout in proportion'. 'God grant that my children may look as they do now', she writes, joyfully expecting her husband's homecoming. 'Brought all my young ones in perfect health to town and had the satisfaction to see all the servants I had left behind surprised at the children's looks, and affirming they were grown fat and tall and more improved than they could have conceived it possible.'

Admittedly there was one bad patch when all three children were ill at once, the girls 'with coughs and fevers occasioned by teeth which were lanced immediately' and the boy with 'a violent and never ceasing cough'. Mrs. Boscawen suspected measles and trembled for 'poor Fanny', barely two years old, 'whose breath and lungs were so oppressed that 'twas pain to hear her, and the slut would not drink anything though she was dying with thirst'. She tried to tempt the little girl with tea, water with a roast apple, a drop of wine in warm milk and jelly, only to hear the plaintive cry: 'No, no, no, cant.' However they all made a good recovery. Mr. Burgess, the apothecary evidently, for Mrs. Boscawen said, 'I have no doctor', did 'vastly well for us'. His powders soon reduced the fever and a white mixture he sent 'did much good to the cough'. It would be interesting to know what was in these medicines.

Fanny Boscawen had some enlightened ideas on the upbringing of the young. She herself declared that her aim was to procure for the children 'a sound mind in a healthful body'. She believed in plenty of fresh air—the children are often described as playing out of doors,[1] making hay, going for walks, or as being 'settled with maids on the lawn'—and she took a furnished house for £25 a year at the top of Hendon Hill, 'Tis a fine air for the nursery', so that the children should not be confined in London.

An unfortunate idea prevailed at this epoch that raw fruit and vegetables were bad for children, though Locke had recommended a diet for them of fruit, brown bread, water gruel and flummeries. Their diet was plain, sometimes even meagre[2]; it was probably often too stodgy. Mrs. Boscawen says that when returning to her London house from the country, she took the precaution of ordering chicken broth for the children, which sounds good, but another time 'two immense pieces of bread sopped in very weak tea' were brought in for the nursery supper.

Sugar was still an expensive commodity, and as far as the children were concerned was more of a treat than a normal part of their diet. The children of hardy Highland families, were 'nourished with good and substantial cheer not with Dates and Sugar Plumbs' (though a Highland lady, Elizabeth Grant remembered having brown sugar with her nursery porridge), but the household accounts of at least one Scotch family had the kindly entry, 'Sugar candy for the bairns when sick'.

All kinds of delicious things came out of the 18th-century stillroom, apples in syrup, preserved oranges, and dates, sugar plums, candy, and sugared almonds, which might find their

---

[1] She would probably have agreed with Dr. Buchan that girls who were allowed to romp about as children make the best mothers.

[2] The Wesley family had three meals a day (no tit-bits allowed between meals) of which breakfast and supper consisted of one dish (or bowl more likely) of liquid food. Dinner was more substantial.

way into an indulgent grandma's silver comfit box, and from there into eager young mouths.

Country-bred children would be well acquainted with syllabub, that mixture of milk, wine and sugar, all warm and foaming, whose very name conveys the essence of rural (almost Arcadian) 18th-century England.

Jam was not made much in the early part of the century. What jam was to the Victorian and Edwardian child (many modern children seem indifferent to it) gingerbread in all its forms was to the 18th-century child. Gingerbread 'books' with the alphabet stamped on them for ½d. a slice were cried in the streets of London, and every fair, besides the great gingerbread fairs held every year in Birmingham, sold gingerbread toys, in the shape of animals, ships, human figures and a variety of everyday objects.

At Easter, instead of the elaborate chocolate eggs that children look for nowadays, the 18th-century child received a hard-boiled egg dyed a bright colour.

England, in the 18th century, resembled France, Spain and other European countries nowadays, insomuch that water was hardly considered a drinkable proposition. Even small children were given wine to drink, and the Wesley children whose diet was as strictly regulated as the rest of their lives, were allowed to drink as much small beer as they liked.

When Jean Jacques Rousseau declared in *Emile* that 'the limbs of a growing child should be free to move easily in his clothing . . . there should be nothing tight, nothing fitting closely to the body', he was only saying what Locke had said fifty years previously. But parents had not taken any notice of Locke on this point, or if they had his influence had been slow in making itself felt.[1] By the time that *Emile* had burst on a startled world, children's fashions were, as we have seen, already showing a tendency to become simpler and more comfortable. Whether Rousseau's advice hastened up this process, it is impossible to say. He went a good deal further than most parents at that time or nowadays would be prepared to do, declaring that his imaginary Emile should wear his summer clothes all

---

[1] The Russell girls when less than ten years old had dresses sewn with yards of gold and silver braid.

winter, and go barefoot. (The children of the Highland gentry, in fact often did.) 'Why should my pupil be always compelled to wear the skin of an ox under his foot?' he asked. He conceded that the precaution might be taken of removing any broken glass that might be lying around.

The emancipating change in children's clothes that took place about the middle of the century has been commented on; its beneficial effect on their health and spirits can easily be imagined. But it was a gradual change, following, or perhaps as James Laver has pointed out, anticipating adult fashions.[1] For instance, Mrs. Papiendieck in her diary for 1777 described how her small brother aged six was breeched. He appeared 'in a pair of breeches with a buckle at the knee and coat with a falling skirt, collar hanging over, and waistcoat with pockets long over the thigh and a cocked hat', which gives us a picture of an 18th-century mannikin. As a pendant to this, a little girl, dressed to go visiting, is described as wearing 'a silk slip with lawn apron and lace tuckers and small cap with narrow borders of lace neatly quilted round'. She also had 'a rosebud in her bosom and held her silk hood and tippet'. She sounds like one of the lady-mice in *The Tailor of Gloucester*. So does George III's daughter, Princess Amelia, who on her third birthday wore a robe coat covered in fine muslin; a dressed close cap and white gloves and carried a fan.

Even when children's fashions closely copied those of their elders, there were certain modifications in the style. Little boys seldom wore pleated full-skirted coats, but a long jacket coat of the kind still worn by the boys of Christ's Hospital. Then again it is rare, it seems, to find a portrait of a little girl wearing a sacque, even when these were the mode.

It seems strange to us that a little boy should be kept in what really amounted to baby clothes till he was six years old, but as Rosamund Bayne-Powell has pointed out[2], this may have been for economical reasons as clothes were expensive. It was not uncommon for a visiting tailor to cut down grown-up

[1] Dr. Buchan, writing in the 80's thought it necessary to condemn stays, 'the very bane of infants', though he conceded that 'the madness in favour of stays seems, however, to be somewhat abated'.

[2] *English Children in the 18th Century.*

clothes for the children of the family. In 1722 a tailor 'made down father's scarlet breeches for Jimmy'.

By the end of the century the age limit for this sartorial change was lower. Tom Fremantle was only three years old when his mother wrote: 'Tom changed his dress today and looked very pretty in his nankeen jacket and trousers.'

The charm of the later 18th-century fashions for children can hardly be exaggerated; it is tempting to wonder if the more indulgent attitude of adults towards the young, was partly influenced by them! Little girls, unless they were like poor 'little Harriet Howard' who, Betsy Fremantle described tartly as 'the ugliest little Ape I ever saw' must have looked adorable, while the styles for little boys were both manly looking and pretty. How dashing Viscount Althorp aged four, looks in his portrait by Reynolds. He wears a nankeen jacket buttoned down the front and the short trousers that had been adopted for boys since about 1760. A blue sash and a large hat are concessions to masculine vanity.

A charming group 'The Sackville Children' by John Hoppner, shows the little girls in high-waisted muslin dresses the hems well off the ground. The elder girl has a coral necklace and a pair of very saucy striped shoes. The smaller girl, Lady Elizabeth was painted with bare feet, to her indignation. Her younger brother is trying to keep her in order. He wears a little jacket tucked under his trousers, and a double frill of fine muslin round the neck.

4

Imagine what it was like to be a little girl living in the first half of the 18th century—'as well a sweet-tempered as a Pretty childe' (for why not choose an attractive little girl while one is about it?)—a little girl dressed in her best. Her 'dust gown' or pinafore of calico or serge has been taken off, and she wears a long-skirted, stiff-bodiced silk gown, her hair is dressed high on her head with a little lace cap, for she is staying with her aunt and has been brought down to the drawing-room to make her curtsey to her aunt's guests. When they have petted and admired her and let her dip into their comfit boxes, she sees that they are no longer attending to her, being absorbed in their incomprehensible grown-up chatter, and she slips away to investigate the doll's house or Baby-house as it is called, which stands in a corner of the drawing-room. It was presented to her aunt in her childhood by the tradesmen of the town near which her father, a large property owner, lived. The aunt, when she married at the age of fifteen, brought her cherished baby-house (as well as her 'babies' or dolls) with her to her new home, and it was such a work of art that it has been kept ever since in the drawing-room to be admired by guests.

It is mounted on a separate stand which makes it more than five feet high, so that the little girl must stand on a footstool if she is to reach the top storey comfortably. She gazes for a few minutes at the handsome oak façade—the hall door has a carved pediment of swans' necks (if only she could make herself as tiny as a doll and walk through it!) but a young lady who has been watching her with amusement, bends down and shows her how to open the two hinged doors, each side of the central fixed panel, with their glazed windows, and smiles at the child's cry of joy and amazement as she sees what is within. She is transported instantly into that little private world that children desire ('I am tired of this world. I want a world of my own', a little girl of four once told me). It is so minute, so compact that she can comprehend it in a few enraptured glances—while she plays here she is complete mistress of this small domain—yet it has the charm of familiarity, for it is a perfectly proportioned replica of a real house of the time. Everything about it is deeply right and satisfying. The little girl hurries from one discovery to another, looking up now and then with a triumphant, beaming smile at her sympathetic playmate. The drawing-room upstairs has a hand-embroidered carpet, and walnut chairs upholstered in brocade; it has a tiny silver chandelier hanging from the ceiling, a japanned cabinet decorated with carved ivory and a little card table. Two lilliputian ladies are seated at it. The dining-room has no carpet, thus following the custom of the time, but its walnut furniture is handsome, and like the drawing-room it has a mirror above the fireplace. Best of all there is a minute knife box and set of cutlery, and a fairy-like set of silver toys, a coffee and tea set, which Aunt bought from

11. A Mid-Victorian Perambulator

12a.   12b.

12c.
From a Mid-Victorian Family Album

time to time after her marriage at a toy shop and added to her baby-house. Three little gentlemen in brocade suits are seated round the polished dining-room table.

Upstairs in the bedroom, a maid doll in a print gown and mop cap is making the fine tester bed with its blue damask curtains that draw to and from so smoothly like those of a real bed, and its quilted cover. The walnut chest of drawers with brass handles has drawers that pull open and shut, with a complete outfit of doll's clothes inside, and on it a delightful pin cushion. But it is over the kitchen that the little girl lingers most fondly. It is so neat and exciting with its high dresser, pewter dishes and copper pans, its spit above the fireplace which has a portable grate, and the little pestle and mortar on the table.

But her aunt's waiting-woman has come to fetch her. It is time for her to go to bed. The doors of the baby-house are closed. Reluctantly with a yearning backward look she allows herself to be led away. Aunt has promised that she shall play with it tomorrow, but tomorrow is a long way away when you are five years old.

When the company has left, and the candles have been extinguished and the drawing-room left silent and empty, will little pin-points of light appear behind the windows of the baby-house; will the ladies play cards, the gentlemen drink their port, the maidservant put the tiny copper warming pan into the little bed? The baby house is cosy, but it is mysterious too.[1]

There were even more elaborate dolls' houses as the century went on, such as the beautiful one made in 1740 by the estate carpenter at Nostell Priory, Yorkshire. It is the replica of a really imposing three-storied country house with Doric pillars in bas relief flanking the front door, and with ornamental urns on the balustrade round the roof. It has a fine hall and staircase, a drawing-room, dining-room and two other sitting-rooms, all beautifully decorated and furnished, two bedrooms and a kitchen.

As will be seen, these baby-houses whether they were designed for children or made by adults for their own amusement were

[1] This account of a doll's house is based on Mr. G. Bernard Hughes's description of the Westbrook Baby-House in *Country Life*, October 19th, 1951.

almost collector's pieces; they were not available to the general public. It was not till about 1760 that model houses were sold in the toy shops, and became the delight of less privileged children. There were also models of grocer's and butcher's shops and of milliner's and dressmaker's counters. Then there were separate pieces of furniture. Many of these beautifully designed and finished little objects—bureaux, writing-tables, tallboys and wardrobes—were obviously not toys, being too large for dolls' houses, but were made as models by skilled craftsmen as a leisure time occupation or to sell to adult collectors. However some of the smaller ones may very likely have been given to children, or found their way into baby-houses.

The same reservations apply to the exquisite toy dinner and tea services in Staffordshire, Bow and other ware. The sauce boat in one of these sets has 'Miss de Vaux 1770' on it, so it was evidently made especially for some little girl. Mrs. Delany wrote of her little great-niece's raptures over a set of 'young Nankeen China' which the Duchess of Portland gave her. It was 'very fine and pretty' consisting of '12 tea cups and saucers, 6 coffee cups and tea pots; sugar dish, milk jug, two bread and butter plates. . . . They have been produced for the entertainment of my company every afternoon,' Mrs. Delany said.

It is a curious thing that though dolls were called 'babies' or 'children's babies' (the earliest reference to the word 'doll' appears in a *Gentleman's Magazine* of 1751) nearly all 18th-century dolls have mature faces. A wooden doll dating from Queen Anne's reign has a narrow adult body encased in a flowered dress and apron; her face, framed by a cap which ties under her chin, is full of benignity, determination and character. One feels that she is a doll that a child could turn to in a crisis. Another jointed wooden doll, dating from 1720, has a laced bodice to her dress, and wears a cloak and hood. She is rather tight-lipped with inscrutable eyes. It is a face that would not easily be forgotten.

A group of 18th-century dolls, a family party consisting of husband, wife, nurse and child, described as having 'compo' faces and hands and human hair, are to be seen in the South

Kensington Museum. The lady wears a drab-coloured dress and vest, laced across and a wide-brimmed hat. The man has a fawn-coloured coat and a high stock, and the nurse is in pink and white dimity. Yet another 18th-century doll has a quilted cap and petticoat. A wax doll dressed as an old woman—most unusual this—and seated in a chair, dates from the very end of the period.

Fashion designers in France at this time sent their fashion dolls to England and America, as they had been doing (as far as England was concerned) for some centuries; these dolls had skilfully modelled wax heads, and by the end of the century, the wax doll, queen of the nursery, had begun her long reign.

Eighteenth-century dolls were usually not more than 7–14 inches high, though there is a record, in a print, of one doll, late in the century, that was nearly as large as its little owner.

Besides these elaborate dolls, which could cost as much as six or even 10 guineas, there were other humbler but certainly no less loved dolls—the Flanders 'babies' that were imported into England from the Low Countries, and the 'Bartholomew babies' that were sold at Bartholomew fair, also the dolls (and animals) made of bread with currants or comfits for eyes. An extract from a Scotch account book reads 'China-babies 7/–'.

That dolls could and did arouse the most unbridled maternal passions in little girls is shown by the print, "'Tis my Doll' which shows two moppets in white muslin dresses and sashes, one wearing a mop cap and the other a cloak and hood, disputing fiercely over a jointed doll. One is struck by their over-fed appearances. The little girl who is clutching the doll by its leg and dress in an endeavour to tear it away from the other child, looks almost apoplectic.

The roar of motor traffic is the voice of modern London; in the 18th century it was the street cries, rising like discordant music above the rumble of the wheels. A street cry that must have gladdened the heart of innumerable children was that of the pedlar woman who sold little woolly lambs on a tray, crying out:

'Baa lambs to sell, baa lambs to sell,
I've got white pretty baa lambs to sell.'

There were other animal toys that gave delight; the denizens
of the Noah's Ark, which was allowed on Sundays even in
strictly pious households, a wooden horse on wheels, a stick
with a horse's head and bridle and reins, and of course the
spirited rocking horse itself. Where the modern child plays at
cars, planes or spaceships, the little 18th-century boy instinct-
ively 'made believe' at riding or driving. Lady Mary Wortley
Montagu, writing to her daughter, imagines her little grandson
riding on a poker. Mrs. Boscawen went to Ascot Heath races
'on purpose to delight my boy, who has a very great passion for
chaises, wheels and carriages of all sorts, down to a wheelbarrow, so I fancied he would be vastly happy in the midst of
so many, and indeed he was.'

Models of coaches survive; one has six horses with a coachman and postilion and is made of carved wood, painted and
gilt. Another model of a stage coach has miniature luggage on
the roof.

The age of the mechanical toy had dawned. The French and
Swiss toymakers led the field in this respect. I have read a
description of a little coach belonging to the reign of Louis XV
which was worked by clock work. It had a coachman, two
negro lackeys, a postilion, and six dapple-grey horses with
plumes on their heads. Inside this fairy-like equipage sat a lady
and gentleman made of Venetian glass. In 1748, Mrs. Boscawen
described a toy that a friend gave her little boy. The kind lady,
unknown to Mrs. Boscawen put into her coach 'a silver ship
made in India, a very curious thing and has gone by clockwork,
but the spring is now out of order'. All the same it was as Mrs.
Boscawen repeated, 'a very fine thing'.

For little boys there were lead soldiers, first made at Nuremberg. The flat figures which were mostly used in the 18th
century, were older than the rounded variety.

All the old favourites reappear; bows and arrows, drums,
whistles, kites, tops, paper windmills, the Jack-in-the-Box (mentioned by Rousseau as a means of dispelling a child's idle fears)
and the battledore and shuttlecock and hoops. Six shillings and

a penny were paid in 1753 for 'paint and print' for Lord Tavis-
toke and Lady Caroline Russell. There were new amusements
too. Magic lanterns, said to have been invented by Roger Bacon,
were the forerunners of the film in the entertainment way, and
probably gave the children of that time as much pleasure as a
visit to the cinema does to the modern child. The magic lantern was alluringly described in 1719 as 'a little optical machine
which enables one to see in the dark on a white wall, many
spectres and frightful monsters of a sort that those who do not
know the secret believe it to be done by magic art'. By the way,
does anyone amuse children nowadays by making shadow
pictures on the wall with their fingers, or have grown-ups lost
this accomplishment?

How many people of today have heard the sound of a musical
box? I had one as a child before the 1914 war. I have no idea
how old it was. One of the tunes it played was the Imperial
Russian anthem, 'God the All Terrible'. Its tinkling notes
linked my nursery with those of the 18th century, for musical
boxes were invented it is supposed by a Swiss, Louis Favre,
early in the century.

An engraving of a picture by Hamilton called 'The Parachute' shows a very chubby little boy in late 18th-century dress,
wearing a fancy hat with a feather, beneath which his long hair
falls on to his shoulders, and a suit with a frilled collar, watching
a miniature balloon descend. Montgolfier's celebrated ascent
had brought these toys into vogue.

Fireworks and crackers livened up the nursery regime. These
were pastimes that were enjoyed by adults as well as children;
fireworks displays were a regular feature of entertainments at
Ranelagh and Vauxhall. In this century as in earlier ones,
though to a lesser extent, one is struck by the childishness of
some of the adult pastimes. It is surprising for instance to see
depicted a party of grown-up people building card houses, an
occupation that one considers only suitable for children, and
young ones at that, though as a matter of fact it requires a very
deft and steady hand, and strong nerves, to get beyond the
first story.

Educational toys, that had already appeared in earlier times
in the form of alphabetical bricks and a pack of 17th-century

grammatical cards, reared their uninviting heads more vigorously in this century. There was a horrible arithmetical card game, historical cards dealing with Roman history, geographical cards, also a pack of cards, dated 1788, designed for 'the amusement of youth', which tried to combine entertainment and instruction or more accurately, edification. For instance the Rocking Horse was pressed into service to exemplify the duty of obedience:

> 'The *Rocking Horse* performs its courfe,
> Directed by your hand.
> Children should thus their friends obey
> And do what they command.'

Children being what they are, little Master Tommy or Miss Charlotte no doubt happily ignored the moral, fastening their attention on to the delightfully familiar picture of the rocking horse.

Card playing was the great recreation of 18th-century society; for many people in fact it was the chief occupation and passion of their lives. The taste for it was acquired early. After lovely, vain Lady Coventry's death, George Selwyn, who was as fond of children as he was of attending executions, described her motherless little girls playing cards together in their nursery, and discussing how they would receive their new 'mother-in-law' (stepmother). Little Lady Fanny flew into a passion if her cards were not good and threw them into her sister's face. The young gamesters were most likely playing Pope Joan, Roly Poly, Post and Pair, or 'My Sow's pigged'.

There is not a great deal to record about nursery games in this century for the reason that the old games and pastimes were still in favour. Contemporary prints show children playing hopscotch, Puss in the Corner, Hot Cockles, Trap Ball, Hop, Skip and Jump and Frog-Jump, and disporting themselves on swings and see-saws. They are shown playing at Bear baiting. One child is on all fours being baited by his companions with slaps from knotted handkerchiefs, a game that died out with the brutal sport it mimicked. Other popular games mentioned in John Newbery's *Little Pretty Pocket Book* were Hoop and Hide

(Hide and Seek), King (of the Castle) I am, Blindman's Buff, Tip cat, 'I sent a Letter to my Love' and 'Thread the Needle' (a chase game).

'Here we go round the Mulberry Bush', and 'Ring o' Roses' are still played at toddlers' parties, but 'How many miles to Babylon' has survived only as a nursery rhyme.

The 18th-century child had few organized amusements. If it lived in London it might be taken (towards the end of the century) to see Philip Astley's Equestrian performances. The circus too became popular during the second half of the century. But the London streets provided plenty of amusement for the town child; the street criers and orange sellers, the pedlars and ballad singers, and Punch and Judy Shows. There was the Lord Mayor's Show to brighten up the foggy gloom of November, and in May the chimney sweep's festival, when they walked in procession round the Jack in the Green, a perambulating mass of green branches on a frame. On the same day the garlanded milkmaids had a parade, leading a cow decorated with flowers and ribbons.

The country child's amusements were even more unsophisticated—helping with the hay, and the harvest, bird nesting blackberrying, riding ponies. But these pastimes, with the exception of bird nesting, which has fortunately fallen into disrepute, still give pleasure to the child of today, and one trusts may continue to do so for generations to come.

The town child could have a cat or dog, a caged bird or even a dormouse as a pet, but the country child could have the additional richness of a pet lamb or a calf that it had helped to rear.

These items from the domestic accounts of the Russell family deal with the children's pets.

'Feb. 12th, 1752. Gave the dog doctor for coming to Bouncer 5/-. May 29th. Paid Isaac Smith a bill for bird cages for Lord Tavistock and Lady Caroline, £1 14s. od. July 19th. Paid for three peewits for Lord Tavistock, 2s. 6d. April 3rd, 1753. Paid for a new door to the dormouse's cage, 6d.'

Large family parties were sufficient to themselves—there were 19 young Wesleys, though nine of them died in infancy, Lord Edward Fitzgerald was one of seventeen children, with the addition of two step sisters. Families of this size provided ready-made teams for prisoner's base, and even small females in muslin dresses and sashes could be pressed into service for cricket and rounders.

Then there were junketings at Christmas—mummers, carol singers, the house to be decorated with holly and greenery ('. . . a Merry Xmas with a kiss to the little Rogues', a Verney writes) and parties at Twelfth Night, with tickets to be drawn for the title of King and Queen. With Christmas still uncommercialized, present giving was far less of a ritual than it is nowadays. In a general way children were given presents at any time during the year when grown-ups felt so inclined—there was a pleasant custom of giving children new clothes on New Year's Day.

5

1744 was an important date in the history of the nursery for it was then that John Newbery came to London from Reading and began publishing children's books in a large way. The first of these books was called (to give it its full superscription) *A Little Pretty Pocket Book, intended for the Instruction and Amusement of Little Master Tommy and Pretty Miss Polly, with an agreeable letter to read from Jack the Giant Killer, and also a Ball and a Pincushion, the use of which will infallibly make Tommy a good Boy and Polly a good girl*. Price of the Book, 6d., with a Ball or Pincushion, 8d.' It was published at the Sign of the 'Bible and Crown' near Devereux Court, London, and was a judicious mixture of very mild entertainment and instruction, with the former predominating. The moral was one that re-occurred in 18th-century children's books, 'Be good and you will be happy'. The good boy ends up riding in a coach; the good girl is given a handsome gold watch.

There had of course been reading matter suitable for children long before this. Since the 17th century, chapmen had travelled the length and breadth of the land carrying in their packs the chapbooks which, crude as they were in style and illustrations, kept alive the old traditional stories: 'The Babes in the Wood', 'Jack the Giant Killer', 'The Seven Champions of Christendom', 'Robin Hood', 'Dick Whittington', 'The Two Children in the Wood', and so on, to entertain simple country folk and children during the long winter evenings. '9 little books' are entered at a cost of 2d. in an 18th-century account book.

Then in that same significant year, 1744, a collection of nursery rhymes for children was published by someone called Cooper, one copy of which survives in the British Museum. It is called *Tommy Thumb's Pretty Song Book* Vol. II.

However, these were the swallows to John Newbery's summer. His *Little Pretty Pocket Book* was followed by *The Lilliputian Magazine, Christmas Box, New Year's Gift, Goody Two Shoes* and others. These little books only measured 3 inches by 4½ inches, a convenient size for small hands, and were for the most part charmingly bound in coloured (sometimes embossed) paper with flowery patterns of red, blue, green and gold.

By the reign of George III, children's books were firmly established as a branch of the publishing business.

John Marshall, who published about seventy children's books during the decade between 1780–90, made a point of the fact that his publications were 'entirely divested of that prejudicial Nonsense (to young minds) the Tales of Hobgoblins, Witches, Fairies. . . .' Fairies were not too well regarded in the 18th century, being still under the shadow of 17th-century Puritan disapproval, and later being condemned by earnest theorists of the Rousseau school of thought, and by strict moralists like Thomas Day, who was so concerned at the 'total want of proper books for young children while they were taught the elements of reading' that he was inspired to write his celebrated and much mocked at *Sandford and Merton*. If a fairy was allowed to intrude at all, as in Lady Fenn's *Fairy Spectator*, it was most likely a moralizing fairy guardian. Fairy tales were described as 'fantastic visions' and (bizarre criticism) as 'not useful'. Imagine a 'useful' fairy story. What a monstrosity!

Kindness to animals was a constant theme in children's books of this period. Mrs. Trimmer's *Fabulous Histories, Designed for the Instruction of Children, respecting their Treatment of Animals* is an example of this type of story. In fact one is left with the unpleasant impression that cruelty to animals was a recognized fault in children in those days (not surprising perhaps when one remembers that cock fighting and bull baiting were popular adult sports). A child nowadays who was addicted to pulling the wings off flies or tormenting kittens would surely be hurried off to a psychiatrist.[1] It would be interesting to know to what extent children's attitude towards animals were influenced by books that attributed to animals the characteristics and speech of human beings, like the enchanting Beatrix Potter books. Dorothy Kilner's *The Life and Perambulations of a Mouse* written at the end of the century was a story of this type.

Rousseau had some scathing things to say in *Emile* about contemporary methods of teaching. 'You will be surprised,' he said, 'to find that I reckon the study of languages [for young children] among the useless lumber of education. . . . I do not believe any child under 12 or 15 ever really acquired two languages.' As for dead languages. 'The children have scarcely learnt their primer by heart, without understanding a word of it, when they are set to translate a French speech into Latin words . . .'. He considered the smattering of Latin that children acquired quite valueless. He was equally contemptuous of the conventional methods of teaching geography and history to the young. Nature, he contended, had not given the child 'plasticity of brain' to have imprinted on it 'the names and dates of kings, the jargon of heraldry, the globe and geography, all those words without present meaning or future use for the child, which flood of words overwhelmed his sad and barren childhood.'

In spite of Rousseau's views, precocity in the young was still much applauded throughout the century. Not every child could be expected to be as advanced as Dr. Malkin's little sons who were 'linguists at 3, profound philosophers at 5, read the Fathers at 6', but children were encouraged and expected to emerge as soon as possible from babyhood. Betsy Fremantle, it is true, protested when her husband wanted to take Tom (aged 5) to sea with him—'I have endeavoured to dissuade him from

[1] Even the pious mother in *The Fairchild Family* as a child, teased her aunt's dog, pinching him and pulling his tail till he howled. She also 'planted' a plate that she had broken on a blameless tabby cat and 'was glad that poor puss was beaten instead of me.'

it—the poor child is certainly too young'. Little boys of six years old had tutors, and 'Perdita' Robinson the Prince of Wales's (George IV) mistress, claimed that before she was seven she could 'correctly repeat Pope's "Lines to the Memory of an Unfortunate Lady" and Mason's "Elergy on the Death of the beautiful Countess of Coventry".'

None of Mrs. Wesley's children were taught to read till they were five years old, but then they were expected to learn their letters in a day, after which they worked for six hours a day, from 9–12, and from 2–5. By the age of six they were all able to read. In Scotland children were set down to their lessons at 7 a.m.

With the increase of cheaper printed books, the horn book which had been the first sign-post on the road of knowledge for generations of children, fell into disuse, and was eventually to be found only in the village dame school. Tots in the early years of the century learnt their alphabet from the famous jingle which began:

> 'A was an Archer who shot at a frog,
> B was a Butcher who had a great dog.'

Their grandchildren learnt from *Reading made Easy*, price 6d. published in 1786 that:

> 'A was an acorn that grew on an oak,
> B was a boy who delights in his book.'

(Poor substitute for the frog-shooting archer and the butcher's 'great dog'.)

Cocker's spelling and arithmetic books were hardy survivals from the 17th century. Then there was *A Little Lottery Book for Children containing a new Method of* playing *them into a Knowledge of the Letters, Figures, etc.*, 1768, probably published by John Newbery. In spite of its dashing, almost rakish title, it was nothing more than the alphabet illustrated by small blocks. The young reader as he learnt the letters could prick them with a pin.

In 1789, Andrew Bell thought out a system of teaching children to trace in sand instead of using books and slates. One way and another it is clear that educationalists were beginning to acknowledge the fact that the average infant did not particularly want to be educated, and that lessons must be made attractive to it.

Little girls had other burdens besides that of learning the alphabet laid upon them. Deportment was still an important part of a young female's education. Small girls curtsied to visitors when entering or leaving a room. Backboards were worn by small girls to give them an upright carriage, and one reads of a governess who pinned sprigs of holly to the front of her pupils' pinafores to make them hold up their heads. A family legend tells of a little ancestress who was taken round Europe in a coach by her parents, and never once lolled back against the seat. (I am not sure of the date of this feat. It may have been as late as the early 19th century, but it was certainly in the 18th-century tradition.)

A tiny china plate had 'A Prize for Sewing well' inscribed on it. Plain needlework was still one of a female child's first lessons.[1] Though 18th-century samplers do not reach the high standards set by earlier specimens, they were part of the nursery routine. The letters of the alphabet, numerals and Biblical verses were worked on fine canvas by small fingers, helped one suspects by kindly nurses. A sampler with pictures of houses and trees, birds and human beings is 'signed', 'Made by me Barbara Jones 1723'. One almost hears the triumphant sigh as Barbara worked the final '3', and the task which at times seemed unending was finally completed.

Mrs. Boscawen's eldest boy, not quite four wrote this letter to his naval father:

July, 1748.

Dear, dear Papa,
    Pray come home, I have made you a great many ships to come in, and Mama says you will bring me something pretty, and pray do Papa, for I am very good Your dutyful son,
                                                    E. H. B.

His proud mother admitted that only the signature was his

[1] Dr. Buchan again: 'Miss is set down to her frame before she can put on her clothes, and taught to believe that to excel at the needle is the only thing that can entitle her to General esteem.'

own unaided handiwork; 'the rest was of my guiding, his dictating', which is what one would expect of a (barely) four-year-old from almost any century.

As early as 1715, Isaac Watts, inspired by the wish to introduce children to the 'great delight' of learning 'truths and duties' through the medium of verse, wrote his 'Divine and Moral Songs for Children.' He has been described by Harvey Darton in his *Children's Books in England* as 'a Puritan of the previous generation become delightfully gentle, tolerant and persuasive'.

It is true that he was responsible for these horrifying lines:

> ''Tis dangerous to provoke a God!
> His pow'r and vengeance none can tell.
> One stroke of his almighty rod
> Shall send young sinners quick to hell.'

Children who disobey their father or mock their mother's word are threatened with a gruesome fate:

> 'The ravens shall pick out his eyes
> And eagles eat the same.'

But later come the lines:

> 'Let Love thro' all your actions run,
> And all your words be mild.
> Live like the blessed Virgin's Son,
> That sweet and lovely Child.'

It is not easy to get a clear picture of the religious upbringing of the 18th-century child. On the one hand there were worldly and fashionable households where the observance of religious duties was perfunctory and formal, and the parents took little interest in their children's spiritual welfare. On the other hand there were intensely pious families like the Wesleys where the children were taught to say the Lord's Prayer as soon as they could speak and trained to sit quiet during family prayers. Later, when rising in the morning they conducted what practically amounted to a short private morning service, prayers, collect, a brief catechism and readings from the Scripture.

But the atmosphere at Epworth Rectory was permeated with the fervent devotion of their mother, Susanna Wesley.

Even in less fervently Evangelical circles, Sunday was observed with a strictness that appalled foreigners. Toys, with the blessed exception of Noah's Ark, were put to one side on the Lord's Day, and only good books were read. Here again, Bunyan's *Pilgrim's Progress* must have seemed a merciful dispensation of Providence. William Godwin as a child was rebuked by his father for fondling the cat on the Sabbath!

Sermons were very long, lasting for anything from an hour to three hours, but children were expected to sit through them from an early age, though, oddly enough, they were allowed the solace of sucking sweets.

The Lindsay children though kept in rigid subjection by their mother Lady Crawford, had 'heaps of sweets' of all kinds on their dinner table, given by their father.

Sentiments of this kind (embroidered on a late 18th-century sampler):

> 'The Lord delights in them that speak
> The word of truth, but every liar,
> Must have his portion in the lake
> That burns with brimstone and with fire'

must have been terrifying to nervous children (especially as these are perhaps the ones that are inclined to be untruthful?) but it is hard to imagine that Mrs. Boscawen's children—'the most lovely babes in the world' she considered them—were frightened with brimstone and fire. Mrs. Boscawen told the Admiral: 'Your son has also been to Church every Sunday and has behaved extremely well. Mr. Gore asked him if he could sing Psalms. He said no, but that he could sing the Rakes of Marlow [Mallow] if that would do.'

6

The child has now emerged from infancy. We have watched it at play, at its first lessons and praying at its mother's knee. This might be the moment to record some random impressions of its life as it begins to join in the adult life around it. Here is

Miss Cave, aged six (very early this in the century) who 'everyday at dinner Drinks a health to Claydon, Stanford, the Queen and Church, to Sir Sachevrill and her maid Betty of whom she is very fond'. I like to picture that plump little Tory and Churchwoman, in her laced bodice and flowered petticoat, drinking this nice assortment of toasts in small beer or negus, which consisting of wine, hot water, sugar and lemon was thought to be suitable for invalids and children.

A little Boscawen boy, midway through the century, is also seen drinking toasts while having a '*tête-à-tête* upon a chicken' with his mother. Having drunk his father's health, his mother 'advised him to drink that of brother Boscawen'. He did so and 'leaving something in his glass, he returned again, took it up and said, "Now I'll drink myself sharn't I ?" '

The Boscawen children are depicted by their fond mother as robust young creatures—'stout, robust, bold and comical'— 'such a sprightly cub' she calls one of her little boys, certainly not in the least repressed. 'If you hum a tune' to little Bess, 'instantly she seizes her frock at each side and falls a dancing'. Frances, too, was a great dancer, but when Mr. Glover paid 'a civil visit', the girls were asleep, and Edward, aged nearly four, could not be prevailed upon to perform what he called 'a hornpike', which according to his mother he did 'vastly well'. He made an attempt to oblige but was overcome with shyness and came running back after the first step saying, 'Mama I am ashamed, don't ask me to dance'. But he promised himself 'great pleasure in dancing before dear Papa. He would do anything for you, loves you excessively and remembers you perfectly'. The little boy drew ships for his father to sail home in, and houses for him to live in. He was, Mrs. Boscawen assured her husband, so 'well informed that if you asked him who beat the French, he will immediately bawl out "Papa"'.

A naval officer, Captain Palliser, called on Mrs. Boscawen to collect a letter for the Admiral which she was entrusting to him. Before he left, he was taken to see the children at their meal, so that they might see the man who was to see their father. He, tactful man, admired their good looks and appetite. 'He asked your son what to say to you, who answered with his chops full, "I want Papa at home".'

After a journey to Alton in Hampshire, William, aged 5, who had not slept in the coach, was put to bed and covered up 'most neat', and the room darkened. But William was tough. He had not been five minutes in bed 'before he called out that he had no posts, that 'twas a silly bed, and that he did not want to lie in it, but rather to see those pictures that hung in the passage'. His mother reported that, as she wrote to the Admiral, he was 'making a great riot in the galleries'. One suspects that William was over-ripe for a taste of naval discipline.

Imagine what it was like being boxed up for hours in a coach or chaise with a restless or fretful child. The Verney clan's enjoyment of the company of their 'sweet babes' never seems to have flagged. On a journey 'young Verney filled up the bottom of the Chaise and diverted us in the journey much'. But Betsy Fremantle, I feel, found family journeys exhausting—'It was past eleven before we could get away, what with Nurses, Children and Lumber'—even though 'Tommy behaved very well in our post chaise all the way'. (Her baby girl Emma was 'with the women in a back chaise'.) On a later occasion, the Fremantle family had a gruelling drive down to Portsmouth where Betsy was meeting her husband, 'I suffered much from the heat and dust, as well as the poor children and arrived at Portsmouth quite fatigued at seven o'clock [a journey of twelve hours] . . . the children being cross and tired, Nurse ill and obliged to go to bed where she was soon terrified at being attacked by a regiment of Bugs'. (This contrasts oddly with Betsy's assertion that the house she had rented was 'extremely small but tolerably clean'.)

Travelling, even in the British Isles, could be worse than tiring. 'The morning Northampton,' wrote Mary Lovett in 1710, 'the Coach was overturned two hours before day, which frightened me extremely for my poor little boy's sake, but I thank God we were none of us hurt.' No wonder that Mrs. Boscawen told her husband, '. . . you know how I can never trust anyone in a coach with my children but myself'.

Lucy Aitkin's earliest recollection was of the rigours of a journey that she made with her family from Warrington to Yarmouth. Her grandmother and the grandmother's maid, Lucy and her little brother were in the post chaise, her father

13. From a Mid-Victorian Family Album

14. A Little Boy of the early 1870s

was on horseback. They travelled through heavy snow, and such was the cold and fatigue of the journey that the poor grandmother died from the effects shortly after arriving at their destination.

It is not surprising that children were left at home as much as possible—'It be very troublesome to remove children from place to place' as one mother put it. A child recovering from a serious illness might be sent to drink goat's milk and whey in the country, or, as the century went on, to the seaside for sea air and bathing.

A picture by Beechey of 'Children relieving a beggar boy' shows a little girl in a muslin dress and bonnet, and a small boy in pantaloons and jacket with a frilled shirt, wearing a plumed hat on his long hair, and an insufferably smug expression, bestowing alms on a taller boy in rags. The contrast between the beggar boy's cringing attitude and the complacent and patronizing air of the rich children (which seems to have communicated itself to their pet dog) is nauseous to modern ideas. The picture illustrates vividly the growth of class consciousness during the century and of a condescending snobbery that tainted even the children of the well-to-do. Society was beginning to wear a purse-proud look. Excessive value was attached to wealth, social influence and worldly possessions. The easy familiarity between the classes, that had existed in rural communities anyhow, was fast disappearing.

It is true that the misery that the Industrial Revolution had brought in its train, had led to a considerable amount of organized philanthropy. Miss Sarah Holroyd writing to her niece in 1787, described a Sunday School that was held in Bath Cathedral (Abbey) 'Nine hundred children in perfect order . . . so quiet you could hardly have heard a pin drop while the clergyman was reading . . . most of them taken out of the streets untaught, and actually almost savage, cursing, swearing and fighting in the streets, and many without a home at night. Most of them not only ragged and starving, but without a chance of being put in the way to earn their bread.'

What a horrifying glimpse this gives of the abyss that lay beneath the suave exterior of late 18th-century society. She

goes on to describe a school of Industry, 'thirty or forty little
things may be seen knitting. They begin to knit garters at three
years old. . . . Here I often go with great pleasure and would
have carried you.'

Beneath her undoubted benevolence, the implication is clear.
The poor, even when they are toddlers, must be busy and
industrious. The attitude considered suitable to the poor child
was summed up in one of Watt's verses:

> 'What tho' I be low and mean,
> I'll engage the rich to love me,
> While I'm modest, neat, and clean,
> And submit when they reprove me.'

I have left to the last an aspect of nursery life which should
perhaps have come first, because of its importance, so much
else hinging upon it. The fact is that I find it the most interesting, and believe that my readers may do so too. It is the
attitude of adults towards the children.

The 18th century was in this respect as in many others a
transition age, the meeting place of the old and of the modern
world. ('I had the curiosity to goe to see him dye,' someone
wrote of Lord Derwentwater's execution, adding, 'but the
sight was very terrible.') Children were sometimes kept under
rigid discipline, in other cases they were spoilt and indulged.

Swift describes the son of rich parents thus: 'He is taught
from the nursery that he must inherit a great estate and hath no
need to mind his book, which is a lesson he never forgets till
the end of his life.' A child like this would have expensive
clothes to wear, elaborate toys, and relays of servants to wait on
him. Mrs. Boscawen's style of living was comparatively simple,
yet her son had a little black boy to wait on him. He had been
brought as a present by a naval lieutenant who had dressed him
in the Boscawen livery. 'Your son took to him immediately and
whispered he should be his servant. Accordingly he walks out
in the garden with him, plays up in the nursery, waits upon him
at table.'

According to Maria Edgeworth, nurses were responsible for a
good deal of the harm, as they hoped, by indulging the child to
gain the parent's favour. Here again we see a marked contrast

between the 18th-century nurse and the best type of Victorian Nanny, with her inflexible standards of right and wrong.

But in many circles the spartan ways still prevailed. Mrs. Wesley believing as she did that self-will was the root of all evil, trained her infants from the word 'go' to absolute obedience. From a year old they were brought up 'to fear the rod and to cry softly', with the result that 'the odious noise of the crying of children was rarely heard in the house'. They were never allowed to eat between meals, nor was anyone allowed to sit up with them at night till they fell asleep. Yet she was not the unsympathetic martinet that all this suggests. She was scrupulously just. Her children were never punished or scolded twice for the same fault. A promise to be good, accompanied by signs of sincere repentance, was always accepted. Her children loved and trusted her. When one of them called her 'Madam' she remonstrated in horror, 'There is more affection and tenderness in the name of mother than in all the compliments and titles in the world'. Moreover, outside the rigid routine of daily devotions and lessons there was time for some cheerful little family parties. It was not a household that I personally would have chosen to have born into, but it was good of its kind.

I have read that discipline by means of the rod began to go out of fashion in the time of George I. As proof of this, the story was told of how Queen Caroline, then of course Princess of Wales, was whipping one of her children. Sarah, Duchess of Marlborough, interceded for it, whereupon the Princess said, 'Oh, see there! you English are none of you well-bred because you were not whipped when you was young'.

English, and particularly Anglo-Irish parents, were considered to be exceptionally indulgent towards their children. Old-fashioned discipline still held firm in many homes in Scotland, where the children were made to stand in the presence of their parents. One of Lord and Lady Balcarres' daughters, Lady Anne Lindsay described her childhood home as being 'a sort of little Bastille, in every closet of which was to be found a culprit, some were sobbing and repeating verbs, others eating their bread and water, some preparing themselves to be whipped'. It was Lady Balcarres who was the tyrant. Lord Balcarres occasionally tried to intervene with an 'Odsfish, Madam! you will break the spirit of my young troops. I will not have it so.' But as a matter of fact their spirits were far from broken. One day, goaded beyond endurance, they all ran away. An old shepherd rushed to Lady Balcarres with the news that 'all the young gentlemen and all the young ladies, and all the dogs are run away'.

Scotch parents were not by any means all cast in such a stern mould. Mrs. Scott, the wife of the British Envoy in Hanover, believed in teaching small children, as her own mother had done with her, by telling them stories. She disapproved of children's duty (i.e. reading the Bible) being turned into a punishment. Children she said should never be called names by their elders. They 'do not forget these little affronts'.

Enough has been said earlier on, to show the pleasure that the Verney family (which includes their relations and even connections) took in their offspring. Sir Thomas Cave, in particular, positively revelled in his paternity. 'Our stock of Enfans being now seven, we don't fail of Domestick noise and diversion sufficient and at this instant you'd fancy the House full of Bears.' Evidently no one was 'taught to cry softly' in the Cave household. A little boy is described by his father, Ralph Palmer, as 'the life of the house'. Children are tenderly called 'the little fry', 'all the little Olive branches round your table', 'my Flock', 'your sweet little ones'.

Mary Lovett certainly found her children a worry at times, but she, poor woman, was in very low spirits, having recently been widowed. She wrote to her father, Lord Fermanagh, 'I am very much obleiged to you and my mother for desiring them, [the children] but while I live in this world I will be as little troublesome in it as I can, and I am sencible children are very much so, but mine shall be as little as they can.'

I am sure that it never occurred to Mrs. Boscawen that her children could be troublesome—'the most beautiful, the most healthful children that even were seen, with the most tractable tempers and the most engaging behaviours', she considered them.

Yet, when she took them to stay with her father, though he duly commended them as the finest children that ever were seen, he surprised her by 'not choosing to bear their noise (that is their play for they never cry) a minute'. She warned the Admiral that his boy would tell him that 'Grandpapa says I was born in a storm because I talk so loud'. A great-aunt aged 88, who they visited later, stood the test better. She was 'vastly fond of all the children and has always one or two of them playing in her room.' Perhaps she was deaf?

It must be admitted that Mrs. Boscawen doted on her children to the point of infatuation. One of her favourite pastimes, as she admitted to her husband, was comparing them with other people's children, invariably to the latter's disadvantage. 'I must have one observation ... the comparison of our children with your brother George's. ... What a difference! ... she is as far from an agreeable child as she is from a pretty one. Ours is both, in the highest degree, and so everyone thinks.' 'Your son maintains his superiority over Neddy Meadows, than whom he is taller by 2 inches, though the latter is turned five years old, and our jewel is three and a quarter. Bess too is a jewel that has not its fellow. There never was such a girl ... Frances is a charming little plump, blue-eyed maid that would pass for a beauty in any house but this.'

Her son 'towers above' all Lady Romney's children both in height and learning, 'which is no small honour to him and me, since the elder Marsham will be six years old next spring, and there is more pains taken with them than with most children. Nevertheless your child beats him to nothing.' Then, 'Little Augusta is reckoned a fine child but my little Bess spoils me for admiring any child'. She also relates a triumph that she had over a Mr. Mason who had rashly claimed that his son was a great deal taller than the Boscawen boy. Not only did Mr. Mason's boy prove to be 'half a head shorter than mine', but badly behaved into the bargain. Mr. and Mrs. Mason 'seemed mortified', and Mr. Mason exclaimed, 'What a joy it must be to the Admiral to see such a lovely, such an interesting child', which in the circumstances was, I think, rather generous-minded of him.

I am afraid that Mrs. Boscawen, excellent woman as she was, cannot have endeared herself to other mothers, by this over-weening pride in her children. But of course it must be remembered that her letters were intended for her husband's eyes alone, and that she was endeavouring to console herself for his long absences by absorbing herself in her children's existences. They were constantly with her. She could hardly tear herself away from them even for a few days, which on one occasion at least exposed her to the mirth of her friends. 'But till they have such a lovely boy as mine, they cannot tell how they would dote on it.' Another time she went on a visit to Oxford, but only after she had 'sworn all my maids that they would never once go out of the place till I return, and that two of 'em viz. the two nursery maids and Marchfield will watch and attend the children night and day.' As an extra precaution, the apothecary was to call every evening to see if they were well, and the butler was to send a daily bulletin. Mrs. Boscawen, by the way, was only absent for a week!

Yet, doting mother as she was, she could be firm with her darlings. William got out of hand as a result of his inoculation —'it is unknown how perverse and saucy we are, and how much we deal in the words, wont, cant, sharnt'. There was a tussle over breakfast, but in the end Billy capitulated, the bottom of the porringer was revealed, and he admitted that 'indeed he could not but say it was very good milk'. Another time there was 'a misunderstanding between Billy and his pudding'. Mrs. Boscawen records that 'T'other son received discipline this morning'.

She kept her children to a regular and sensible routine. As soon as she got up she went out in the garden 'the boy in my hand, and by the time his shoes are wet through with dew (which never gives us any cold) we come into breakfast'. One would imagine from this that Mrs. Boscawen was a believer in Rousseau's hardening system, if the date of the letter, 1748, was not more than a decade earlier than *Emile*. Immediately after breakfast came lessons 'a ceremony never omitted nor broke into, whether I have company or not—by which means he has made a considerable progress since we came into the country'. Lessons were followed by another little walk before dinner, at two. Afterwards in a grove, 'my son and his sister make hay beside us, Mrs. Smythe having presented him with a rake, fork and spade, and I treated him with a large wheelbarrow'. The rule, strictly kept to, was that 'hay never peeps into our green parlour, but stays in the grove, which is full of dead leaves and twigs, so that it could not be kept neat which the rest of the garden is in an eminent degree. . . .' Tea was at six, and bed-time at eight.

A Verney mother earlier in the century was less sensible in her arrangements. She wrote asking Cousin Peg to get her a pair of leading reins. These were for John or 'Jak' Verney. The unfortunate child was four years old, but his mother 'never let him be a moment out of my sight, so I have been never out since but he has been with me at church and scolds every day for his Papa to come home'. No wonder!

Though a new interest in children as such, and some acknow-ledgment of their special needs, was growing up among adults, it was still felt very strongly that their main purpose in life was to be a joy and comfort to their parents. Sir Thomas Cave, writing in 1705 to his father-in-law, expresses the hope that his new-born son will prove 'as great a comfort as a present joy to your Lordships dutiful son and servant'. Mary Lovett in a letter to her father, trusts that her 'little Betty will be a good child, and hope now she will begin to have some sense and mind to be obediant to you and my mother, to whome I am extreamely oblidged for all her kindness to her'.

Towards the other end of the century, an aunt was adding to her loving birthday greetings to her six-year-old niece, the hope that she would 'live to be the joy of Papa and Mama'. She exhorted her to be 'good, gentle and obliging to everyone . . . little girls that are not so always pass for vulgar, ill-bred children and are despised and unhappy'. But the pill of this little homily was coated with jam. 'Your Grandpapa sends love to you, and if he were able, would go two hundred miles to see you.' Grown-ups were no longer afraid to show children that they were desired and precious.

Children were being brought forward and receiving atten-tion in circles outside the immediate family. Betsy Fremantle mentions, 'A little boy not four years old that plays very toler-antly upon the pianoforte'. When she visited Stowe, she records with satisfaction that 'Lord and Lady B. [Buckingham] were exceeding kind to me and insisted on having Tommy down to coffee', also, 'Tommy is taken a great deal of notice of and much admired'.

The attitude of the Fremantle parents towards their large brood (or 'brattery' as Betsy called it) was affectionate but unsentimental. Betsy alludes to her children as her 'brats', and to other people's children in even less complimentary terms. 'Mrs. Howard and her nasty children'—'. . . the ugliest little Ape I ever saw'—'Mrs. Le Mesurier who is as big as a house, and her three ugly little brats, the eldest only three years old.' One suspects that Betsy was not a child lover.

Her description of her small daughter Louisa as 'a little love-ugly' is cool—some people may find it refreshingly so—after Mrs. Boscawen's raptures.

Fremantle refused to rhapsodize. 'My dear little baby grows exceedingly . . . I think him a pretty child but Fremantle calls him an ugly dog.' But he was a devoted enough father, writing of 'the dear little brats', and saying, 'You cannot imagine how desirous I am to see little Louisa, I hope I shall not spoil the monkey'.

It would be a long and tedious business to try and trace the influence of Jean Jacques Rousseau's *Emile* on the parents and instructors of the young in the second half of the 18th century. Perhaps it will be enough for the purpose of this book to give a brief outline of Rousseau's theories, as they affected the young child, and this may best be done by quoting some of the key sentiments in the early chapters.

'Education comes to us from nature, from men, or from things,' he declared, and 'Life is the trade I would teach him' [his imaginary pupil Emile]. From which it will be gathered that it was his aim to free children from the artificial restraints and rules that surrounded them from their cradles, and of which the 'senseless and unnatural custom' of swaddling was a symbol. 'Civilised man is born and dies a slave' he said . . . 'all his life long man is imprisoned by our institutions'. Priests, philsophers and doctors were all anathema to him. '. . . as I never call in a doctor for myself, I will never send for one for Emile, unless his life is clearly in danger, when the doctor can but kill him', he says cynically.

Again and again he stressed the importance of bringing the child up hardily. 'He must be taught to preserve his own life when he is a man, to live at need among the snows of Iceland,[1] or on the scorching rocks of Malta. . . . Teach him to live rather than to avoid death . . .' Later he exhorts parents to, 'Fix your eyes on nature, follow the path traced by her. She keeps children at work, she hardens them by all kinds of difficulties, she soon teaches them the meaning of pain and grief. . . experience shows that children delicately nurtured are more likely to die. . . . Accustom them therefore to the hardships they will have to face, train them to endure extremes of temperature, climate and condition, hunger, thirst and weariness.' 'A feeble body,' he believed, 'makes a feeble mind.'

He deplored the fact that for the first six or seven years of his existence, the child was in the hands of women, 'the victim of his own caprices and theirs'.[2] After they had burdened his memory with words he cannot understand or 'things which are of no use to him' or 'stifled nature' by the passions they implanted in him, 'this sham article' was handed over to a tutor. Rousseau strongly emphasized his belief that it was the duty of the mother to be the children's nurse, the father to be their tutor. (Strange are the inconsistencies of human nature! Rousseau's own children, as I have already mentioned, were consigned to a foundling hospital.)

Though Rousseau advocated a hardening system that might seem at times to verge on harshness, he was insistent that the child should be spared any unnecessary irritation. 'Take the greatest care to remove from them any servants who tease, annoy or vex them.'

He dismissed Locke's maxim, 'Reason with children' with the tart comment that 'those children who have been constantly reasoned with strike me as exceedingly silly'. This led him to the revolutionary idea that 'It is no part of a child's

[1] Was he thinking of Greenland?
[2] Most parents will agree with me, I think when I say that small children are never happier or better behaved than when they are in the company of gardeners, farm workers, sailors and so on—in other words, of men who treat them as fellow-workers and are too busy with their own jobs to bother them.

business to know right and wrong'. Few English parents can have agreed with this, but though the book must have shocked and even appalled many people, it must also have stirred parents into considering anew their relationship to their children, and the essential characteristics and needs of childhood.

Its influence, though gradual must have been far-reaching. But it would be a mistake to imagine that all children before the publication of *Emile* led repressed, constricted lives. Here is a glimpse of the childhood of one of the most fascinating women of the 18th century, Lady Sarah Lennox, who might have become Queen of England if George III had not sacrificed his personal inclinations for what he considered to be his duty. Lady Sarah was the result of an exceptionally happy and romantic marriage. Her parents the Duke and Duchess of Richmond were married at the age of eighteen and thirteen respectively, to cancel a gambling debt between their fathers. Young Lord March, as he was then, was so little attracted by his first sight of his youthful bride that he broke out rudely, 'Surely you are not going to marry me to that dowdy?' After this unpromising beginning, he was whisked away by his tutor on the Grand Tour, while his bride remained with her parents. Three years later Lord March returned home reluctantly to take up his duties as a married man. At the playhouse that first evening he saw a bewitching young girl seated in one of the boxes. Eagerly he asked her name, to be told, 'You must be a stranger, sir, to the town if you do not know its reigning toast the beautiful Lady March'. Many years later, the Duke of Richmond, as Lord March had then become, was reported by the omniscient Horace Walpole to be sitting all evening at a ball by his wife's side, kissing her hand.

Lady Sarah, one of their younger children was born in 1745, so she was only five years old when she had her encounter with George II in Kensington Gardens. She and her sister Louisa were walking with their governess when the royal party came in sight. 'Sha-Sha' as Sarah was nicknamed in her family, bounded up to the King, and speaking French (for her father had been Ambassador in Paris and she had not yet learnt to speak her native language) said: '*Comment vous portez vous,*

Monsieur le Roi? Vous avez une grande et belle maison ici, n'est ce pas?'
The peppery King was so delighted with the little creature's
gay audacity that he invited her to come and see him at Kensington Palace. On one of these occasions when they were playing hide and seek together, the King had a sudden whim to test
Sarah's courage, and popped her into a large china jar and put
the lid on. But there was no plaintive outcry, only a small voice
trilled out:

> 'Malbruc s'en va-t-en-guerre,
> Miroton, Miroton, Mirotaine.'

V

❖▶

Nineteenth Century

DATES have a significance for us immeasurably greater than their real importance. They are man-made conceptions devised to make more bearable the profound mystery of time. We know this, but we cannot feel it. The year 1800 means something special to us (even though in fact it was, as the purists point out, the completion of the 18th century, not the beginning of the 19th). To us, it can never be just a year like any other year; it is the dawn of that century that links us so amazingly with the 'historic' past. Its closing years are well within living memory, yet there must have been very old people living on into its first few years, who were born in the reign of the last Stuart monarch—Queen Anne.

The panorama that unfolds itself before our mental vision is bewildering in its complexity—the years of conflict and victory—Trafalgar, Waterloo—the years of prosperity and unrest which were the birth throes of industrial England—the Reform Act, the Chartist Riots; then the picture stamped on our minds by nursery history books, the eighteen-year-old Queen, a shawl thrown over her dressing gown, her hair falling over her shoulders receiving the homage of Archbishop and Lord Chamberlain.[1] These are the 'old times' still; mail coaches, Dickensian inns and Christmas jollities, men in fancy waistcoats wearing their hair in waved locks, and women in demure bonnets and bell-like skirts. But the modern world is rapidly

---

[1] It is disconcerting to read that she was wearing a nightcap at the time.

172

taking shape; railways supersede the ancient highways as the chief means of communication; at sea, steam takes the place of sail; the candles are extinguished, the gas lamps lit; women demand higher education and political rights. The Crimean War and the Indian Mutiny are livid scars on the prosperous and complacent face of the century.

In family albums, handsomely bound in leather with metal clasps, we see photographs of our Victorian forbears, sitting in bountiful family groups on verandah steps, or posed, book in hand by a carved table or a plush-upholstered chair. They are shown playing croquet or in tennis 'rig' (why, one wonders is that young man wearing football boots and a boater hat?). Their names are known to us—'That is your great-grandmother. That's Great Uncle Bill who went out to Australia. That must be his sister Mary who died young. . . .'

Like a train that goes faster and faster as it nears its destination, the century rushes towards modern times, its unsuspecting passengers little guessing at the terrors that lie ahead.

Before Victoria, 1800–1837

I

A child who was old enough on January 1st, 1800 to use a pen, might be encouraged by its mother or nurse to write the momentous date at the top of its copy book, so as to impress on its mind the interesting fact that the 18th century was over. For the rest of its life (in spite of the encouraging example of Methuselah in Holy Writ) it would head its letters or journal with those numerals 18–.

Yet in actual fact the little boy or girl in question would, of course, continue to look and behave just the same as it did yesterday on December 31st, 1799. And for some years to come its younger brothers and sisters would be, to all intents and purposes, 18th-century children, the little boys in their nankeen trousers and frilled shirts, the little girls in the simple muslin or Indian calico dress, with a coloured sash, that was practically uniform attire for upper- and middle-class 'misses'.

It has been said that 18th-century ways of thought and habits persisted till the accession of Queen Victoria.[1] Time cannot be sliced up like a piece of cheese and tied into neat parcels (the absurdity of trying to do this was brought home to me when I was taking notes for the 18th-century part of this book from the Wynne Diaries, and felt obliged to stop when I strayed more than a few years into the 19th century). Yet it is certainly true that the 18th-century atmosphere and outlook—'climate' as it is called nowadays—lingered on long after the calendar had consigned the 18th century to limbo.

This makes it difficult to give an account of nursery life in the early years of the 19th century without a good deal of repetition that would be as tiresome to write as it would be to read. Confinements were still often difficult and dangerous. The doctors could not save even so exalted a patient as Princess Charlotte, the heiress and hope of England, when she gave birth in 1817 to a still-born son. It is generally believed that her accouchement had been badly bungled, and the unfortunate physician Dr. Croft, who was in charge of the case, afterwards committed suicide in a patient's house, though Miss Dorothy Margaret Stuart's medical researches in her book *The Daughter of England*, show that the Princess was not as healthy as her appearance suggested, and that in the state of medical knowledge, as it was then, the disaster could hardly have been avoided.

Large families were still the rule. Elizabeth Ham was governess to the eight Elton children from 'little Jane just beginning to prattle' upwards, and Mrs. Elton was expecting a ninth. The times were long past, however, when fecundity was considered an unmitigated blessing. Not only did celibates like Miss Weeton (another governess) deplore the fact that a married couple, the Armitages, had 'foolishly contrived to increase and multiply', so could not afford to keep a carriage (there were six young Armitages, the eldest girl just seven years old, and another on the way, when she wrote—eventually there were to be fifteen) but Captain Fremantle, himself the father of a large family, wrote:

'I am very sorry Mrs. Henley is likely to increase her family,

[1] *London in the 19th Century*, Sir Walter Besant.

that is a misfortune that happens in other families as well as hers, and one must have patience.' His sister-in-law Eugenia told of a Mrs. Manners who 'talks cooly of riding to procure a miscarriage, and this because he [her husband] hates children and beats her for having some'.

Infant mortality was still high, as many an early 19th-century memorial on a church wall sadly testifies. A drawing-room in a country house might have a marble memorial statue of a dead child. Fortunate were the parents who escaped without the loss of at least one young child. This no doubt explains the attitude of the bereaved mothers and fathers. Their grief cannot for a moment be doubted—it is conveyed to us across the years in pathetic letters and epitaphs—but they accepted these nursery tragedies as one of life's expected hazards rather than as a cruel catastrophe. Captain Fremantle was a fond and indulgent father, 'What is there in children,' he asked, 'that gets such possession of our hearts?' with a particularly soft spot for his little daughters—'What is it that makes me think so much more of my girls than of my boys?' Yet, in his reply to his wife Betsy's letter telling of the death of their five-year-old Louisa at Brighton (in particularly poignant circumstances as 'measles or scarlet fever being apprehended', Betsy who had a young baby dared not go to her) after expressing his severe distress at the news, he went on to write at some length about other subjects. It is difficult to imagine a modern father, as devoted as Fremantle was, disposing of a much-loved child's death in a few lines.

Aunts were even more stoical: 'How are your little ones?' Miss Weeton wrote to her brother in 1807. 'Do they escape the whooping cough? Great numbers have it here, and it is very fatal. Many die of it, several children are gone blind with it, and some thrown into fits . . .' (encouraging news this for parents!). Later she expresses concern over a sick nephew thus: 'Poor sweet little suffering angel. . . . I hope his days are not *so soon* to be terminated.'

In Mrs. Sherwood's inimitable book *The Fairchild Family*, little Emily and Lucy Fairchild talk together of 'heaven where their cousins Emily and Ellen, with all their infant brothers were with their parents in a state of everlasting glory'. As a result of this holocaust of young relations, their father Mr. Fairchild had succeeded to a large estate. Lucy when she heard the news, clasped her hands and exclaimed with tears, 'Oh, God! help us to use these riches well.'

It is startling to realize that there was an outbreak of cholera not only in 1831–32, but as late as 1867.[1] But vaccination was winning the battle against smallpox. 'Cowpox appears to be the universal practice, and I believe that Doctor Jenner is going to have a premium in Parliament for having Discovered so useful a muzzle for the dreadful disease' wrote Lady Jerningham in 1802. The Reverend Benjamin Newton, a country parson, recorded in his diary early in the century, 'Vaccinated three or four [children] on Saturday'.

Fevers were still very prevalent however, which was hardly to be wondered at, considering the primitive sanitary arrangements in many houses. Water closets only came into general use about 1830 in the better type of houses, and were so defective as to be a positive menace to health. At as late a date as 1844, fifty-three overflowing cesspools were discovered under the august foundations of Windsor Castle. A facetious attitude was adopted towards bad drainage; weather prophets considered the smell resulting from it a convenient warning of bad weather.

2

In picturing to oneself the background against which these pre-Victorian children lived, one must visualize house interiors that still retained much of the impress of the 18th century. It was not till after the Queen's marriage and particularly after the 1851 Exhibition, that the typically Victorian style of decoration became general—a style now beginning to acquire the glamour of age, so that Victorian 'pieces' have been described as 'the antiques of the future'.

Certainly the average early 19th-century nursery, where for

[1] It is curious to note that rubber hot-water bottles, or 'bags' as they were called were 'in great esteem' during the 1831–2 epidemic, but for some reason quite inexplicable to me, they did not come into general use till many years later.

15a. A Nursery party at the turn of the Twentieth Century

15b. Eighteenth-Century Child's Chair

16. A Baby, 1900 and his eldest brother

some years after Waterloo, naughty children were frightened by their nursery maids with the threat that Boney would come and take them, was bare to the point of austerity, with deal tables and rush-bottomed chairs (the cry of 'Chairs to mend' still resounded in the streets) a big press for clothes, a toy cupboard, and the dreariness of uncurtained windows. Here the head nurse, in a mob cap, or in a more modest household the single-handed nurse, reared her large brood. One may imagine her sitting in the firelight, rocking her charge to sleep in a cradle of the type to be seen in the Victoria and Albert Museum. This is fitted with a clock-work spring, and is made of joined and turned wood. The walls of the crib are formed by parallel, vertical wooden bars which slope outwards. The posts of the cribs and the stand to which it is attached, are topped with carved knobs.

Elizabeth Ham mentions a friend who disliked her monthly nurse and insisted on sending her away. 'Her husband I believe was the better nurse of the two, and he was certainly very attentive to her at that time', but in another household the 'young fry' were under the care of an old Nurse who 'had been at the birth of every one of them'.

A nurse of the Nanny type who presided over a country house nursery in the second decade of the century was nicknamed 'Gish' by the family. She married the bailiff when she was in her fifties, and her devoted charges continued to visit her when they were grown-up.

A nurse in a household of any pretentions would have one or more nursery maids in attendance. In 1830 one of these girls was paid £10 10s. a year, and one may be sure that Nurse told her how fortunate she was. 'In my young days etc. . . .' In the *Jerningham Letters* it is recorded that 'Lord Bute's new little girl goes out on airing with these nurses, and two footmen behind the coach'.

Wet-nurses were still in demand and the custom (an unnatural one as it seems to us) of putting a child 'out to nurse' persisted. An acquaintance of Elizabeth Ham's, a Mrs. Dennis, wife of an Irish clergyman, was convinced that one of her children 'a heavy, rickety looking child' whose unprepossessing appearance contrasted strikingly with that of another of her

children, 'a sweet, engaging little prattler', had been changed
at nurse. 'Nothing could make her believe that he was her
child', she told Elizabeth Ham, which shocked Elizabeth very
much.

Mrs. Dennis's nursery arrangements seem to have been peculiar even for an Irish household. She had a little crib in her
room for each of her four children, who all slept on straw to
keep them healthy. In a recess in a corner of this stable-like
apartment, the nurse had her bed. Only the baby was allowed
a pillow, Mrs. Dennis believing that pillows made children
round-shouldered.

Elizabeth Ham tells the tragic story of an over-anxious
mother. She had gone sightseeing to the top of a ruined castle
with her first-born baby and its nurse. On the way down, not
trusting it to the nurse, she insisted on carrying it herself. She
lost her footing in the dark and fell; the poor baby was taken
up dead, and the distracted mother went temporarily out of
her mind.

Careless and ignorant nursemaids could be a menace.
Elizabeth Ham's own little niece, Emma, pulled a basin of
bread soaked in boiling water, which the nursemaid had prepared for her supper, off the table and over herself. The maid
bathed the scald with vinegar and said nothing to the parents,
and the little girl died in a matter of days from 'inflammation
of the chest'. The fact was that in those days of cheap domestic
labour any mother who laid claim to gentility employed a girl
to look after her children, without always making sure of her
suitability or efficiency.

The same thing applied to governesses. Miss Weeton complained that her employers the Armitages, 'never examine the
progress their children make—they are totally unaquainted
with a great part of what their children learn. . . . For anything
the parents might know, I might teach the children to be Deists
or Atheists, or what is even worse, might never teach them
anything like religion at all.'

Incidentally, governesses were often expected to look after
children of nursery rather than of school-room age. Writing of
the 'utter loneliness of the life of a governess', Elizabeth Ham
described 'the dreary winter day, and the still more dreary

evening, confined to the dull school-room, with the reeking towels [on the fireguard] in the morning, and the noisy young children in the evening, for those who were too young to be my pupils were not thought too young to be turned into the school-room to play. They would not be amused by any quiet pastime, and I had not the heart to check their young spirits by any undue restraint.'

In one place she was in, she was warned by her employer that the head nurse might be jealous of her, but luckily 'Mrs. Mary' turned out to be a simple, honest creature and gave her no trouble.

In *The Child in Fashion*, Mrs. Langley Moore, an authority on the art of fashion throughout the centuries, gives the exact measurements of the babies' long clothes from her collection. These (from shoulder to hem) were 46 inches in 1815, and a couple of inches less in 1830. Lawn or batiste was the most popular material for baby clothes, but christening robes were often rather sumptuous, as will be seen from these extracts from a letter written by a young mother to her sister in 1836. She confesses that she 'cannot overcome the wish to have Georgey christened in a mantle though I have persuaded myself not to have a seven-guinea one. But I mean to have a white satin one covered with Indian muslin and I should be very much obliged to you to get me five yards of *faultless* white satin. It must be a most luscious article, soft as down and white as snow, with a *soupçon* of a pink blush upon it. . . . All these virtues, they say, can be got for six or seven shillings a yard. . . . It must be trimmed either with silk fringe or swansdown. . . . Swansdown seems to me a beau ideal but I leave it to your discretion when you see them together, and yet it sounds as if Bunting would look so *very* pretty in satin and swansdown.' (One imagines 'Bunting' looking quite furious as boy babies are apt to do in christening finery.)

White satin pincushions were favourite christening presents, and Mrs. Langley Moore describes one in her possession dating from about 1814, with the following inscription worked on it in pin heads:

'Welcome thou little darling heir
Of heavenly bliss and mortal care,

Oh may thy Parents live to see
Their fondest hopes fulfilled in thee.' [1]

Little boys under the age of six or seven still wore dresses and
continued to do so well into the Victorian era[2] *The Fairchild
Family* grandmother, when a gushing maid described little
Master Henry as being an honour to the family, retorted with
tart commonsense: 'as to little boys in pinafores doing honour
to their families, you must know that is quite out of the
question.'

It seems that Henry (who was not quite eight) was partially
breeched, as he spilt beer from a picnic hamper on to his white
trousers. He still wore however a petticoated jacket, though his
mamma intended to have a boy's cloth jacket made for him
soon. Meanwhile he objected strongly to wearing a shawl while
travelling, saying that he did not want to be dressed like a
girl. A little boy is shown in a fashion plate of 1830 wearing
a long tunic coat with a belt, light-coloured trousers and
a high-crowned muffin-shaped hat. His hair is worn rather
long.

By 1817 little girls were also wearing trousers below their
dresses—an odd fashion when one comes to think of it. Even
an uninhibited modern child might feel some mild embarrassment if her knickers came down in public, yet these 19th-
century trousers or pantalettes were presumably a modesty
measure designed to conceal the ankles. Sometimes they were
only shams tied on at the knee.

The fashion for white which had prevailed among adults and
children for so long, was on the wane. By 1827, brighter colours
began to appear, while even ten years or more before this,
skirts became fuller, sleeves were puffed and trimmings more
elaborate. Classical simplicity was no longer the vogue. Emily
Fairchild, dressed up by a worldly young cousin (who like the
ill-fated Augusta Noble was of the school of thought that it was

[1] Readers of Dickens will recall the immortal words of Mrs. Gamp:
'Don't say it's you, Mr. Whilks, and that poor creetur Mrs. Whilks with not
even a pincushion ready. Don't say it's you, Mr. Whilks!'

[2] A miniature, dating from this period, shows a little boy of five wearing
a low-necked and sleeveless white dress with a blue sash. His wavy, golden-
red hair, cut in a fringe, hangs down below his shoulders.

'time enough to be religious you know, when we get old and expect to die') wore a frock which was a mass of frills diminishing in size to the waist with short petticoats displaying her ankles. She had on a velvet spencer, and wore her sash tied in front instead of behind (evidently this was considered rather depraved). Her bonnet was profusely trimmed, and her delicate lavender gloves were sewn with black. Altogether she was very 'starched and bustled out'. *The Fairchild Family* by the way was written between 1812–13 and published in 1818.

A portrait of Queen Victoria at the age of four (a regal tot if ever there was one) shows her wearing a large feathered hat and a fur tippet with her outdoor coat.

Till the middle of the century little girls were dressed on the whole in light-weight materials, muslins, lawns and ginghams —the female ideal was to be airy-looking and graceful—though for cold weather there were also warmer stuffs such as soft cashmere and merinos, and for out-of-door wear, a cloth or velvet pelisse with a cape collar trimmed with fur, a bonnet to match and a fetching little fur muff. (Every little girl should possess a muff, I think.)

Short hair, worn either in an 'urchin cut' or in clustering curls, was common among little girls during this period. Caps were worn, too, and straw hats or bonnets tied under the chin might be worn over the cap.

Nursery food was plain and monotonous, and there was still an unfortunate prejudice against fresh fruit. Boiled mutton and plainly cooked vegetables, with rice pudding, and bread and milk or porridge for breakfast and bread and milk for supper was the staple diet.

Children in smaller households who ate with their parents probably fared much better. Mrs. Fairchild's piety was rather too much of a good thing, but she certainly fed her family well. In between homilies on the utter wickedness of human and particularly child nature, discourses on death and hell, and prayers 'adapted for the state of well-wishing but thoughtless young people' or 'for unholy friends', there is cosy mention of cheese cakes, custard and apple pies, currant turnovers and puffs, and other toothsome eatables. The children joined their parents in a supper that consisted of 'a nice smoking leg of lamb, peas, and young potatoes, and a hot currant and raspberry tart'. What could be nicer? After evening prayers on Sundays, they had baked apples or, in the summer, strawberries or raspberries and cream. It must have been this appetizing and wholesome diet that gave the children the stamina to endure, without apparently any serious damage to their nervous systems, Mr. Fairchild's little chats on death and corpses, and the gruesome expedition when he took them (little Henry being carried by the man servant) to see the gibbeted body of a murderer—as a warning against fratricidal anger.

Mrs. Fairchild's store cupboard was stocked with good things. A story entitled, 'The All-Seeing God' tells how Emily stole some bottled damsons from it. In this case her conscience, after inflicting her with 'horrible dreams' (some indigestion here, too, perhaps?) and a fever drove her into confession. She may have remembered Dr. Watt's formidable lines:

> 'Then let me always watch my lips,
> Lest I be struck to death and Hell,
> Since God a book of reck'ning keeps,
> For ev'ry lie that children tell.'

That Mrs. Fairchild also provided good teas, we may surmise from a remark made by the clergyman who had officiated at the funeral of the poor little rich girl, Miss Augusta Noble, who was burned to death as a result of her disobedience: 'Mr. Fairchild, if you are going home, I will take a seat with you in the coach and drink a dish of tea with Mrs. Fairchild this evening; for I feel in want of a little Christian society.'

3

It may seem absurd under the heading 'Before Victoria' to write of Victoria's own toys, but of course in a sense she was pre-Victorian before she ascended the throne. As a young Princess living in Kensington Palace she was well equipped with dolls, in fact she had 132 of them, some of them grand dolls, others tiny little wooden figures, such as might have been owned by the humblest of her future subjects. Of course she had a doll's house, and she also had a pretty little toy sofa in painted wood, upholstered in white satin, and a toy village.

The Germans were renowned toy makers by now; perhaps it was one of the Princess's many German relations who gave her the miniature roadway with trees, along which a figure only $2\frac{1}{2}$ inches high moved, or the little stage with tiny figures of dancers that pirouetted to the tinkle of a musical box. This was enclosed in a rosewood box with a strap, so that the little princess could play at being a travelling showman.

Those austere early 19th-century nurseries were well stocked with toys. One may imagine the little boy in his pinafore riding a splendid dappled rocking horse, covered in real cowhide, with an audacious eye and silky white mane, or playing at English and French on the floor with toy soldiers. Some of these were mounted on a leaden base so that when they were knocked over they automatically righted themselves, and were called 'The Invincible Army' in consequence.[1] His little sister would almost certainly have a wax doll. One of these dolls, dating from about 1820 is a beautiful creature $20\frac{1}{2}$ inches high with luxuriant hair, and wears a bonnet, and a shawl over her dress.

The early 19th century was an important era in the doll world. There were dolls that could open and shut their eyes, and a Parisian doll-maker took out a patent in 1824 for a doll that could say 'Papa' and 'Mamma'.

As well as wax dolls there were dolls with composition or porcelain heads; some had wooden legs and bodies stuffed with sawdust. When, by some mischance the stuffing came out, the little owner in her muslin frock and sash must have felt that her beloved doll was dying, and rushed to her mother or nurse for help. There are some things that don't change throughout the centuries. Here is a child writing to her mother in the early 19th century. What mother has not had a similar epistle with its mixture of cajolery, stern reminder of a promise and breathless determination to get the longed-for present?

---

[1] In my youth I possessed an 'Invincible Bear' which worked on the same principle, having a heavy rounded base instead of legs. In an unlucky moment, both for the under-matron of my preparatory school and for myself, I had the idea of balancing it on the top of the half-open door when that lady was due to come into the dormitory.

15 Lower Park Street,
Bath.

My dear Mama,

Will you get a Doll for me with her eyes to open and shut—Beautiful Black hair, wax arms, legs, feet and Toes, and to cost one Guinea because a cheaper doll would not be so nice, and besides you promised me a Guinea Doll.

Believe me to be your affectionate Daughter,

Catherine Odell.

For the amusement of children at this period there were toy peep shows, kaleidoscopes and the clumsily named Phenakistecope, which consisted of revolving discs which were looked at through a peep hole.

The fascination of toy theatres is something that must be felt not described. That toy theatre prints were published as early as 1811 shows that these enchanting playthings were in use early in the century, but they reached the zenith of their popularity after Queen Victoria came to the throne, so really belong to the next section.

Henry Fairchild had a tiny boat that sailed about by means of a magnet in a large soup plate; instead of a boat he might have had a fish, a duck or a tortoise.

The year 1951 was a melancholy date in the history of toys. For it was then that Morel's most fascinating toy shop in the Burlington Arcade was closed down. It was established in 1820 and never passed out of the ownership of the same family. Surely in a properly constructed society something should have been done to preserve this unique, this fairy-like shop which has given delight to generations of children and grown-ups? It specialized in miniature toys of every description, 'toy' being used in the 18th century as well as modern sense of the word; it was almost impossible to tear oneself away from its window. Few women, and certainly no child can resist the allure of lilliputian objects.

There is little that is fresh to tell about children's games and pastimes, for in essentials these remained the same as they had been in the 18th century. One can only note a few actual examples in the early part of this century as shown in contemporary pictures. Children are seen skipping, sitting on a garden swing and see-saw, playing at frog-jump, hop-skip-and-a-jump and hunt the slipper. Two little girls are playing at shuttlecock.

Queen Victoria as a child drove about the grounds of Kensington Palace in a donkey chair, the donkey being decked with blue ribbons. There were dog curricles too, for young children (what happened when the dog caught sight of a rabbit or a hare?).

The old customs survived. Betsy Fremantle in her diary for January 6th, 1806 recorded: 'Twelfth day kept in the most charming manner for the amusement of the children and toutes les jeunes personnes. . . . My brats danced and enjoyed themselves,' but there were more up-to-the-minute entertainments too. Two children in 1816 were taken to see the Menagerie at Exeter Change in the Strand where they saw not only the lions but also an accomplished elephant who rang a dinner bell with his trunk. Even nursery fare of boiled mutton and cold rice pudding would seem palatable, one fancies, if announced in this charming way. They also went to Astleys to admire the illuminations, and to Vauxhall to watch a puppet play.

4

These lines from Isaac Watts' *Divine and Moral Songs for Children*:

> 'Let children that would fear the Lord
> Hear what their teachers say;
> With reverence meet their parents word
> And with delight obey'

summed up the prevalent attitude of serious minded adults towards the young who were under their care. Yet at the same time these parents and teachers were growing more and more aware of their obligations towards the children. Rousseau and Locke had not written in vain. Rousseau's theory that children should be allowed to learn by experience rather than by admonition—if a child breaks a window let him sit in the draught (must Grandma sit in the draught too?), if he dawdles while getting dressed let him miss the treat—was gaining ground and is reflected in Mrs. Edgeworth's *Moral Tales*.

One may mock at Mr. and Mrs. Fairchild's educational methods, and feel how discouraging Mrs. Fairchild's dictum that 'All children are by nature evil', must have been to a sensitive child, but undoubtedly they were devoted parents, and believing, as they firmly did, that the pilfering of damsons from a store cupboard, would set the child's feet on the downward path to hell, their threats and warnings were only a measure of their conscientiousness, or as they would have put it, showed that they were 'pious and prudent parents'. 'Parents must be kind and patient or children will be afraid of opening their hearts to them', Mrs. Sherwood, creator of the Fairchilds wrote, and her ideal was a relationship of perfect trust and candour between parent and child.

Mr. Fairchild, of whom it has been said that his only apparent recreation or means of livelihood was to sit under a tree reading the Bible, evidently considered himself a genial father. 'I am amused with anything that entertains my family,' he said, 'I make a point of enjoying everything which they do as far as I can.' Admittedly these pastimes were sometimes peculiar. An old gardener dies, and Mr. Fairchild asks his children, 'Have you any desire to see the corpse, my dears? You never saw a corpse I think?' 'No, Papa,' answers Lucy eagerly, 'but we have a great curiosity to see one.' Mr. Fairchild warns her that 'death is very terrible. A corpse is an awful sight'. 'I know that, Papa,' says Lucy sturdily, 'but we would like to go.'

The Fairchild Family was, as the sub-title stated, calculated 'to show the Importance and Effects of a Religious Education', and nearly every incident in it was pressed into service to point a moral. Even when little Henry nearly met a sad death by falling into the pig-wash though he was not actually to blame (as the pious manservant admitted reluctantly) the reader is left with the impression that this disagreeable experience was sent to him to correct his pride—'It was in this disgraceful plight that the little heir to this great estate and fair property was first presented to the astonished servants'.

Mrs. Sherwood's views must have been extreme even for her age—the popularity of her book which endured till nearly the end of the century was due to her skill as a writer, and her vivid and fascinating attention to detail.

A more authentic picture of parents and children at that time is surely provided by Jane Austen, a connoisseur of happy as well as not so happy family life, in several of her novels.

Emma Woodhouse's brother, the sardonic Mr. John Knightley, counts 'the sacrifice of his children after dinner' as one of the evils of dining out. (Then follows the superb tirade which begins, 'A man must have a very good opinion of himself when he asks people to leave their own fireside, and encounter such a day as this, for the sake of coming to see him'.) It is evident that he considered his children's society, in small doses anyhow, to be one of the day's enjoyments, and that he was keenly disappointed when he had to forgo it.

Gentle Mrs. John Knightly on her visit to Hartfield contrived (with the aid of nursemaids) that her five small children should have 'all the liberty and attendance, all the eating and drinking, and sleeping and playing, which they could possibly wish for' without allowing them to be a disturbance to their hypochondriacal grandfather.

The two little Musgrove boys in *Persuasion* are robust little creatures, obviously being spoilt by their ineffectual mother who complains . . . 'They are so unmanageable. Little Charles does not mind a word I say, and Walter is growing quite as bad.' Their aunt Anne had a better hand with them. 'They loved her nearly as well, and respected her a great deal more than their mother.' She was in the embarrassing position of being everyone's confidante. 'I hate sending the children to the Great House', her sister grumbled to her, 'though their grandmother is always wanting to see them, for she humours and indulges them to such a degree, and gives them so much trash and sweet things that they are sure to come back sick and cross for the rest of the day.' But her mother-in-law, the elder Mrs. Musgrove, had quite a different story:

'Oh! Miss Anne, I cannot help wishing Mrs. Charles had a little of your method with those children. They are quite different creatures with you; but to be sure, in general they are so spoilt! It is a pity you cannot put your sister in the way of managing them. They are as fine healthy children as ever were seen, poor little dears, without partiality; but Mrs. Charles knows no more how they should be treated!—Bless me how troublesome they are sometimes!—I assure you, Miss Anne, it prevents my wishing to see them at our house as often as I otherwise should . . . you know it is very bad to have children with one, that one is obliged to be checking every moment; "don't do this, and don't do that"—or that one can only keep in tolerable order by more cake than is good for them.' A refreshing contrast to Mrs. Fairchild's austere sense of duty!

Jane Austen described the toddler, Walter's appearance in his mother's 'pretty little drawing-room' in a few masterly sentences: 'The younger boy, a remarkable stout, forward child of two years old, having got the door opened for him by someone without, made his determined appearance among them, and went straight to the sofa to see what was going on, and put in his claim to anything good that might be giving away! There being nothing to eat, he could only have some play' and not being allowed to tease his elder brother (who was lying on the sofa with a dislocated collar bone), he fastened himself upon his aunt in such a determined manner, taking no notice of her orders and entreaties, that it required naval intervention to free her, in the person of Captain Wentworth who bore the little boy resolutely away.

Though it is obvious that Jane Austen did not approve of spoilt children, she was evidently tolerant of boisterousness in the young. The 'domestic hurricane' caused by the happy, noisy Musgrove children is described with humorous indulgence, 'It was a fine family piece'. Jane Austen's attitude towards children was, as one would expect eminently sensible, kindly and level-headed. She herself was the beloved aunt of a large family of nieces and nephews, and had ample opportunity to observe the ways of parents and children with a kindly if satirical eye. The Lakeland poets took a more sentimental view of the young, particularly of little girls.

Elizabeth Fry that noble woman and philanthropist wrote in her diary, 'I am at home with my nine children, a great and very precious charge; at times they appear too much for me, at others I greatly enjoy them'. Which probably sums up the feelings of most mothers of sizeable families, whether early 19th or 20th century.

John Ruskin was not an ordinary child, nor was his upbringing as described in his book *Preaterita* a usual one (how much the first fact was related to the second is hard to say) but it is worth mentioning as it shows the austere lines along which an early 19th-century child could be reared. (He was the only son of a well-to-do wine merchant.)

His playthings were so few that they impressed themselves indelibly on his memory—a bunch of keys, a cart and a ball and, when he was five or six years old, two boxes of well-cut bricks. His chief amusement as a little boy, dressed in the fashion of the time in a little white frock with a blue sash and shoes to match, was to study the designs of carpets, dresses and wall-papers. He remembered being given three raisins by his mother out of her store-cupboard, also his first taste of custard when he was allowed to finish up some that his father had left.

If he cried, did not do what he was told, or stumbled, he was whipped. Sunday was a day of gloom. His best story books were taken away from him in the morning, and he found 'the bottom of the pew an extremely dull place to keep quiet in'.

Looking back at his childhood from the viewpoint of an elderly man, Ruskin analysed dispassionately its advantages and its drawbacks. Its blessings, in his estimation, were that he was taught the meaning of peace, of obedience and of faith. Peace, because he never heard his parents wrangle or quarrel, or heard a servant scolded, obedience because he was trained to obey his parents as 'a ship her helm', and faith because nothing was ever promised him that was not given, or threatened that was not inflicted nor told him that was not true.

Finally he learnt concentration, and an 'extreme perfection in palate and all bodily senses, given by the utter prohibition of cake, wine, comfits or, except in carefullest restriction, fruit, and by the fine preparation of what food was given me'.

But the 'calamities' as he called them, of his childhood, were serious indeed. 'First that I had nothing to love.' He explained, that his parents were to him visible powers of nature, 'no more loved than the sun and moon'. Secondly he had nothing to endure, and thirdly was taught no precision nor etiquette of manners. Those who have read of his disastrous marriage and melancholy old age may well feel that the first drawback was overwhelming in its gravity.

189

In spite of the efforts of Isaac Watt, Mrs. Sherwood and other moralists to inculcate obedience and docility in the young, spoilt children seem to have been fairly numerous at this period. Miss Weeton who had a post with the Armitage family (they were one of the oldest families near Huddersfield, well-to-do clothiers and coal owners) took rather a sombre view on the whole of her young charges, who were really of nursery age, as the eldest girl 'Miss A' was only seven. In Miss Weeton's opinion she was 'the black sheep that infects the flock; punishment or reward make no lasting impression; I fear she is naturally depraved. Though seven years of age, she has no ideas of common modesty; it is a wrong thing to inure children to stript entirely in the nursery, whilst washing.' Miss Weeton taught this 'depraved' little creature to dance, and 'a sweet boy of five years' to write. The children's ignorance appalled her. When she came to them, the two eldest could only read a few words of three or four letters, the third child (aged four and three quarters) words of only two, and the fourth (three and a quarter) 'has his alphabet to learn'. They were 'so indulged that they seem not to know what obedience was' and out of their parents' sight were 'as unruly, noisy, insolent, quarrelsome, and ill-tempered a set as ever I met with'.

However they became quite attached to her—they confessed to her, before she left, that they called her 'ugly-face' at first, but liked her now because she was so good to them and told them so many things—and she was quite 'upsides' with them. When George asked her, 'Why does God make lions when they do nothing but kill and eat us?' she promptly replied, 'If flies could speak, George they would say, "Why does God make little children, who do nothing but kill us for sport?"'

Later on she went through another bad patch with them. She wrote almost in despair of, 'Their perverse and violent tempers. . . . Such screaming and shouting and incessant loud talking, and such incessant quarrelling' (not much 'Children should be seen and not heard!' there). The two little boys flew into 'violent fits of passion' when they attempted to say a lesson, 'screaming dreadfully'. At last she was driven to use the rod 'notwithstanding it is so repugnant to the present mild system of education' (a significant remark this). The children retaliated by screaming as though they were being killed, though Miss Weeton claimed that she was only hitting their clothes. The eldest girl went on strike for a week and refused to do any lessons. Miss Weeton 'requested, persuaded, insisted' all in vain. The infuriating child only smiled carelessly and tossed her head.

As a last resort the hard-pressed governess kept her in during her play hours. This produced cold looks from Mrs. Armitage, 'Sarah Anne's health would suffer, she thought, I thought so too, but something must be done, and as Mrs. A. did not propose any better way, I persevered . . . and I think I have conquered. Miss A. is again not only tractable but affectionate.'

Certainly something seems to have been very wrong with the contemporary system of education, the well-meaning but inexperienced Miss Weeton's methods, or, more likely with the Armitage children and their parents, but what it was exactly I don't feel competent to say!

In large establishments, children were kept out of sight and hearing in the nursery quarters, but the fact that a friend took all the Elton children away to stay when their mother was having another baby, so as to keep the house quiet, shows that in the average household the children were neither banished entirely to their own quarters nor unduly repressed. In short as is so often the case in life, practice fell very short of preaching, and fact of theory. The official attitude of adults towards the young was summed up in Nathaniel Cotton's lines:

'Our babes shall richest comforts bring;
If tutored right they'll prove a spring
Whence pleasures ever rise.
We'll form their minds with studious care,
To all that's manly, good and fair,
And train them for the skies'

but it did not always work out like that!

5

These wilful tots who could barely read at the age of five would have been accounted shameful ignoramuses by these Elizabethan and Stuart parents whose children were reading

Latin and Greek at the same age.[1] Yet by now quite a nursery literature had grown up. Children were no longer dependent for their reading on suitable adult books or on the cheap and sometimes squalid little chap books.

To go fully into the matter of children's books in the early 19th century would be too weighty a proposition for our purpose. Perhaps it is enough to give an indication of some of the 'juvenile' books that might have been found on nursery shelves during the first thirty-seven years of the century.

Maria Edgeworth, who has been called 'The novelist of the nursery' by E. V. Lucas—herself one of a family of eighteen children—stands pre-eminent as the chief children's writer of the period. She was a didactic but lovable and very readable author with a sense of humour. (At last, after many years I have traced in Maria Edgeworth's *The Purple Jar* the source of a story that my mother used to tell me about a little girl who clamoured for a purple jar in a chemist's shop, only to find when her request had been granted, that, emptied of its contents, it was made of plain, colourless glass.)

A lighter touch than had been usual in children's books was introduced by two sisters, Dorothy and Mary Jane Kilner, as some of the titles of their books suggests: *The Life and Perambulations of a Mouse*, *Little Stories for Little Folks*, *History of a Great Many Little Boys and Girls of four and five years of Age*, and *Memoirs of a Peg Top*. Some of their books date in fact from the late 18th century, but were favourite nursery reading for fifty years or more.

Animal stories, pale forerunners of Beatrix Potter's little masterpieces, were making their appearance—Mrs. Pilkington's, *Marvellous Adventures of the Vicissitudes of a Cat*, 1802, and *The Adventures of Poor Puss* by Elizabeth Sandman. There was also *The Adventures of a Donkey* (1815) by 'Arabella Argus'.

The rather ominously named *The Infant's Progress* was written by Mrs. Sherwood in 1809–10, and had a strong missionary flavour. Earlier in 1804 a book of children's poetry had been published, called *Original Poems for Infant Minds*—by several young Persons (among them was a pair of sisters, Ann and

[1] They would have approved of Mr. Fairchild who 'thought it proper to teach Henry Latin as he wished to bring him up as a clergyman'.

Jane Taylor). There is a caressing note about some of these poems that is a pleasant relief from the endless moralizing of other authors.

Ann Taylor in a little poem called 'Washing and Dressing' says to the imaginary child:

> 'It is not to tease you, and hurt you my sweet
> That I wash you, and dress you, and make you
> look neat,
> And comb out your tanglesome hair.'

Any mother in any century, combing her little girl's hair might say something of this kind, or encourage a toddler in the words of 'Learning to go alone' in the sequel 'Rhymes for the Nursery' (1806).

> 'Come, my darling, come away,
> Take a pretty walk to-day;
> Run along and never fear,
> I'll take care of baby dear;
> Up and down with little feet,
> That's the way to walk, my sweet.'

This is the mother-child talk that may seem absurd to outsiders, but it is not to be laughed at for it is not intended to be overheard.

The Taylor sisters' poems were deservedly popular.

The monitory note was still loud. Elizabeth Turner, the author of *The Daisy, or Cautionary Stories in Verse adapted to the Ideas of Children from four to eight years old*—1807, produced this remarkable warning of the fate that overtakes children who were cruel to animals:

> 'But all such boys unless they mend,
> May come to an unhappy end,
> Like Jack who got a fractur'd skull
> Whilst bellowing at a furious bull.'

(Almost pure Hillaire Belloc this last line!)

But at the same time an attempt was being made to provide literature that was gay and fresh for the very young, like the frolicsome poem 'The Butterfly's Ball' which begins:

'Come take up your Hats and away let us haste
To the Butterfly's Ball and the Grasshopper's Feast.'

'The History of Sixteen Wonderful Old Women' (1821) contained a pleasing stanza about an Owl:

'There was an Old Woman named Towl,
Who went out to Sea with her Owl,
But the Owl was Sea-sick,
And scream'd for Physic;
Which sadly annoyed Mistress Towl'

(the first appearance, Harvey Darton, the author of *Children's Books in England*, says, of the Limerick which was later made famous by Edward Lear). While on the subject of owls, one can forgive Mrs. Sherwood quite a lot for that endearing line in *The Fairchild Family*—'an owl in the garden called Ralph'.

6

Lurking in the shadows behind these prosperous nurseries with their pampered, spoilt, or sweet and 'engaging' little inhabitants, one can discern the starveling, ragged figures of the Other Children—the children of the slums, the little chimney sweeps, and mine- and factory-slaves, whose martyrdom had now reached its zenith. The conditions under which these most unhappy children toiled read like some tale from a barbaric past. But, as I said in the preface, these forlorn waifs knew nothing of nursery life (it was computed that in the early years of Victoria's reign the age for starting regular work throughout the country as a whole, was between seven and eight) and thus have no place in this book. But their pitiful ghosts cannot be exorcized. Their plight had begun to stir many consciences. As early as 1803, if not before, there was an 'Association for Improving the Situation of Infant Chimney Sweeps', but it is doubtful if the full monstrosity of that concatenation 'Infant Chimney Sweeps' struck the kindly ladies, devoted mothers many of them no doubt, who subscribed to the association. It is a salutary thought to realize that we may seem no less callous to future generations.

As early as 1773, the philanthropist, Jonas Hanway, had

drawn attention to the miserable condition of the chimney sweeper's young apprentices, and the dangers to which they were exposed, but nothing was done about it for some years. The writer of *The Diary of a Country Parson* recorded in 1797 that the chimney sweep 'had a new boy with him who had likely to have lost his Life this morning at Weston House in sticking in one of their Chimnies. Gave the poor boy a shilling', which probably summed up the attitude of most people towards this matter. At last a Parliamentary Committee of 1816–17 produced appalling evidence of these boys' sufferings. Yet several years later in 1819, Sidney Smith, while writing compassionately about young chimney sweeps in an article in the *Edinburgh Review* was able to say: 'After all, we must own that it was quite right to throw out the Bill for prohibiting the sweeping of chimnies by boys, because humanity is a modern invention, and there are many chimnies in old houses that cannot possibly be swept in any other manner. But the construction of chimnies should be attended to in some new building act; and the treatment of boys watched over with the most severe jealousy of the law.'

It was not till 1834 that an act was passed to safeguard these children, and later, further acts (1840, 1864 and as late as 1875) prohibited their employment. So it took nearly a hundred years after Jonas Hanway's protest before this abuse was entirely swept away.

Charity to the poor, and even consideration ('How sweet it is when persons of a higher rank take thought for the small comforts of those below' says Mrs. Sherwood) was taught as a matter of course to well-brought-up children. But it was taken for granted that a divinely-ordained gulf, almost as great as that which separated Divies and Lazarus, divided the rich and comfortably-off from the poor.

The child in Watt's *Divine Songs for Children* remarks complacently, when rendering 'Praise for Mercies, Spiritual and temporal':

> 'How many children in the street
> Half naked I behold;
> While I am clothed from head to feet
> And covered from the cold.'

In another poem entitled, 'Good Resolutions', the child, prepared for all eventualities, resolves:

> 'Should I e'er be rich or great
> Others shall partake my goodness;
> I'll supply the poor with meat.'

Then comes those remarkable lines:

> 'What tho' I be low and mean,
> I'll engage the rich to love me,
> While I'm modest, neat and clean,
> And submit when they reprove me.'

To be charitable and polite to their social inferiors was the duty of the rich; the poor, in return, were expected to be modest, neat, clean and above all, submissive.

The child-workers or child-slaves, as one might call them, of England, were to find a doughty champion in Lord Ashley (afterwards Lord Shaftesbury) whose own childhood had been unhappy and lonely, due to the neglect of his fashionable, heartless parents.

There was another class of people whose wrongs were brought to the public notice at this time by one of their members, that is to say the women whose marriages had broken up, through no fault of theirs, and yet were separated by law from their children. Lady Jerningham in a letter (1808) tells about Lady Bovingdon, who before eloping with Sir Arthur Paget 'went to the nursery and kissed the children before she went away'.

In this case she was the party at fault (it seems that she had made no secret of her liking for Sir Arthur Paget either to her father or her husband) but as far as her children were concerned, it would have made no difference if she had fled from her husband because he had brutally ill-treated her or kept a mistress in the house. The children would still have remained in his custody.

Caroline Norton was one of the brilliant Sheridans, a beautiful, emotional woman, who married at the age of nineteen the Hon. Richard Norton, a blackguard in the real early 19th-century style. She was miserably unhappy with him, he beat her, and eventually she ran away from him; though his efforts to divorce her for 'criminal conversation' with the Prime Minister, Lord Melbourne, failed dismally, she lost her children. They remained with their despicable father. Poor Caroline, almost beside herself with 'pain, exasperation, helplessness and despair' campaigned unceasingly, with the help of sympathizers, notably Mr. Talfourd, to bring about an amendment of the law regarding the custody of infants.

Her impassioned appeal, 'A Plain Letter to the Lord Chancellor' was written under a masculine *nom de plume* which Caroline hoped would carry more weight. 'You cannot get the Peers to sit up till three in the morning listening to the wrongs of separated mothers' she said bitterly. 'They are disturbed by the preposterous importance set by women on the society of their infant children. What I suffered regarding those children, God knows, and he only. . . . I *really* lost my young children, craved for them, struggled for them, was banned from them, and came too late to see one that had died, except in his coffin.'

People disapproved of her. She was called a 'she-devil' and a 'she-beast', but her efforts and those of her supporters were ultimately rewarded by alterations in the custody laws. It is interesting to compare her complaint with that of Lady Hungerford in similar circumstances: 'Touching my children they are as strangers to me.' This was written in the year 1570; it was 1839 before guardianship rights over children were granted to women.

Victorian, 1837-1870

I

To be able to assess the personal influence of Queen Victoria on the domestic life of her subjects, one must glance back at the family history of the monarchy for some fifty years previous to her accession. It makes sorry reading. George III—'Farmer George'—and his plain little German Queen, in the early part of their married life certainly presented an edifying picture of conjugal happiness with their simple, respectable tastes and their fine family of fifteen good-looking children—nine princes and six princesses. It sounds like something out of a fairy tale, but alas! there was no 'happy ever after' for the 'Royals', as Mrs. Delany nicknamed them. Behind the cosy domestic façade a melancholy, one might almost say sinister, drama developed of bitter family quarrels, frustrated unhappy daughters, dissolute, undutiful sons, and the long-drawn-out tragedy of the King's insanity. George IV's marriage to his cousin Caroline of Brunswick was a disaster and a source of scandal from the wedding night.

No wonder that the nation looked to his daughter, Princess Charlotte, young, fresh, and spirited, as the only hope of a monarchy that had sunk to its nadir in public esteem. No wonder that black despair fell like a funeral pall on the nation when it heard that her happy, pathetically brief married life to Prince Leopold had come to an end with the birth of a dead boy. Even the cynical Byron was moved to lament the 'fair-haired daughter of the Isles' whose death had 'laid in the dust the love of millions'.

There is something very pathetic not only in Princess Charlotte's untimely end, but in the longing of the British people for a sovereign whom they could love and respect.

After tragedy came farce, as three of George IV's middle-aged brothers, who had been living for years in a domesticity bordering on respectability with their mistresses and illegitimate children, were more or less ordered to take unto themselves German princesses in the hope of providing an heir or heiress for the English Crown.

As Canning put it bluntly in a speech, proposing that the Duke of Clarence's allowance should be increased when he married Princess Adelaide of Saxe-Coburg-Meiningen, 'Into this alliance His Royal Highness entered not for his private desire and gratification, but because it was pressed on him for the purpose of providing for the succession to the throne', a remarkable statement that was greeted by the House with loud and derisive laughter.

William IV and his wife lost both their little daughters, one at birth and the other—who if she lived would have been Queen Elizabeth II—at the age of three months.

The Duke and Duchess of Cumberland and the Duke and

Duchess of Cambridge had sons, but they were not long in the running for the English throne, for in the same year Victoria was born—'the most upright child I ever knew and yet arch', so her State Governess the Duchess of Northumberland was to describe her.

Nothing could have been greater or more piquant than the contrast between the girl-Queen and her predecessors. She was so very young, only 18, not uncomely looking with her pink and white complexion and rather prominent blue eyes, and very homely and simple—'she blushes and laughs in so natural a way as to disarm anybody', and yet already showing signs of that impressive dignity that was to develop into the rather formidable majesty of her later years. She was fond of gaiety and dancing, and devoted to her handsome, kind, middle-aged Prime Minister Lord Melbourne, but it was all as dewy and innocent as a spring morning, and the gentlemen at her Court were told that they must not remain at table drinking after dinner for more than five minutes before joining the ladies.

Her injudicious preference for the Whig party, and the Lady Flora Hasting's scandal soon dimmed the brightness of her early popularity; it was rumoured that she was obstinate and hard, but Prince Albert with his beautiful eyes and whiskers, and his fine, earnest if humourless character arrived on the scene and all was well. The Queen herself said that her marriage had brought her into a 'safe haven' and after a few tiffs (for she could not forget that she was after all, the Queen of England as well as Albert's wife) his influence over her was paramount. He not only brought order into the royal household, but trained his wife in the arduous and delicately balanced duties of a constitutional monarch.

The Court became a model of morality and decorum (and it must be confessed, of dullness). The personal tastes of the royal couple were atune to those of their upper middle-class subjects. The Prince Consort did not find favour among the aristocracy because he neither hunted nor raced, and was interested in music and science (also he had the disadvantage of being a foreigner, strictly decorous in his life and stiff in his manner). Though it was fortunate for the country that he occupied his high position, one imagines that personally he would have been happier had fate made him a professor.

The Queen and he were devoted and conscientious (perhaps too conscientious) parents. When their numerous children— nine in all—were young, Prince Albert for safety's sake himself kept the keys of their apartments at night. Though a great Queen, Victoria as a girl, wife, mother and broken-hearted widow, set a pattern that both inspired and harmonized with the prevailing tone of society. Security, prosperity, morality, idealism—these are some of the thoughts that come to one's mind in connection with the word 'Victorian'.

2

It is rather startling (such are one's preconceived ideas on the Victorian outlook) to find recorded under the date 1841, the following entry in the diary of Mrs. Clive, a clergyman's wife:

'Nothing remarkable, except the appearance of eight Severnes, six offspring and a father and mother, two boys having preceded them to Thenford, whither the whole family are flitting. Archer [her husband] was very much shocked at the appearance of so much domestic felicity, and declared it not fit for the advanced civilization of the nineteenth century. Lady Harriet Mitchell he thought was quite justified in running away with a lover from a family of eight children'—the last sentiment that one would expect to hear from a clergyman, and an early Victorian clergyman at that. But one must remember that Victoria had only been on the throne four years, and the raffish days of the Regency were not yet quite dead. The Clives anyhow were mildly advanced in their views. They themselves had a 'pigeon pair', but Caroline Clive was not young when they married.

In a general way, large families were accepted as what one might call 'a necessary blessing' (something between a blessing and a necessary evil!) Child mortality was on the decrease, at any rate among better-class families, and in the country (it was still appalling in the poorer quarters of the cities) and though it appears from statistics that four to five children was the natural rate of fertility during this period, there seem to have been a great many families of nine or ten or even more.

Childbirth, though less lethal than formerly, still ranked as one of the more dangerous occupations. Lucy Lyttleton (1857) writes of, 'Poor Mr. William Harcourt who four months ago lost his young wife in her second confinement, her first beautiful baby having died the year before'. Her own mother died, worn out it seems by child-bearing, some months after the birth of her twelfth child. Again nine years later in 1866, Lucy Lyttleton by then Lady Frederick Cavendish, recorded in her diary the death of Lady Fortescue in her confinement, leaving thirteen children.

The doctor, who called on Mrs. Clive after the birth of her child for what would nowadays be called 'a check-up', asked if she loved the child, and said he had seen many instances in which there seems no maternal feeling. He had frequently known the mother very indifferent to the infant being still-born. She was vexed perhaps if its life was of importance for an heirdom but not for itself.'

Caroline Clive was certainly not one of these indifferent mothers. 'My child, thank God, my child, thank God, thank God,' was her rapturous exclamation when her daughter was born, and her husband was a devoted father to their two children. He 'shed tears of joy' at hearing that his wife had been delivered of a son—their first-born. Both he and his wife had wished for a boy, but had not ventured to ask for this in their prayers. He had prayed daily for his wife's safety but 'had felt it presumptuous to add male or female, or to say more than "Thy Will be done"'. In the light of modern gynaecological knowledge, one knows that it would have been useless as well as presumptuous, the sex of the child being determined at a very early stage.

'I desire to record my hearty thanks to Almighty God for the prosperous confinement of my dear wife and the birth of a daughter in my house,' he wrote when their second child was born. 'Caroline is delighted with her baby. Meysey [their little son] does not know what to make of her. He at first was frightened, then bribed with a sugar plum to kiss her, and now continues the practice in the hope of the same reward.'

The anxious endeavours of modern parents to prepare their older children for the arrival of a new baby would not have commended themselves to the average Victorian parent. I think it is unlikely that in most families, children if they were old enough to be observant, were not given a few hints that a brother or sister was being despatched from heaven, but in some cases the new arrival would come as a complete surprise, pleasant or unpleasant.[1] Lucy Lyttleton told in her diary for 1857 of the birth of her mother's twelfth baby. As a girl of sixteen, she herself was of course aware of the impending event, and being of a devout nature, wrote out a short prayer for her younger brothers and sisters when she heard that the baby was arriving. 'Little they knew of it all!' When they were told that they had another brother they were 'utterly incredulous, and then over the moon! had known nothing about it'. Led by elder sister Lucy they knelt while she read earnest thanksgivings. The father, Lord Lyttleton's reactions were 'a delighted chuckle' and a 'Another boy! What in the world shall we do with another boy?' Luckily one thing they did not do was to call the baby 'Duodecimus' or 'Octavius', names that were considered as being 'appropriate' but were rejected.

It was not until 1847 that we hear of anaesthetics being used for childbirth. Some doubt was expressed as to whether this was in accordance with the Divine Will as it would enable women to escape the curse pronounced against Eve in the Book of Genesis. Queen Victoria set an example of good sense when she had anaesthetic for the birth of Prince Leopold in 1853.

Caroline Clive however had her children too early to benefit by this wonderful new discovery. She was seriously ill after the birth of her son in 1842, had a relapse, but was given brandy and sal volatile and happily recovered. She nursed her baby, ate fruit and vegetables while doing so, and managed very well on it, although she had been told that this diet would disagree with the baby.

[1] Children have a natural preference for drama and mystery. I have heard a modern child who had had the elementary facts of childbirth carefully explained to her, firmly assert that God had 'dropped' her on the hospital where she was born. (Possibly she had a parachute rather than a stork in her mind.)

The monthly nurse carried on the age-old superstitions. She asked Mrs. Clive if she had had any unsatisfied cravings during her pregnancy, 'as the baby had a habit of licking his lips and rolling his tongue' and she supposed my unsatisfied longing reappeared in him. As a remedy she recommended a little drop of sacramental wine for the baby. As a cure for thrush, she advised a frog sewn into a muslin bag, and its head put into the child's mouth so that the child should suck it. This was supposed to draw away the thrush. According to the nurse the unfortunate frog always died—of shock I suppose.

The little Clive boy cried just enough at his christening, which took place about six weeks after his birth, to satisfy the nurse who said that if he had been absolutely silent, she would have had to pinch him, because children who did not cry at their christening soon died. This superstition in a milder form has persisted till today. Now it is said jokingly that unless a baby cries at the font, the Devil won't be chased out of him.

After three months, Mrs. Clive gave up nursing him, and a wet-nurse had to be found. There was the usual difficulty over this, or as she put it in her diary, 'it was eight days before we succeeded in getting him another cow. The cow is the mother of a calf seven weeks old, who went first to a woman with a baby of thirteen months, and next to a dry nurse, when the thirteen months baby insisted on returning to its mother. Both of these processes were prohibited for our child, but the poor little plebian does perfectly well'—an entry which in spite of the date is more Regency than Victorian in spirit and style.

When he was nearly a year old 'Babkin' developed a swollen gum, Mr. Love was summoned and 'made light of it'. The Clives were due to go on a visit, and 'so we left our Babkins. I was very broken-hearted but Archer was rational'. Next day they received a good account of their son, and the gum was lanced.

Two decades have passed, and in the *Amberley Papers* we have a glimpse of a serious and high-minded young couple, Lord and Lady Amberley preparing themselves for the birth of their first child. With delightful solemnity, they 'sat for some time in the field talking about the religious education of our children; we both want them unbiased but of course would wish them to believe what we believe ourselves and to have a religious mind'. (One imagines them, she in her crinoline and demure pork-pie hat and chignon, he in a sack coat and hard round hat.)

Theological problems were quite literally table-talk in their circle. 'We discussed the question of whether unbaptized persons should be buried in churchyards at breakfast,' wrote Lord Amberley, with a pleasant disregard of syntax.

There is no mention of chloroform or ether in Lord Amberley's rather detailed account of his young wife's confinement in August, 1865, but this may have been because the whole thing was over in barely three hours, the doctor arriving only ten minutes before the baby was born.

Nursing difficulties began at once, and drove the poor young parents almost distracted. 'Baby would not suck, and had to be fed by Mrs. Potts, whose child is four months old.' Things were no better next day, and the young father, who made the mistake of expecting Nature to be as rational as he was, complained, 'It seems very badly managed by nature that little babies should not find it as easy to suck as little puppies; but if this is one of the arrangements that was made in consequence of Original Sin, we must not complain of it. Baby, though obstinate, is a dear little fellow and it is a great happiness to look at his face and feel he is our own, mine and my darling wifie's.'

But the strain of the situation began to tell on his nerves: 'I was annoyed at the nursing not being successful and did not feel so happy as the first days.' Meanwhile the young mother was feeling very low and weak, and so no doubt was the baby. 'K. [Kate] cannot bear the notion of a wet-nurse. I dislike it nearly as much', but finally, ten days after the baby's birth they gave up the harassing struggle. 'A terrible disappointment to her, for we both care very much about ladies nursing.'

Three more days passed before Kate's mother Lady Stanley found a suitable wet-nurse, who fortunately for the Amberley's baby, if not for morality, had been confined less than three months after her marriage. But before another three days had gone by, the new wet-nurse was whisked away by her husband who had not been consulted about the arrangement.

On September 5th, Lady Amberley noted that the distracted baby was frowning too much, 'but he has been so bothered since his birth. This is the 5th woman he had since birth.' Enough to turn him into a misogynist! 'Dear baby does fret and cry so awfully' she writes, adding rather surprisingly, 'but is perfectly well and wonderfully strong'. The whole affair seems to have been badly muddled, though the Amberleys were the most devoted and conscientious of parents.

The unfortunate baby's trials were not yet ended. A satisfactory wet-nurse, Lizzie Williams, had been found, but it was not long before she was warning her young mistress of the 'nasty brutal conduct' of the baby's other nurse Davies, ('The *good, trusted, clever* Davies' as Lady Amberley called her in bitter retrospect). All the servants knew that Davies was ill-treating the baby and in their disgust complained to Lizzie. Lady Amberley, very agitated, wrote to consult Mama, who said 'send her away at once'. A not surprising reply considering that one of Davies 'horrid ways' was to stuff a sponge in the baby's mouth when she was washing it, (she also thrust her fingers down its throat, said that she hated it and wished it were dead). Unmasked and given three hours' notice, the malignant Davies showed up in her true colours, declared that she would have been leaving anyhow in March, as she hated the child and did not think the place good enough. She claimed that she had been accustomed to double her wages (£25 a year) by selling baby clothes.

Her furies might have affected Lizzie's milk, and Lady Amberley was thankful to get rid of her and to carry on temporarily with Lizzie 'till I get a nurse. . . . I shall not get another in a hurry and without great investigation, but shall feel afraid for Davies was so praised and so sensible and nice spoken to me. Of course I shall not recommend her.' (I should hope not!)

Mrs. Carlyle, condoling with Lady Amberley over the misdeeds of 'that Ogresse' Davies, wrote: 'Poor little child! I can specially sympathize with him under the *gin*; for my own nurse used to put *me* into a deep sleep with whiskey, when she had assignations outside.'

Another nursery crisis threatened when the Amberleys were thrown out of a dog cart. At the sight of her mistress being carried upstairs, Lizzie Williams had 'bearing down spasms', and it was feared that her milk would be affected. The next entry shows that even in those days of plentiful domestic help, fathers did not have as easy a time as one might suppose. 'Dear Amberley got up all night to take her [Lizzie] medicine, and see how she was and to attend to me.'

It is comforting to know that in spite of all these vicissitudes the baby survived and even flourished. On December 19th his proud young mother recorded: 'Baby is 2 feet 2 inches in height; he is so strong that he lifts up my work box with brass fastenings on it in his hand, quite high up and holds it a long time. It had several reels of cotton in it and weighs $3\frac{3}{4}$ lb. He now screams for all he sees and does not like to be taken away from anything he is playing with.'

Against the repellent picture of Davies one may set another one of a loving and much-loved Nanny portrayed in Mary Carbery's evocative book, *Happy World*. The author was born in 1867 so was writing about the early 70's of the century. Their Nanny was a tower of strength and kindliness (her photograph shows a face as square and as plain as Mrs. Noah's but with an expression of great sweetness). She was strict but patient and gentle—never talked in a silly way to her charges, never slapped nor whipped them, and was free herself of fears and superstitions. Her own education at a dame's school had been limited but sound. She could read aloud beautifully, write and spell perfectly, and sew finely. She also knew the Bible well and could repeat many hymns and poems. It was a heartbreaking moment for the children when she had to go away to look after her mother. She was followed by a Nurse who smelt, not without reason, of gin, and then by a Welsh nurse who was 'clean and kind and lively and deceitful'. She could also dance a jig, but even so was a poor substitute for the original Nanny.

Sometimes not an aged mother, that bugbear of employees, but a suitor removed a cherished Nanny from her adopted family. 'The beloved Williams was married at half-past nine . . .' Caroline Clive wrote in her diary in 1846, '. . . the children cried, Williams cried and so did I. She had been perfect in her state. Archer gave her £20 and £5 to buy a gown. We also gave her a cap, and a locket with the children's hair.'

3

It is time to picture to ourselves the nurseries that could be a little heaven of cosy security or a place of torment, according to the character and temper of the nurses who presided over them.

The austerity of the early 19th-century nursery was gradually being replaced by some degree of homely comfort.

It was not till mid-century that the taste for the heavy opulence in furnishing and clothes that we associate with the Victorian era was fully developed. The early Victorians favoured flowered chintz, muslin and dimity in spring-like colours, pink, white and blue, for bedroom curtains, and for the 'petticoats' of dressing tables. There is a connection, as James Laver has pointed out between fashions in clothes and fashions in furnishing, and this was an appropriate background for the figures in tulle and tarleton that flitted across it.

It is unlikely however that these refinements of taste were to be found to any great extent in the nursery, which was still used as a receptacle for furniture and pictures that had been rejected for other parts of the house. It was not till much later that an attempt was made to decorate and furnish the nursery in a distinctive style of its own. The Lyttleton nursery in the 1840's is described as being a large room filled with massive furniture. There was a large white cupboard for toys, and a towering white wardrobe for the children's clothes and the nursery linen. Another cupboard of dark wood, also very lofty, held the breakfast, dinner and tea things in its bottom drawers. A round table, covered with a heavy fringed cloth, was an important piece of furniture. Round this the children would gather for their solid plain meals, or for cards and cutting out games on wet days (this was the heydey of the scrapbook; grown-ups too, amused themselves compiling them). There was a heavy carved chimney-piece, and half-way up the wall two large bookshelves with grotesque china and other ornaments that were only played with on special occasions, also a few books, prominent among them a family medicine book. The walls were hung with old prints of foreign men and women, presumably in national costume, a picture of the Queen and the Duchess of

Kent, and a large map decorated with birds, beasts and fishes. The carpet and the wall-paper were brightly coloured, so the general effect cannot have been uncheerful. It seems that 'in early times a swing hung from the ceiling', an entertaining but perhaps not very safe arrangement.

Every self-respecting nursery would have a high fireguard in front of the nursery fire, on which night-gowns and towels were aired, and a rocking chair, and would be well provided with such items as pin-cushions, sewing baskets and powder boxes. There would be a hip bath for bathing the children, and this would be placed on a blanket in front of the fire and filled with hot water from brass cans which were brought up flights of stairs and along corridors by a nursery maid. That is to say if the children were lucky enough not to be born into one of those spartan houses where cold baths were the rule for the young with one hot bath a week on Saturdays. Lady St. Helier in her *Memories of Fifty Years*, told how in a Highland household, the children often had to break the ice on the bath water in winter.

A country vicarage in the 1850's—to take one example of a medium-sized household—had no bathroom, and all the hot water had to be carried upstairs from the kitchen and scullery, but in spite of this, the children had hot baths every day.

The nursery medicine cupboard would almost certainly have on its shelves, Dr. Gregory's powder to be taken in jam, syrup of senna, rhubarb, castor oil, liquorice and the fearsome sounding brimstone and treacle. Far too much dosing took place in Victorian nurseries, according to modern ideas. There might also be blackberry syrup for coughs, tar water and cinnamon, borax to be rubbed with honey on the gums of an infant suffering from thrush. Individual nurses had their favourite remedies in whose efficacy they had unshakeable belief. The Nanny in *Happy World*, kept lily petals soaked for weeks in brandy to be used for cuts and bruises, and used camphor balls for chapped hands. A piece of coral, rubbed with carrot juice, was recommended for the gums of teething infants.

I have written of the nursery in the singular as though it were only one room, but of course, except in small households, it consisted of two rooms, the day and the night nurseries. A child would have to be ill before it was considered necessary to light a fire in the latter.

No doubt in some families cradles dating from an earlier generation were still used, but a typical contemporary cradle of the 60's (as seen from the viewpoint of twenty years later) would be 'a good old-fashioned wicker-work cradle, with a deep hood and daisy fringed flounces'.

The nursery quarters were set apart from the rest of the house, often behind baize doors (I must admit that I think the Victorians showed wisdom over this!) and in theory at least were self-sufficient, except (and it was a big exception) for the ministrations of the servants who toiled up and down stairs with trays of food, coal and hot water from the basement. In practice there was often constant tension, amounting to a state of hostility between the nursery staff (which in a large establishment might amount to a head nurse, a french *bonne*, and several nursery maids) and the rest of the domestic staff. Maids and footmen disliked waiting on the nursery—not altogether surprising when one considers that the nursery was usually located at the top of the house—and were apt to give slovenly and sulky service. Cooks, even if they were not actually at 'cuts' with Nurse (and they often were) grew bored with preparing the nursery menu of boiled mutton, plain vegetables and milk and batter puddings, and made this even more unpalatable than necessary by careless cooking.

This may explain why it became the habit in the 50's and 60's for the older children, supervised by a governess, to join their parents at luncheon in the dining-room, while in medium-sized households, it was usual to carve the joint in the dining-room and send the nursery its portion direct from there.

While on the subject of diet, delicate or ailing children were cosseted with chicken, roast veal, jellies and sips of claret. Even children who were not ill might be given a glass of ale for luncheon, and hot wine and water at bedtime.

A distrust of fresh air still persisted. It was thought enough to air the nursery when the children were out of it and a cold or wet day was sufficient reason for the children to be kept indoors. This, of course is a generalization. There must have been many hardy mothers and nurses, especially in Scotland, who believed in their charges braving the elements. But undoubtedly the general tendency was to muffle up children when they were exposed to fresh air.

Babies in particular were still overloaded with clothes—tight binders, little linen shirts, flannel and linen petticoats, long embroidered robes (these measured about 42 inches by 1870)[1] and for out of doors, a pelisse and a bonnet or cap according to sex (I have put the ladies first). Even indoors the baby would wear a lace-trimmed or embroidered cap.

Little boys were still dressed like their sisters. A picture of the Prince of Wales in 1842, shows him wearing a very *décolleté* dress, displaying plump little shoulders, with a necklace, a sash and a large hat worn over a frilled cap. About a decade later a small boy (my father in fact) was wearing a low-necked muslin frock with a tartan sash, the feminine attire contrasting amusingly with his boyish and roguish expression.

Mrs. Langley Moore in her invaluable book, *The Child in Fashion* gives a clear and detailed picture of the clothes worn by the Victorian child, and one cannot do better than to take her as a guide. By the early 40's she tells us, shirts were worn shorter, soft lawn and cambric had been replaced by cotton which could be starched and worn over stiff petticoats. Sprays of flowers or little designs in dark colours on a white ground were favoured for children's dresses. A little boy in the early 40's wears an odd get-up, partly masculine, partly feminine, consisting of lace-edged pantaloons which came just below the knee, and a skirt and little jacket.

It has been said that the fashion for white has a social, or snobbish, significance, indicating that the wearer belongs to the leisured classes. Certainly much washing and ironing was necessary before little Miss Alice was able to trip downstairs in her second-best muslin dress and bronze shoes, and sit on Papa's knee during dessert. The muslin frock with sash and coral necklace remained the nursery vogue throughout the 40's, but by the end of that decade, white simplicity was giving place to vivid colours and complicated trimmings. A little girl wears a frock of shot green taffetas with a gathered bodice and fichu, and pinked frills. Instead of the slippers which had been worn

[1] *The Child in Fashion*, Doris Langley Moore.

for generations by girls, she wears a pair of black merino half boots and white stockings.

By 1855, the well-to-do female child is as starched and bundled up as her mother. Her muslin or taffetas dress is supported by a number of undergarments—chemise, cotton slips, drawers, a flannel petticoat for warmth and a starched under-petticoat and stiff muslin top petticoat to give her dress the required overblown effect. (Crinolines for children were rare.) One must remember of course that these were best clothes; for everyday wear there were plainer dresses in woollen or holland, according to the time of year.

The Queen's and Prince Albert's love for Balmoral and the Highlands led to a rash of tartan in nursery fashions. 'Highland costumes which are not only prettiest for boys and girls, but also the most healthy' made their startling appearance. A tartan sash for a muslin frock was fair enough, but one wonders what a genuine Highlander would have said to the small boy (1857) in a tartan dress with a lace collar, long stockings and red shoes laced up the leg.

Mrs. Langley Moore has in her collection a tartan frock of alpaca, a favourite Victorian fabric, which one might easily mistake for a girl's, with its full skirt, shaped bodice and white ruched sleeves. Only the little glengarry cap asserts its wearer's sex—he is in the favourite nursery expression 'A young Turk'.

A little boy of the same date looks boyish and attractive in a pair of trousers, cut away coat and waistcoat of buff cloth. He has a turned-down collar and a floppy tie. In spite of his manly attire he is probably still under Nurse's care, for patterns of boys' frocks in a magazine of this period are given as 'from three to six years old'.

A boy in a contemporary illustration of the same date is dressed more formally. He has a peaked cap on his hair which he wears as long as a present-day woman's style, a long-waisted coat of dark material and light trousers. His young sister who has short hair (it might equally well be twisted into sausage curls) is dressed in a silk dress lavishly trimmed with braid, with a low-necked tunic bodice, and a short full skirt. White under-sleeves appear below her three-quarter-length sleeves, and frilled knee-length pants below her skirt. This 'ensemble' is completed by a low-crowned hat with a curved brim, and striped socks.

These juvenile fashions have the charm of 'quaintness' to modern eyes, but they were undoubtedly a retrograde step from the simple clothes of the late 18th and early 19th century as far as comfort and practical considerations went. Mrs. Langley Moore gives, as an example of the complete unsuitability of children's clothes at this time, a picture and description of a tiny girl's 'toilette'. It consisted of a dress of dark mauve glacé, with a black pin-stripe and black ribbons, rosettes and ruchings (of all colour schemes, but amethyst and other shades of light purple with black trimmings were often used for little girls). Of course there could be no question of washing it, but luckily the dry-cleaning process had been known since the 18th century. One must not forget to mention the absurd little black hat, something in the shape of a fez, adorned with a bunch of feathers in front, and the cross-gartered satin boots that completed this toilette of a tot of the mid-sixties. Elastic-sided boots were much worn.

A charming and comfortable fashion for little girls at this time was the red ridinghood cloak for outdoor wear.

4

The nursery is a little world apart. Imagine it on a winter's evening, the red curtains drawn against the wind and the rain outside, the coal fire burning brightly behind the high fire-guard, Nanny sitting in her rocking chair, working through the pile of mending in the basket by her side. To see her sitting there like a rocking graven image, stout and comfortable in her print dress and her voluminous white apron, you would suppose her nearly immovable, at the best slow-moving. But let some nursery crisis occur—Miss Florence bellowing from the cupboard into which she has been locked by her angel-faced toddler sister, the adenoidal nursery maid dropping a kettle of scalding water over her foot, and Nanny is all speed and commanding movement.

Now and then as she rocks, she looks up and admonishes her charges, when they become too noisy or quarrelsome—'Dogs delight to bark and bite' she says, biting off a thread—or to issue directions to the nursemaid, who has been allowed as a great favour to hold the latest baby in her arms.

A splendid dapple-grey rocking horse with a long silky mane is King of the Nursery toys; the beautiful wax doll which a kind aunt brought from Paris is the Queen (the doll, Josephine, travelled with her trousseau in a tiny trunk; she has a change of everything and her own brush, comb and mirror) but the nursery floor is littered with lesser personages, a rather battered but beloved cat on a wheeled platform which nods its head as it is pulled along, a Jigging Irishman also on a wheeled platform, a Jack-in-the-Box (Charlotte is frightened of him, but then she is only three) and a party of little penny china dolls dressed by Mama in scraps of silk and velvet from her workbox, also a platoon of wooden soldiers given by Uncle Arthur before he went out to die of cholera in the Crimea (the whole nursery except the baby went into mourning for him). There is a fine doll's house in one corner of the nursery, its rooms filled untidily with doll's furniture, and with the odd, inappropriate assortment of toys that children insist on keeping in dolls' houses—marbles given in a moment of open-handedness by a schoolboy brother, a top, and part of a set of building blocks, designed to teach biblical history.

But it is time to tidy up the toys—Nanny insists on this every day—and tidy up the children for their descent into the adult world. Faces and hands are washed, hair combed and brushed unmercifully (what a pity that the effect of Miss Lucy's nocturnal curl papers have always worn off by the evening), holland pinafores discarded, the little boys changed into their tidy suits or frocks, the little girls into their billowing 'second-best' dresses. Nanny transformed by her black silk and her mourning brooch, with a piece of her dead mother's hair in it, into a figure of ineffable dignity, wraps shawls round the shoulders of her little ladies.

Lord Frederick Hamilton, writing of his childhood in the 60's in *Days Before Yesterday*, recalled his dread of the 'Terrible Passage' that had to be passed through on his way down from the nursery to the hall of his Ulster home, for he was six and considered old enough to go downstairs by himself. Eerie in the dim light of colza oil lamps, it was haunted, to his childish imagination, by a fearful assortment of bogies—a stuffed crocodile that came to life at the sound of his scuttling little footsteps, grizzly bears (can there have been a huge stuffed bear there as there was in the hall of another Ulster country house in my childhood? It held a tray for visiting cards in its paws, but was none the less intimidating for pretending to be a butler) and a wicked little hunchback who was somehow associated in his mind with the outbreak of 'garrotting' in London, of which he had heard his elders speak. Yet, with the mysterious resilience of childhood, once down in the cheerful, lighted hall, these fears were forgotten.

Escorted by all-wise, all-powerful Nanny, who has no use for bogies, the children from our nursery scamper fearlessly along chilly passages and, with a final injunction from Nanny, to mind their manners, into the big dining-room, where the younger ones scramble on to Papa's and Mama's knees, and the older ones cluster round to be given grapes, candied fruits, almonds and raisins and sips of wine—delicious treats after the sameness of the nursery fare. Such 'goodies' as dates and tangerines were still a luxury in the late 60's.[1] This was the moment in the day when grown-ups, well-fed and well-wined, were at their most genial.

It was the traditional point of contact between the Victorian adult and child, but of course not the only one. Victorian parents were by no means as aloof or unapproachable as they have been portrayed in fiction and drama. After all most of them loved their children and liked being with them—within reason! Lucy Lyttleton writing of her childhood in the 40's, told how her parents often went through the nursery on their way to each other's rooms, Mama greeting her children with a smile and, 'You little pigs', Papa with 'Absurd little monkeys'.

Fashionable young mothers met together to display their babies and compare notes (rather in the spirit one suspects of

[1] The theme of a child stealing jam or sugar or some other delicacies from its mother's store cupboard (the plot of one book I remember, seemed to turn almost entirely on the small girl's passion for strawberry jam) occurs so frequently in Victorian children's stories as to indicate some serious deficiency in their diet.

the gardening expert who I heard saying with unconcealed satisfaction, 'There is only one other plant like this in England. Lord —— has it. Last time I saw it, I am sorry to say it was *not* looking very well'). Lady Amberley wrote in her diary for June, 1866, 'Baby went to Dover St. at four for a baby show. There was Rosalind's, Blanche's, Bessy Melville's, Addy Biddulph's and E. Peel's . . . Lady Russell was there and thought ours the nicest of all.'

Victorian memoirs are full of nostalgic reminiscences of shoping expeditions in the barouche with Mama (a less affluent Mother whose stockbroking husband's income fluctuated alarmingly, took the children for drives in Hyde Park in a hired victoria) of country walks with Papa, of 'joyous home-gatherings' at Christmas, and family theatricals when the children performed before an audience of grown-up relations.

It is probably correct to say that few parts of the house were actually out-of-bounds to the children except at specified times, or when the forbidden quarter harboured some aged, invalid relation like Lucy Lyttleton's grandmother who lived 'quite secluded' in her apartments, and was hardly ever seen by the children who not unnaturally considered her 'an awful mystery'. (Another grandmother—'Granny' as opposed to 'Grandmama' was more in evidence, and gave charming presents of sashes, etc.)

Many Victorians, looking back on their childhood must have recalled with pleasure the sweet exotic smell of their parents' conservatory—a fairyland so it would seem to them of maidenhair ferns and palms, verbena, geraniums, myrtle and cyclamen, or remembered the click of croquet balls on the lawn during hot summer afternoons (the summers of childhood are always fine). There was the clandestine delight of peeping through the banisters into the hall below when parents were giving a party, seeing the guests arriving in all their finery, or passing in dignified procession into the dining-room, two by two, male and female, like the animals going into the Ark. The more audacious ones, on these occasions might venture down into the pantry and, with the connivance of a friendly butler, carry off delectable booty left over from the long, elaborate meal.

In some respects the children in a large establishment knew more of what was going on behind the scenes than their parents did, being often on very friendly terms with the domestic and gardening staff. The friendship of housekeepers, in particular, with their stores of figs, dates, dried apricots and crystallized sugar was always worth cultivating. Lord Frederick Hamilton as a little boy believed that the heating furnaces in the basement of his Irish home were the 'Gates of Hell', but as they had to be passed to get to the housekeeper's room, he braved them, sustained by the clasp of a kindly footman's hand.

Naturally the smaller the household the more the children saw of their parents. The Clive's in their country rectory were constantly with their young son and daughter (this was in the 40's) gave them their first lessons, played with them (the little boy had 'very little notion of Play' 'Why don't you run? Daddy is playing with you.' 'Oh!' said the little boy, 'I did not know') and took them with them to visit friends. On one such occasion the children 'were delighted with shells, butterflies, pebbles, models of shops, the garden, the nuts and the apples, and all the kindness they received . . .' They also begged their hostess to play a piece of music on her harp imitating the approach and the retiring of a village band.

But even in these less formal circles there was some segregation. 'Dinner is at six on Sunday' (at a relation's house) 'so that the children may come to dessert and play at Scripture characters.'

The very size of the average family demanded some division between adults and children. In some cases families were so large that the generations overlapped. Lord Frederick Hamilton had four nephews when he was born. An entry from a diary of 1861 records, 'We are a large party, 30 in at prayers last night— 35 slept in the house'. 'The dear old house is chocked, over-flowing, echoing with children,' Lucy Lyttleton wrote in 1857. 'The meals', she considered, 'are the fun.' Breakfast was two tables, several loaves, besides plates of bread and butter, two teapots, a dish of meat, a dish of bacon and a full toast-rack. Fun these nursery meals may have been, but one cannot help feeling that the grown-ups did well to avoid them.

Seaside holidays were now an accepted and eagerly looked forward to part of the nursery year, and one of their pleasures, perhaps, from the children's point of view was that they entailed an almost complete collapse of the usual nursery routine and a lowering of the barriers between parents and children. Papa and Mama released from frock coat, top hat, watch chain, from crinolines or bustles and clad in voluminous bathing dresses were brought endearingly closer to the children's own level of carefree informality. It was all part of the delectable seaside atmosphere, the cart that took them out to the bathing boxes, the clear water lapping invitingly, but a little alarmingly, on the bathing box steps, the biscuits after the bathe, the sand castles, bucket and pails and shrimping nets, 'The tight fit is great fun', Lucy Lyttleton wrote of the seaside lodgings at St. Leonards, where four of the children slept in one 'little hole of a room'.

Christmas, of course was the chief family festival when adults and children joined together to worship, to merrymake and to eat. The Lyttleton children roused their elders in the early Christmas morning with 'Hark the Herald Angels', then scrambled on to their parents' bed for kisses and 'Merry Christmas', after which, surrounded by a circle of admiring maids, they partook of coffee and tea cake in the nursery where the holly gleamed in the firelight. Church and a late dinner with all the rich food, plum pudding, mince pies, snapdragons, proper to the season, were the two main events of the day, which ended as it had begun with carols.

One often reads that Prince Albert brought the Christmas tree to England, but I wonder if this is correct? The 18th-century Mrs. Papiendieck considered having a Christmas tree at a children's party, then decided that her children were 'too young to be amused at so much expense and trouble'. In any case, it certainly came from Germany, and owed its popularity to the Prince Consort, for which children should remember him with gratitude. What magic and poetry there is in that dark tree, exile from the Northern forests, glittering with candle-light, tinsel and iridescent glass balls! With the Christmas tree came the giving on a large scale, of Christmas presents. Before mid-century, though we know that presents were given at Christmas, there were no mysteriously bulging stockings at the end of the bed, or piles of parcels round the breakfast plate.

As the Christmas season approached, the toy shops in

Lowther Arcade in the Strand and in Regent Street did a brisk trade. (Imagine what it was like choosing presents for a Victorian quiverful of children, and dozens of young nephews and nieces.) Their shelves were stacked with toys not only from England but from foreign countries—Germany, France, Switzerland—there were skipping ropes and hoops, tops (humming, peg and lashing), clock-work toys and musical boxes (the grand ones had drums, bell, castanet and flute effects) dolls of all kinds (baby dolls it seems were an English speciality), dolls' houses and furniture, model farm yards, Noah's Arks and toy soldiers, and the fascinating toy theatres which were at the height of their popularity in the 1840's, and were popular for at least another forty years. The two chief shops for the sale of toy theatres were Webb and Pollock, and the expression 'Penny plain, twopence coloured' comes from their black and white or coloured sheets.

Parents shopping for presents for the Christmas tree itself, had a choice of a variety of little objects, tiny dolls, puzzles, purses, fans, whistles, little animals and ships, money boxes and sheets of brightly coloured, glossy pictures for scrap-books.

They might buy a magic lantern for the Christmas party, excusing themselves for the extravagance on the grounds that it was educational as well as entertaining. This would be the high-light of the party, but there would be games as well, Hide and Seek, Blind-man's-buff Ring o' Roses, all the old favourites. Imagine the little girls in their billowing white muslin dresses and coloured silk sashes, or later, dressed in cinnamon or amethyst silk with ruches and flounces, playing at Hunt the Slipper; or the small boys in kilts falling over the toddlers (as small boys do at parties) as they break into a game of tig. For supper there are sponge and iced cakes, sugared biscuits, jellies and ices, and bread and butter sprinkled with multi-coloured 'hundreds and thousands'.

Lady de Rothschild, the mother of two small daughters, considered that 'Once or twice a year is, I think, as much as children ought to go out to *real* parties; the excitement, if they are amused, cannot be good for them, and if bored, discontent, envy and other unamiable feelings are brought into play'.

The London child had the best of it as far as treats went, with

Christmas circuses and pantomimes, and visits to Madame Tussaud, the Crystal Palace and the Penny Bazaar, and the panorama of the London Streets, which with their street sellers, Punch and Judy shows and hurdy-gurdies, still had much of the variety of the 18th century. But the country child had the freedom of the garden and farm and fields, and of a countryside where many of the old customs remained, and big attics to play in with their chests full of dim treasures and dressing-up clothes. Country children rode, fished, practised archery and helped (or hindered) the gardener—one such child had a little mahogany wheelbarrow.

5

For both town and country children, new vistas of pleasure had opened out in the landscape of books. The fairies, banished by the early 19th-century educationalists, had staged a triumphant come-back. In 1841, under the name of Felix Summerly, Henry Cole, a friend and adviser of Prince Albert's, and a staunch supporter of the old traditional tales, brought out the *Home Treasury* which consisted of the old favourites, 'Cinderella', 'Red Riding Hood', and so on, in little 6d. and 1/- booklets.

The year 1846 was a notable one indeed. Not only did it see the first Christmas card, sponsored by the same Henry Cole, but also the first English translation of Hans Andersen's fairy tales, under the name, *Wonderful Stories for Children*, and the publication of Edward Lear's rapturous *Book of Nonsense*.

Three years later came an anthology, *Fairy Tales of all Nations*; during the previous year Hoffmann's *Struwelpeter* appeared as *Shockheaded Peter*, a book which I believe has given pleasure to generations of children. As a child I found it frightening and repulsive. Thackeray's original and light-hearted fantasy, *The Rose and the Ring* came out in 1855, Charles Kingsley's *Water Babies* in 1863. Tiresome as the do-as-you-would-be-done-by moralizing is in it, Kingsley certainly was able to convey the fascination of water better than any other writer. There is a translucent quality about his descriptions of the river and sea that reminds one of Milton's *Sabrina Fair*,

> 'Listen where thou art sitting,
> Under the glassy, cool, translucent wave.'

The book was also a salutary reminder of the plight of little chimney sweepers who still ran the constant risk of falls and suffocation. Lord Frederick Hamilton in his memoirs mentions that the 'barbarous habit' of sending climbing-boys up chimneys still persisted in the early 60's, and writes of his fear when he met one of them unexpectedly in a bedroom, for his nursery maid used to threaten him that the sweep would take him away if he were naughty.

Then came the *annus mirabilis*, 1865, which gave Lewis Carroll's (the Reverend C. L. Dodgson's) peerless *Alice in Wonderland*, to English literature. It was six years before it was followed by *Alice Through the Looking Glass* which is almost unique in being a sequel that equals if it does not in some respects excel its prototype, for its atmosphere is even more mysterious and dreamlike.

These were the outstanding achievements in children's literature during this period. There were of course a host of other books, varying greatly in merit. There were the Peter Parley books and their imitators; one of these published in 1838, *Peter Parley's visit to London during the Coronation* was 'Dedicated to the Good Little Boys of Great Britain'. As well as books there was *The Infant's Magazine*, and *Little Folks* a magazine designed primarily to please children not to discipline them. *The Monthly Packet*, a magazine intended entirely for nursery and school-room consumption, came out in 1851, produced by Charlotte Yonge; her *Daisy Chain* appeared in it as a serial. Her stories dealing with family life became firm favourites in the nursery. Moral tales or stories encouraging children in good works were still going strong. The title *Ministering Children* by Marion Charlesworth, speaks for itself, so does the better-known one of *Jessica's First Prayer*, by Hesba Stretton. Stories on the lines of *Froggie's Little Brother* were designed to arouse the compassion of well-to-do children for less fortunate ones, such as crossing sweepers and chimney sweeps.[1]

---

[1] The appalling conditions in which the children of the poor worked was revealed by the 'Parliamentary Commission on the employment of children 1842-3'. Children of six or even younger were employed in the mines. One little boy of that age had to get up at three in the morning for a twelve hours' working day. Female infants of four years old worked at lace-making. The

Children's books were often attractive to look at, bound in bright red or blue or green cloth, with a floral design in gold or little scenes or figures on the cover. They were always illustrated, in colour or with woodcuts or steel engravings, and sometimes by accomplished artists. For instance *Aunt Effie's Rhymes for Little Children* (1852) had illustrations by 'Phiz', and *Songs for Little Children* 1865 was illustrated by Millais.

6

The oppressive dullness that descended on the average Victorian household on Sunday, penetrated like a fog into the nursery. It is commented upon time and again by the authors of autobiographies, who otherwise write nostalgically of their childhood. It was as though the words, 'The Sabbath was made for man, not man for the Sabbath' had never been spoken.

Only 'good' books, such as *The Peep of Day*, *Line Upon Line* or *The Fairchild Family*, or *Pilgrim's Progress* could be read, everyday toys were laid aside (that was where Noah's Ark came into it's own) and harmless amusements such as drawing and painting were forbidden. Lord Frederick Hamilton recalls how a young brother ingeniously evaded this last prohibition. He was very fond of drawing steeplechases, and by an association of ideas was accustomed to depict a steeple in the corner. When remonstrated with and told that a steeplechase was not a 'Sunday' subject, the wily child said, 'You don't understand. This is Sunday and those jockeys are all racing to see which of them can get to church first.'

The child was expected to take part in all the Sunday devotions, morning prayers and a lengthy church service and sermon; in addition to this, a collect had to be learnt and repeated before church. Lady St. Helier described a Sunday in Scotland in her youth as being 'a day full of gloom and darkness'. The two hours' service in Gaelic, followed by another one in English after dinner, was certainly a severe test of infant piety.

Potteries and Glasgow Tobacco works were other centres of misery and suffering for these child slaves. The Sunday Schools which did good work among these children, disclosed the fact that many of them were completely ignorant of the Christian Faith.

According to Lord Frederick Hamilton, the sermon itself at the Scottish Presbyterian Church lasted for an hour and a half.

One must remember however, that children are very adaptable, and in one case at least an early Victorian child was a stricter Sabbatarian than its mother. The little Clive boy repeated with 'great obstinacy', 'Thou shalt do no *manner* of work' when Sunday knitting (knitting was one of his pastimes) was in question. Mrs. Clive tried to modify his ideas of Sunday observance. 'I say hallowing Sunday consists in going to Church, teaching school (Sunday school) reading the Bible, saying more prayers, and that mending my gloves or for a little boy to knit, is by no means dishonouring it.' 'Meysey' Clive, as befitted a clergyman's child showed a keen interest in theological matters. He thought it hard that children should suffer for the father's sins.

Well into the century, children's books of an earlier period with their macabre insistence on death and hell-fire, were still the staple Sunday and religious reading in the nursery, and it is easy to imagine the bad effect that this had on nervous and over-sensitive children, making them magnify their pathetic little misdeeds into mortal sins, and overwhelming them, particularly at night with apocalyptic fears. But there was another side to it. Children are amazingly tough (they need to be, considering how utterly they are at the mercy of adults). Lord Frederick Hamilton's mother, asked one of her small sons, 'What is Emery [the nurse] reading to you about? Is it about Heaven?' 'No, it's about 'ell,' was the cheerful reply. And another Victorian child found the verse from *The Peep of Day*:

> 'Satan is glad—when I am bad,
> And hopes that I—with him shall lie.
> In fire and chains—and dreadful pains'

not only exciting but rather gratifying to her social sense. Then the effect of this grim religious teaching would be mitigated, or even nullified, by the kindlier teaching of a father and mother who would emphasize the love of the Saviour for little children.[1]

[1] This is not surmise on my part but the result of fairly extensive reading in Victorian memoirs.

Belief in the literal though invisible presence of guardian angels was strong and immensely comforting, especially at night. Other children took to good works like ducks to water. 'When I am six, I shall have a ward to visit,' the tiny daughter of the Bishop of London was heard to say.

As I have already indicated, the fond and conscientious mother played an important part in the upbringing of her young children. If she was serious-minded and devout, she was almost painfully conscious of her responsibilities. It makes us smile to read of Lady de Rothschild's misgivings about her daughter Constance, aged four (1847): 'How much fonder she is of dissipation and dress than I was as a child; I must not encourage these faults too much. . . .' One wonders what the 'dissipations' were that tempted a child of four from the straight and narrow path! A little later, she wrote; 'Constance has been rather self-willed and pettish the last few days. She tried to play the tyrant with Annie. How fortunate it is she has a sister and one who does not always give way, for without such a check she would have become very selfish. . . .'

'Sunday was Constance's birthday,' she records, 'heigh-ho, how time flies—she is six years old—the happy age of infancy is over, and she must begin the *labour* of life.'

Caroline Clive, too, confided to her diary (1843) her perplexities about her little son's character: 'Dear Meme [the child's nickname—he was also sometimes called 'Meysey'] shows a disposition to be very passionate. He falls into screams and tears, sometimes from wrath, sometimes from mere excitability, and after any excess of amusement. The fit is soon over and ends generally most abruptly. If quite dispersed he says "All gone" and begins to laugh again.'

Her satisfaction in her daughter 'my precious Alice' was without alloy. 'Alice is the merriest, wildest creature alive, bold, wild, mocking, loving, pretty.'

Princess Beatrice, as a child, does not seem to have been in the least in awe of her father, Prince Albert. 'I was naughty last night,' she said, 'I would not speak to Papa, but it doesn't signify much.'

Some of the punishments inflicted on children of nursery age seem to us not only unnecessarily severe, but also to be tinged with sadism. Lady Frederick Cavendish, looking back on her childhood in the 1840's, recalled that her governess used to take her out walking on the promenade at Brighton with her hands tied behind her back. No wonder that at this stage she was 'very unhappy, very ill-managed and very naughty'. Another punishment was to be put in a large, deep old-fashioned bath that stood in the dark behind a curtain in one corner of the schoolroom.

Even her adored mother, to whose 'gentle and loving care' she paid tribute, used to take her children when they had been naughty, into their father's room and put their small hands under 'a thing for pressing letters together, a bronze hand, which pinched them slightly leaving the dents of the fingers on the back of the hands. This done solemnly, Mama shaking her head.'

Though none of these punishments caused the child any actual pain, they were ingeniously designed to humiliate, and somehow leave 'a nasty taste in the mouth'. Yet it is only fair to add that Lady Frederick Cavendish could write of her childhood as 'a bright, unruffled river'.

The child of nursery age learnt its first lessons from its mother, nurse, nursery governess or an elder sister. Lady de Rothschild employed a writing and dancing master for her little daughter, for as she confessed candidly, 'my temper was not good enough to teach her. . . . I am sorry to say that I have been very impatient lately with Constance at her writing lessons, she has not been very attentive and her mistakes and repeatedly ill-shapen letters irritate and vex me. How happy I shall be when she has a master again for certainly my temper is not good enough to give her writing lessons. . . .' Later she wrote, 'However I must try and be patient with her, and make her lessons as amusing as possible.'

No very high standard of precocity (according to former ideas) was expected of these Victorian children. 'This is dear Meysey's third birthday,' Mrs. Clive recorded, 'he has no learning; hardly more acquaintance with the alphabet than last year at this time, but he is very intelligent.' She admitted that she did not 'observe any strictness about the time' of doing lessons (this was more than three years later) but he generally said himself: 'We have not done so-and-so today. Let us do it now.'

Lesson books dating from the early part of the century, or from the last century were still in use in mid-Victorian nurseries. *The Teacher's Assistant, The Scripture Catechism, Reading without Tears,* and *Aesop's Fables* are titles that occur in accounts of nursery life. The path of education was also made smoother by such devices as alphabet blocks, puzzles, maps, bead frames for counting and other educational toys. One of these 'The Earth and its Inhabitants', dating from about 1850, was in the form of a game. It consisted of a box out of which came hand-coloured pictures of national costumes. It had a tiny globe and a bone teetotum by which the moves of the game were decided.

'The use of the Globes' was considered a very important part of a small child's education, who was also expected to have a good knowledge of the Bible and Prayer Book, and to be able to memorize passages from them. Mrs. Alexander's *Hymns for Little Children* was published in 1848, and must have been a comfort after some of the *Divine Songs* that had been inflicted on the young.

Victorian, 1870–1900

I

Lady Tweedsmuir, writing in *The Lilac and the Rose* about her childhood in what I take to be the late 80's or early 90's, says that the nurseries of that era were severely bare and shabby, furnished with 'left-overs' from the rest of the house, and with no concessions to juvenile taste or stature in the way of pictures of rabbits and squirrels, or in low chairs and tables.

All the same, there does seem to have been a new and lighter atmosphere in the nursery region from about 1870 onwards. By the 1880's, in theory at any rate, some attempt was being made to make the nursery more suitable as a background to the young things who lived in it.

From Kitchen to Garret. Hints for Young Householders, by (Mrs.?)

J. E. Panton, 1888, makes enthralling reading, not only for the breezy style in which it is written ('My dear girls,' she advises young brides, 'you cannot make a greater mistake with your husbands, and later with your sons, than to wait upon them and give in to all their little lazinesses and selfishnesses at home'), but also for the light that it throws on household conditions at that period.

After alluding with horror to the dark and heavy furnishings of 25 years previously ('Even 16 years ago, light was only just beginning to be vouchsafed to us'), the heavy, thick, red damask curtains and monumental sideboards, etc., in whose favour the graceful Chippendale and Sheraton furniture of an earlier age had been banished—she gives some suggestions for an up-to-date scheme for decoration. The graining of wood is to be eschewed at all costs; ebonized New Zealand pine furniture and Liberty bamboo settees in black are recommended, also Turkish embroidered antimacassars (at 2/- each), Japanese paper fans nailed to the wall, tiled fireplaces and potted palms. Mrs. Panton's favourite colour schemes were peacock blue, red and sage-green (she seems to have had a positive obsession for sage-green. She was also very fond of the word 'artistic'.) Such are the mutations of taste that many moderns would almost certainly prefer the Victorian red damask and mahogany to this 'aesthetic' decor.

Working her way upstairs from 'Kitchen to Garret' the author of course has a chapter on 'The Nurseries'. The plural word should be noticed, for she is very insistent that there should be two good nurseries for one child even in 'the suburban villa with five or six bedrooms' where she has domiciled her imaginary young married couple, Edwin and Angelina, and that the extra nursery should not be sacrificed for the sake of having a spare room for an occasional visitor. Upstairs nurseries she condemns, as being inaccessible to the mother, or else the children are down with her 'in and out of season', and become 'little prigs who care nothing for a romp'. 'No doubt,' she complains, 'that children will soon cease to exist at all, and will become grown-up men and women before they have changed their teeth.' In her opinion the nurseries should lead out of the mother's room, which probably accounts for her insistence that loud shrieks and strident voices should be forbidden.

The day nursery, in Mrs. Panton's opinion, should be roomy with a window that opens top and bottom, and that instead of blinds should have 'nice muslin and serge or cretonne curtains'. The room should be cheerful and pretty with bright wall-paper of a faint blue or pink, a cretonne dado with a rail, and varnished and washable paint. Mrs. Panton, incidentally, claimed to have cured 'a young person of five' of damaging the nursery walls by making him pay up 'all his available cash' (pathetic!) for a new wall-paper. But she was a woman of masterly character as will be seen from her remark apropos of not allowing coats and hats in the hall. 'The men of the household can easily be trained to take their own especial property at once into their own rooms.' (I should be interested to know how Mrs. Panton set about this 'training'.)

The ceiling of this model nursery was to be white-washed with a touch of blue in it, the floor stained and polished every Saturday with beeswax. A carpet felt was to be laid down and over it 'a nice square of Kidderminster'. The changed attitude towards the decoration of the nursery is shown by her suggestion that a nursery with coral or rose pink walls should have a pretty flowered cretonne for the curtains, while if the walls were blue, she recommended a blue and white paper at 1/- a piece and a cretonne to match with a pattern of daisies. Doors and cupboards could be papered with cretonne. Altogether it sounded a fresh, cheerful room.

Cupboards were to be flush with the wall to avoid the banging of small heads; there was to be that standby of the Victorian nursery, a solid, round table. ('Please don't faint, all ye aesthetic folk,' she begs, before suggesting that it should be covered with an oilcloth.) There should be a comfortable deep chair for nurse, a chair for each child, as well as extra chairs for visitors, and a sofa for a tired child to rest on, or for a playful child to turn into a ship at sea or an elephant or whatever object its game requires. Needless to say she stressed the importance of having a high fire-guard.

The night nursery could be papered to match the day nursery, but with the addition of 'very dark serge curtains'.

Mrs. Panton had a horror of gas. 'No pernicious gas', should be allowed in the child's sleeping room. She was equally distrustful of candles. A 'good duplex lamp' was all that was required. The night nursery must be properly ventilated with a fireplace and a ventilator.

While Mrs. Panton did not consider it necessary that the night nursery like the day nursery should have a fire as a matter of course in cold weather, she deplored 'the foolish idea' that a fireless bedroom hardened the child's health. Above all, the nursery in her opinion, should be a quiet and peaceful place, a haven of rest for the mother to come to when she wanted to have 'a quiet, confidential talk' with nurse.

Mrs. Panton was nothing if not thorough, and a chapter entitled 'In Retirement' prepared the young expectant mother for what was still considered an ordeal. 'Naturally these times are looked forward to with dread by all young wives.' Why this was so is explained in the next sentences. 'They are fully convinced that they must die, and in fact make themselves perfectly wretched and miserable because of their ignorance, and of their not unnatural dislike to speak of their dreads and fears.' Mrs. Panton adds '. . . though of course I can only lightly touch on these matters in a book which I trust may be widely used and read, I want to whisper a few words to reassure all those who may be contemplating the arrival of No. 1'.

In other words a fog of false modesty surrounded the whole subject of childbirth. Mrs. Vivien Hughes in her autobiography *A London Child in the Seventies* says that her mother had an idea that it was improper to consult a doctor before her actual confinement. Mrs. Panton advises all young wives to procure Dr. Chavasse's *Advice to a Mother* (having previously studied his *Advice to a Wife*), 'possessed of these books,' says Mrs. Panton blithely, 'any young matron can manage herself most successfully without the constant harassment of continually seeing the doctor'. Dr. Chavasse was a pioneer in that line and his works enjoyed a deservedly high reputation, but that Mrs. Panton should consider a personal visit to a doctor unnecessary, shows how little importance was attached to pre-natal care.

Mrs. Panton stressed the importance of securing a good

monthly nurse, and advised against the extreme folly of engaging a lady-nurse, who would almost certainly turn out to be a dismal failure, contenting herself with doing the decorative parts of nursing and leaving the hard work to the servants.

As far as the regular child's nurse was concerned, her opinion was summed up in the incisive sentence: 'No young nurse is worth her keep except as an under-servant.'

As may have been gathered, Mrs. Panton had a brisk way with husbands. In this chapter she begs for some consideration for the mother after her confinement—'for at least three weeks after the arrival of a baby, a wife should have mental as well as bodily rest and be sheltered from all worries and domestic cares'. No one could object to this, though it may seem nowadays to be a counsel of perfection. But she goes on to warn Edwin sternly that he must remember that more care is needed with No. 5 or 6 than with No. 1. 'Angelina is no longer as young as she was; she is tired out and unless Edwin is goodness itself he may so depress and harass his wife by his depression that she may slip out of his fingers altogether, and leave him to himself, that most utterly to be pitied person on earth, a widower with small children.'

For that matter, Mrs. Panton was quite bracing about babies too, begging young parents not to allow themselves to be enslaved by 'long clothes slobberers', or to sink their identities into 'That terrible middle-class "Pa" and "Ma", which seems to swallow like some all-devouring serpent, the prettiness and good taste of so many of our young married people'. She also pointed out to infatuated young mothers that 'Precious, perfect and beautiful as no doubt he [the baby] is, the world is full of others just exactly like him'. Babies 'must be taught to be decent members of society' as soon as possible 'and learn to control their shrieks of anger'. In Mrs. Panton's opinion quite tiny babies began to 'take notice' and size people up and must not be given a sense of super-importance.

It was her frank opinion that a new baby was 'a profound nuisance to its relations at the very first'. She hoped she would not be considered a monster for saying so (the Verneys would certainly have thought her one).

However, the poor little 'long clothes slobberer' must be

properly cared for, and she gave careful instructions as to the layette which the expectant mother should prepare for it. This consisted of 12 very fine lawn shirts, 10 long flannels (6 for day wear of fine Welsh flannel, 4 for the night of rather thicker quality) 6 fine long cloth petticoats, 8 monthly gowns of cambric trimmed with muslin embroideries on the bodices only, 8 nightgowns, 4 head flannels, a large flannel shawl, 6 dozen large Russian diapers, 6 good flannel pilches, 3 or 4 pairs of tiny woollen shoes. It was advisable to wait till the christening before getting the robes, as relations often gave them. Mrs. Panton was strongly against low-necked robes—in fact she was against *décolleté* dresses of any sort even for adults, a fashion that she considered 'foolish and indecent', and wished that Queen Victoria, so sensible in other ways, would abolish them for court ceremonies. Tiny babies, in her opinion should be put into high flannel vests. The long flannel barra-coats should be made with three pleats in the bodice, back and front, and the stay bodice should be lined with flannel. As well as all these garments, four or five strips of flannel, six inches wide and eighteen inches long were required, and six swathes to roll around the infant and give support to its back. She was prepared to meet with medical opposition on this point; 'new fashioned doctors' would try to dispense with it.

For a cradle she recommended a 'hammock berceaunette'. This seems to have consisted of a little bed, quilted and hung on four strong legs, with curtains. For trimmings she did not consider fine muslins and lace suitable, but would prefer plain white or figured cambric edged with touchon lace, with an old gold satin ribbon to tie back the curtains. A 'sweet arrangement of palest blue, palest pink and butter colour looks very French and uncommon'. As for the objection that the 'berceaunette' was easily knocked over, well all Mrs. Panton could say was that she had never known it happen. A more obvious objection to all type of cradles with curtains was the danger of them catching fire from a carelessly held candle, but this does not seem to have occurred to anyone. The 'berceaunette' should have a light hair mattress with a 'nice' piece of blanket, and blanket sheeting which had the advantage over a mackintosh sheeting of being easily washable. The small pillow, shaped to the neck should have fine cotton pillow-cases edged with a tiny cambric frill. The sheet should be a piece of cotton or long cloth frilled, tacked on to a blanket and folded over for appearance sake. A miniature eiderdown quilt with a washing cover of figured cambric edged with touchon lace and decorated with pretty bows was also advisable.

The newly born baby was to be bathed every day in tepid water in a high standing bath in a wooden case. A bath of this kind is illustrated in the Army and Navy Stores' catalogue for 1900. It is oval shaped, costs 19/- to 25/- and the stand has wooden legs resembling a chair or table. Another type of bath called an 'Infants' Hammock' seems to be a deviation from the ordinary type of bath stand. A hammock is suspended inside the tub and the water comes below this level, thus presumably protecting the child from the danger of being drowned by an absent-minded nursemaid!

Mrs. Panton did not believe in treating the baby like 'a very precious fragile new toy'. He (or she) could certainly be 'parked' as one would say nowadays, in the night nursery whenever his mother (in her heliotrope bed-jacket) 'wants to get rid of him' and have her bedroom (perfumed with the smell of joss sticks from the Baker Street bazaar) to herself. She assured her readers that she could write pages about first babies, 'poor little things', and all the ill-advised experiments of which they were the subjects—'the hygienic and stupid clothes, the patent foods, the ghastly tins of milk, and the fearful medicines'.

It is really astonishing, considering what an old-established institution babies are, so as to speak, that perambulators made such a late appearance on the nursery scene. As has been noticed, they were not in general use till after the middle of the 19th century, and in the late 70's no English perambulator was made in which the baby could lie down. A drawing from an illustrated magazine of this date, shows a pretty nursemaid, in rather fancy attire, leaning against the railings of a London square, flirting with a brawny looking butcher's assistant. The pram, of which she is nominally in charge, is shaped like a miniature bath chair, with a hood and large wheels.

The same type of pram, based on the principle of the 'penny

farthing' bicycle, with a small wheel in front and two large wheels behind, is advertised in the Army and Navy Stores' catalogue of 1883. The child faces forward, with its back to the person pushing the pram. The pram is lined with American cloth and certainly has the merit of cheapness, costing only 35/- to 45/-. For an extra sum, the carriage could be fitted with bicycle wheels.

It is probable that by now this upright pram was only used for older children, as a different type in which the child could lie down, was shown in the same catalogue. This was engagingly called, 'The Sociable Vis-a-Vis'. It was made of wicker, cost £5 5s. and had four wheels. The occupant of the pram lay facing the pram-pusher, and the two front wheels, immediately under the baby's head, were considerably smaller than the rear wheels under the handle, which gives one an uneasy feeling that the pram, carelessly handled, might tip over and throw the baby on to its head. The reversible, jointed hood when raised, gave the pram the appearance of a covered wagon in an American film about pioneering days in the Middle West, being about three times the height of the pram itself.

By 1890, the prams offered for sale by the Stores had a more stream lined appearance. The handle was by now behind the head of the child, and the wheels this end were larger than the forward ones. The pram bodies were of wood, except for one monstrosity in the 1900 catalogue with a cane body and excessively complicated scroll designs in relief on the sides. This cost 122/6 as against 60/- to 90/- for the plainer model.[1]

Those who have accompanied me through this story of the nursery will have noticed that all down the centuries it was gener-

---

[1] I know of one young mother who has resolutely refused to buy a pram for her children, and recently I saw another one carrying her large baby along a busy street, in a kind of little seat or support which she wore slung over her shoulder. With the virtual disappearance of nannies from the nursery scene, prams are used more and more for 'parking' the baby in the garden while its mother attends to her household jobs. It may be that the wheel is turning full circle, and that the modern mother, revolting against the high price of prams, will gradually dispense with them altogether, using other devices in their stead, such as Moses' baskets, carry-cots and the ingenious contraptions which enable young parents to take their babies comfortably with them in their cars.

ally assumed that breast-feeding—if not with the mother's milk then with that of a wet-nurse—was the best nourishment for the newly-born child. Now for the first time, one comes across a complete break with tradition in the proposition that a young baby may thrive just as well or better on cow's milk. 'In these days of ours, few women are strong enough or have sufficient leisure to give themselves up entirely to the infant's convenience,' wrote Mrs. Panton.

That breast-feeding had not yet entirely gone out of fashion was shown by her remark that she expected to be told that she was a disgrace to her sex. She was probably thinking of elderly doctors and women of the older generation (we have seen that some twenty years previously the Amberleys resorted to a wet-nurse after Lady Amberley had made desperate efforts to nurse her child), for there seems no doubt that bottle feeding was in the ascendency, and this state of affairs was to continue till well into the next century. This was due, one supposes, to various causes, more hygienic milk and bottles, the invention of patent foods, and the fact that women now had more interests and occupations outside their homes, and were not prepared as Mrs. Panton put it, 'to give themselves up entirely to the infant's convenience'. That the word 'convenience' should have read 'welfare' had not occurred to her, for the crucial importance of breast-feeding during the first few weeks or months of the baby's life had not been made clear to mothers. Mrs. Panton at any rate was all for an Alderney cow, or for Londoners, the Alderney Dairies.

Mrs. Panton had very little use for the contemporary child. 'I confess the child of the period is my chief detestation . . . poor little soul', she said, 'I cannot bear to see poor, innocent babies dressed out to imitate old pictures with long skirts sweeping the ground because they are picturesque, with bare arms and wide lace collars and manners to match, who go out perpetually to luncheon and tea parties, and if they do happen to be passably good looking, are worshipped by a crowd of foolish women until the conversation is engrossed by the child, who very soon becomes an intolerable nuisance . . .'

Her schedule for children's meals, all of which except the midday one were to be eaten in the nursery, was as follows:

breakfast at eight with porridge, followed by eggs and bacon or fish; luncheon at one o'clock, and for this meal she recommended more chicken and fish, and would allow a few pure sweets to be eaten afterwards; tea with jam and cake at five, and milk and biscuits before going to bed. She put in a plea for giving the children a good supply of fresh fruit and jam.

Her advice on health was rather sketchy. Weak backs should be rested on the nursery sofa, and bathed with salt water, which could also be used for weak ankles. Cuts should be dressed with calendula and soft rags. The nursery medicine cupboard should contain plenty of sticking plaster and camphor for colds. In a general way she relied on fresh air and good food to keep the children well.

To our ideas her advice on children's clothes was less sound. They were still to be overloaded with garments, as the following suggestions for dressing a small girl shows. First the child was to wear two pairs of combination garments one in wool, the other in longcloth, a stay bodice made of ribbed material on which a flannel skirt should be sewn in winter, over which another skirt was to be worn, sewn on a bodice, and on top of all this a smock-frock, with tucks, full sleeves and a sash of Liberty silk. No other form of dress was so suitable in Mrs. Panton's opinion for a girl from short clothes to the age of fifteen. She may have been right but how tired the girl must have become of it!

Silence is maintained about little boys' underwear; as their main garment, a 'Jack Tar' suit or a kilt is recommended. That suits with a nautical air (really that is about as much as one can say for them) were being sold for small boys more than a decade before Mrs. Panton's book was published, is shown by the specimen illustrated and described in Mrs. Langley Moore's *The Child in Fashion*. The material is cream flannel and the suit was not as serviceable as it looks, as the broad blue silk collar and bands at the waist, wrists and down the 'shorts' are not washable or detachable. A comic-looking straw hat and laced boots completed the outfit, which cost 12/6 complete with waistcoat.

It was an era when a mother's fancy was allowed full rein when it came to dressing her small son. Another little boy in *The Child in Fashion* is shown, under the date 1873, in a little navy cloth coat, embroidered with coloured flowers and leaves in the Tyrolean style, and a round Tyrolean hat, and as the Irish would say he looks 'a little doat'.[1] A year later an older boy of about seven or eight is in a velvet suit also vaguely suggestive of the Alps. He wears a hat of the shape that one associates with an Italian peasant in the Dolomites, and girlish looking shoes with pointed toes and fairly high heels. (These pointed shoes were fashionable for children of both sexes, though button boots were also popular. To walk with them pointed out delicately, was the stylish carriage for a girl-child.)

Something should be said about the popularity of velvet and its kindred materials for young children during the 70's and 80's. A tiny boy in a photograph dating from 1878, is in a home-made velvet suit trimmed with gold braid. On his head is a peaked cap which his candid sister says makes him look like a monkey on a hurdy-gurdy. (She herself a few years later wore a miniature Swiss peasant's dress and cap, also made for her mother.[2])

Mrs. Langley Moore tells us that velveteen was popular for the young from the 70's onwards. It was a speciality of John Lewis's and could be bought from them for about 1/11 a yard. Plush, too, was worn by children. My mother who was born in the mid-60's, used to tell me that she wore an absurd little bustel, and children's clothes till the mid-80's had what Mrs. Langley Moore calls 'an upholstered look' ('fubsy' might also be a good description of it), partly due to their padded curves and partly due to the materials, such as plush, which nowadays we would associate with furniture rather than clothes. Trimmings of chinchilla, tiny sealskin muffs and 'a panache of cock's plumes' were all considered suitable for young children. A little girl in the 70's wore in the winter, a sealskin hat with an elastic fastened under her chin, a tartan wrap-over and button boots. Dressed like this she bowled a hoop along the pavements.

The wildfire popularity in the mid-80's of Frances Hodgson Burnett's *Little Lord Fauntleroy*, with its nauseating little hero, gave a further impetus to velvet suits for small boys, accompanied by white lace collars and flowing locks, and it may

[1] i.e 'to be doated on'.   [2] Eleanor Farjeaon, *A Nursery in the Nineties*·

have been of this that Mrs. Panton was thinking when she rebuked mothers who dressed their children up to look like old pictures. I do not believe she would have approved either of the little girl in the plum-coloured velveteen dolman coat with narrow cape sleeves and a high collar (in *The Child in Fashion*) dating from 1887. The pretty little puss who is displaying it wears a broderie anglaise dress under the coat and a little toque with ribbons and feathers. She carries a grey-sealskin muff and has satin boots based on an antique style. She looks very feminine and fetching and is, as Mrs. Langley Moore points out, dressed 'to go visiting', but Mrs. Panton I feel sure, would have clapped her into a Liberty smock-frock and a long coat. She would have thought well however of the high collar. As will have been noticed, she had a horror of any form of *décollétage*, and here fashion supported her.

In her memoirs, *The Child in the Crystal*, dealing with her London childhood in the 80's, Lady Sybil Lubbock has a photograph of herself wearing a hat shaped rather like a puff ball edged with fur, and fastened with elastic under the chin, and a coat trimmed with fur. But this was probably for 'best'; for everyday, in the winter, she wore a warm stuff coat with a handkerchief tucked round her neck, a hat with an elastic or a tam o'shanter, and of course gloves. No self-respecting Nanny would allow her young lady to appear in public with bare hands. In summer this toilette was replaced by a white piqué jacket, very much starched, worn over a coloured cotton frock (a white frock was reserved for Sundays) and a floppy straw hat. In another photograph of her at the age of six, she is in a frock with a gathered front, a falling lace collar and elbow cuffs, and a sash. Her hair is cut in a fringe and falls prettily on to her shoulders. A trip to Scotland to stay with relations of Nanny's called for tam o'shanters and knitted jerseys. As a little girl she had a dress of broderie anglaise with a pale blue under-skirt, a blue sash and ribbons to match. This was kept for such special occasions as a tenant's ball in a country house. Most likely she wore bronze slippers on this occasion. Unbleached holland with embroidery insertions and frillings were a favourite combination (Mrs. Langley Moore says) during this decade, and a surprisingly practical one.

The bustle (never however called that in polite circles) was 'out' by now, and the princess line appeared in children's clothes in imitation of adult fashions. At the same time children wore sashes low round their waists. The 'dainty' effect of a white broderie anglaise dress on a little girl would be rather spoilt (to our ideas) by black stockings and boots.

2

It is interesting to set against the theoretical picture of nursery life in *From Kitchen to Garret* the vivid account of a real nursery at the same period (the 80's) as described by Lady Sybil Lubbock in her book.

The London Nursery which she shared with an elder sister, was presided over by a beloved Highland nanny to whose unfailing devotion and simple piety she pays tribute. Her parents were loving, and long-suffering towards childish mis-adventures, and were by no means aloof. Too young to go to school in Sloane Street with her sister, she learnt poetry every morning with her father, had reading, history and geography lessons from her mother and went shopping with her in Sloane Street.

When afternoon lessons and tea was over, the two little girls in starched white muslin dresses with coloured sashes and beads, descended to the drawing-room where they sat with their mother, embroidering a pair of slippers for their father, or dressing penny dolls for the 'Hospital Box' while their mother read aloud to them from Mrs. Ewing, Walter Scott or Miss Yonge. (Reading aloud was one of the chief family recreations in Victorian times.) Or they might make scrapbooks from Christmas cards and from the brightly coloured glossy sheets of pictures sold for that purpose. Their father's return from his work meant race games, backgammon and draughts. When visitors called, the children were not banished from the draw-ing-room but sat quietly at their task in their small chairs under the lamps, making what sense they could of the strange grown-up talk. If they grew bored they could slip away and have a romp in the dining-room with the butler or, descending to the basement, wheedle bits of sugar candy from the cook.

Before they went to sleep, their mother came into the night nursery to give them a 'good night' kiss.

Yet though by no means cut off from the adult world, it remained to the little girl alien and unpredictable. Only in the nursery could real security be found. The figure of Nanny, in her brightly coloured dress (no impersonal white uniform for her) dominated the scene; she was cooking Scotch porridge or potato cakes or griddle scones, or busy putting fine stitches into frocks and underclothes. Her lilting Highland voice brought poetry into their young lives with her old Border ballads and stories of Prince Charlie.

One is struck, when reading Victorian memoirs, by the many obscure terrors that seem to have haunted the children of that period. (Was that because so many things were discussed before them in hushed voices, or because they were constantly in the company of uneducated people?) Lady Sybil, in spite of her happy surroundings, was no exception. She was terrified of 'the Eye of God', burglars, 'Penny for the Guy' urchins, the May Day 'Jack in the Green' and his capering chimney-sweep attendants, mad dogs and gipsy women. These terrors only sprang to life at night, and were soon laid to rest by Nanny who came in with a shaded candle to soothe her. But even Nanny could not cope with the effect on her nervous system of 'Jack the Ripper' of whose nightmare exploits she had gathered something from the whispers of servants. The gruesome tit-bits that she had overheard wrought so much on the poor child's mind that she had to be sent on a visit to a beloved aunt in Yorkshire to recuperate.

Life in the nursery moved with a clockwork regularity. Breakfast was at eight; the staple nursery luncheon still consisted of roast or boiled mutton, mashed potatoes, greens and rice pudding. 'Pomard aveen' (Pomade Divine') was prescribed for bruises, blackcurrant tea at bedtime for colds, when the patient was wrapped in a scarlet flannel dressing-gown; foot-baths of steaming 'potato' water for chilblainy toes. There were weekly dancing lessons at which the little girls practised polkas and valses, (wearing bronze slippers I dare say) or did exercises with indian clubs.

There were pleasant breaks in the routine, shopping expedi-

tions to Harrod's bazaar and Rose's toy shop, where pocket
money (2d. a week) could be laid out advantageously at the
penny stall, and ducks to be fed on the Serpentine. Ball games
were played round the pavement of the Albert Memorial (this
surprised me I must say, being more suggestive of a Spanish
evening, when little girls, dressed like exquisite dolls play about
in the squares, under their young nurses' eyes, than of the
decorum of a Victorian afternoon). Aunts and other grown-up
relations often had 'treasure tables', ladened with tiny curios in
ivory, silver or even in gold, and a well-brought-up little girl
would be allowed to play with these. Relations also took the
children to see the circus or the Christy Minstrels. There were
birthday treats, of course—visits to the Tower of London, the
Mint, Madame Tussauds or the Crystal Palace, or best of all to
an evening performance at the Pantomime. This meant a rest
after luncheon, much scrubbing after tea with the round balls
of 'cherry blossom' soap which were used in the nursery, and
much brushing and curling of hair. Muslin frocks with sashes
and Indian necklaces were worn and of course shawls for the
drive in the four-wheel cab.

An allusion to the May Day 'Jack in the Green', to hurdy-
gurdies with monkeys in scarlet jackets, and to trips to the
Foundling Hospital, remind one that much of the early 19th
century, in fact of 18th-century London still lingered, providing
London children with a wealth of visual entertainment. (There
was music, too, in the jingle of the hansom bells.) Lady Sybil
Lubbock used to go in a horse-drawn bus on those shopping
expeditions with her mother. How could a present-day bus,
great snorting, grinding monster, hope to compete in a child's
favour with the horse-drawn bus, the fascinating clip-clop of the
horses' hooves, and the fun of rushing to the front seat to get a
good view of the horses? I know, because horse-drawn buses
survived at Brighton into my Edwardian childhood.

But the country and the seaside were, as they still are, the
child's paradise. Every now and then the family doctor would
obligingly prescribe a 'change' and sea air as a restorative after
some childish illness, and the two little girls were taken to
lodgings at Eastbourne and sampled all the delights of spades
and buckets, sand castles, shrimping nets, sailing boats, and

coloured balloons and kites, (donkey rides too, and Punch and Judy shows on the sands, one supposes).

In the summer there were country holidays, the freedom of overalls, bare legs, 'chip' hats, and drives in the pony cart. Christmas, too, was often spent in the country, and its joys are nostalgically recalled—first the train journey with foot warmers and bags of biscuits, then the station brougham, then the wonderful country tea, toast and muffins, home-made butter and jam, brown bread and delicious cakes. There were hilarious games of happy families, old maid, animal grab, tiddly winks, and charades and dumb crambo; the mysterious, ecstatic ritual of the Christmas stocking (the children borrowed their father's shooting stockings for this) and the climax of the Christmas tree glorious with crystal ornaments and candles and little parcels tied up in gold and silver paper. Happy memories!

3

I have not mentioned an important part of the Victorian family day, that is to say family prayers. Miss Olivier, in her memoirs, *Without Knowing Mr. Walkley*, says that evening prayers were unusual except in clerical households (and as the daughter of a clergyman she was in a position to know) but the ordinary God-fearing family would as soon have missed breakfast as morning devotions. In fact the two were closely connected, as the prayers usually took place in the dining-room (except in a very large household where they might be held in the hall immediately before breakfast) and the sound of a kettle bubbling away on a spirit lamp was apt to provide a rather distracting accompaniment to the head of the household's petitions. Everyone joined in them; the servants trooped in first in strict order of precedence, and knelt down at the row of chairs provided for them, while the family grouped themselves round the breakfast table. Visitors had to time their descent from their rooms carefully if they were to avoid the embarrassment of bursting in on a room full of worshippers. The children, too, except the very small ones, took part in family prayers, having first had their own breakfast in the nursery. In one household at least, after the prayers were over, the children played with their toys in the dining-room while their elders ate breakfast.

There were families, of course, where the children had no set nursery life. One such household is described in *A London Child in the Seventies* by M. Vivien Hughes. The children had neither nurse nor nursery, but they were given a room to themselves which they called their 'study'. It had all the essential features of a conventional nursery, a large table, a warm carpet, a good fire and a big ottoman, but they were allowed to choose the wall-paper and pictures themselves.

They had to keep to a few strictly enforced rules; there were to be no arguments about bed-time, everything on their plates must be eaten up, they were never to be rude to servants. Apart from this, discipline was not onerous, and there were very few punishments. Sunday however was very tedious, with long services and restricted reading and games, but the parents seem to have been fitting in with accepted custom rather than carrying out their own inclinations. Probably they were as bored as the children.

Toys were few, and a new one was an event. Life, however, the author says, was not dull. A box of plain bricks, a dozen toy soldiers and ninepins and marbles, provided her and her brothers with endless amusement.

The mother, except in a well-to-do family where a nursery governess was employed, was usually the child's first teacher. The author of *A London Child in the Seventies* recalled the lessons in Bible-reading, sewing, writing, French and English poetry, and English history (in the form of little stories) that her mother gave her. Where the family was hard-up and it was an effort financially to send the boys to school, the little girls were taught by the mother till they were well into school-room age.

In the Olivier family, everything was learnt by heart—pieces of poetry, passages from the Bible, History, Geography, French or Latin. After half an hour or so, the children's mother came back to 'hear' them. Then she wrote out stories for them and left them alone for another hour to write them down.

Reading Without Tears occurs in nearly every memoir of a Victorian childhood. Sir Osbert Sitwell recalls (in *Left Hand, Right Hand!*) how at the age of five—this was in the last few years of the century—he flung down his copy of *Reading Without Tears* and ran from the room in a dash for freedom, pursued by a screaming Swiss governess. It was the first real exquisite day of summer. Lady Tweedsmuir as a child learnt to read from a book illustrated by Walter Crane, that dealt with the classic combination of 'a cat' and 'a mat', also from a Kate Greenaway alphabet. The great popularity of this artist with her pseudo-18th-century but charming children endured from about 1875 to the end of the century, and undoubtedly influenced children's fashions.

There was a rich crop of books for the young from the 70's onwards—Anna Sewell's *Black Beauty* which has been wept over by generations of children, Mrs. Ewing's *Flat Iron for a Farthing* and *Lob Lie by the Fire*; Mrs. Molesworth's *The Tapestry Room*, *The Cuckoo Clock* and *Carrots*; George MacDonald's *Princess and the Goblins* (to mention only a few). A gifted artist, Randolph Caldicott illustrated old rhymes and songs, such as *John Gilpin* and *The House that Jack Built*. There were several magazines for children, notably *Sunday at Home* and *Little Folks* which numbered Kate Greenaway among its contributors. Its readers were encouraged to write about their pets and hobbies, and this was symbolic of the more indulgent and more understanding attitude of adults in general towards the young. Yet some habits of thought persisted from an earlier age. It seems strange to us that a very small girl should be taken in to see her dead grandmother.

4

'I had the fortune to be born towards the sunset hour of one of the great periodic calms of history. . . . Everything was calm and still and kindly . . .'

With these words which to one reader at least conjures up a visionary seascape of surpassing beauty, Sir Osbert Sitwell in the first volume (*Left Hand, Right Hand!*) of his superb biography, sums up the atmosphere of the closing years of the 19th century—'that halcyon age' as he calls it. He was born in 1892, so his recollections of his nursery years bring us exactly to the limits of this book.

A family that produced three such gifted writers as the

Sitwells in one generation can hardly be regarded as typical, but their upbringing, allowing for parental idiosyncrasies, followed the traditional lines of their class and period.

Mrs. Panton, as we know, made no bones of the fact that she considered small children a nuisance, and that this attitude was not uncommon among parents is borne out by Sir Osbert Sitwell in the following paragraph:

'Parents were aware that the child would be a nuisance, and a whole bevy of servants, in addition to the complex guardian-ship of nursery and school-room, was necessary, not so much to aid the infant, as to screen him off from his father and mother, except on such occasions as he could be used by them as adjuncts, toys or decoration.'

The children, as he points out, were often unconsciously in league with the servants against their elders. Much of their knowledge of practical life was derived from these domestics, and it was fortunate when they were looked after by someone of the quality of Davis, the Sitwells' nurse, to whose excellence the author pays tribute. He calls her 'our dear nurse who had been nursery maid to our mother' and says that 'Placidity and a comforting trust in the beneficence of God and man were her chief characteristics. Her wisdom was of the blood, not of the mind, and she possessed a great understanding of young people, young animals, and of birds and wild flowers.' This admirable woman always wore black bonnets in the winter. Indoors she wore high white caps covered with lace and trimmed with pink or pale blue ribbons. She too believed in Butler and Crisps *Pomade Divine* for bruises, and in boiled mutton and rice pudding for nursery meals (a child, recovering from croup was fed on sago pudding, blancmange, and calvesfoot jelly), but on occa-sion would relax her own dietary rules to the extent of indulging her charges with a treat of winkles bought on the sly (they were living at Scarborough at the time). 'Anything for peace, Master Osbert' was a frequent remark of hers, and this obviously gave considerable scope to a determined child. One result of it was a delightful visit to Davis's aged parents in Berkshire, the author, aged three, having refused to be parted for a minute from his nurse.

To a highly imaginative and sensitive child, Renishaw that

old 'haunted and haunting house', so beautiful by day, was frightening at night, and it was comforting to the little boy to hear his nurse and the nursery maid talking away together in the day nursery, and even to smell the beer and cheese off which they were supping. The atmosphere of the Renishaw nurseries was impregnated with that of earlier epochs. Even a blanket had the date 1801 on it—how many children long since dead had slept under it! An old rocking horse had the date 1836 painted on it. It would be easy, one supposes, to imagine that at night it rocked gently in ghostly play. The perambulator used by Davis was 'very ancient and wide'.

Such links with the past would, one supposes, be the exception rather than the rule. The 1900 catalogue from the Army and Navy Stores shows the type of folding cot made of iron and brass and trimmed with chintz, sateen or muslin, that would be used in more humdrum nurseries. It was basket-shaped, its mesh sides supported by iron rods, diagonally intersecting, this framework being decked up in enormous quantities of lace and satin trimmings, which left only the legs showing, thus matching the elaborate *toilettes* which the baby's mother will wear for garden parties and other social occasions.

To return to *Left Hand, Right Hand!*; the little boy often saw his parents. He was allowed to wander in and out of his mother's bedroom in the morning: 'I sat on her bed, and upset everything with impunity. I adored her,' and both his parents came to say good night to him, 'it was the high moment of the day, a reception'. They told him bed-time stories. His father's, unlike his mother's, were thought-out, 'It would be something about the crusades, though he was in no way stiff with children, but they existed to be improved and in the meantime to amuse and interest him with their curious point of view.'

His mother stayed with him while he fell asleep, and as she left the room, so beautiful in her evening dress, 'she took the last remainder of all the light that the day held'.

This experience of seeing a mother transformed by the splendour of formal evening dress is one that modern children miss, for they live in such close proximity to their parents, that their mothers' probably hurried change from day to evening clothes when occasion demands (and long evening dresses at the time of writing seem to be worn less and less) is just part of the day's routine.

Yet in spite of these and other contacts with the adult world, picnics and so on, the nursery of the 90's was still a sphere apart, enclosed, if the nurse was of the calibre of Davis, in a charmed circle of affection, security and simple earthy wisdom—alas! that it had to be broken into so soon by governess and tutor.

Families by now tended to be much smaller. Five or six children was considered quite a respectable-sized family, and there were many families with only three children in them. (I have no statistics for this, and — going merely by the families in the 90's of which one has read or personally known.) But the teeming quiverfuls of an earlier generation still survived in the form of uncles and aunts, great-uncles and great-aunts—I cannot resist quoting here again from *Left Hand, Right Hand!* where the author says: 'I will not here, however, unleash on you the whole ancient pack of my great-aunts'—these in their turn had descendants, and so most children were well provided with cousins, and the family to a smaller extent still had that resemblance to a tribe which is often commented upon by the writers of Victorian memoirs.

Moreover children more than ever, were encouraged to fore-gather at children's parties—'Those fearful ordeals imposed upon the young by their elders,' Sir Osbert Sitwell calls them—where they were entertained with conjuring tricks and magic lanterns. Fancy dress parties for children were so popular by the 80's that albums of juvenile patterns for these entertainments were being issued by publishers.

Though nurseries, on the whole were becoming more cheerful places, children's clothes and diet still left much to be desired, according to modern ideas. The stodginess of nursery diet made it imperative for a child to be on friendly terms with the cook. An illness had at least this compensation, that it might produce blackcurrant tea, barley water flavoured with lemon juice, and grapes. Another treat, though officially it was a cure for colds, was a lump of sugar dipped in essence of camphor. Parishes food, too, was agreeable (not so the frightful Gregory mixture) and had the additional attraction of looking like wine. Their starchy diet may explain why many small Victorians look so limp and listless in their photographs.

A dread of cold air persisted, and children were muffled up from babyhood. The baby's tiny face seems to wear an expression of protest as it peeps above the high shouldered, highly frilled bodice of the robe which cascades down along the sofa on which the infant is lying, its front panel consisting of embroidery and lace insertions (*c.* 1890). Out of doors, the same baby is shown nearly extinguished in a cap (which Mrs. Langley Moore describes as having 'a front of finely pleated silk ruchings') and a long pelisse. Both the pelisse, which in winter was made of cashmere or nun's veiling, and in summer of cotton or silk, and the cap were fastened with wide satin ribbon (a girl baby would have worn a bonnet). It can easily be imagined how much handling of the baby all its elaborate under-clothing entailed, and how heavy and constricting the outside finery must have been to its little limbs.

Little boys, once they were out of petticoats, came off best perhaps in the sailor suits which, in some form or other, were almost ubiquitous by now. The frontispiece of *Left Hand, Right Hand!* shows the author, aged three, looking perfectly composed and dignified in a dark reefer suit with brass buttons, and long trousers. A wide-brimmed straw hat of the type associated with Tom Kitten is set well back on his head. He has a white handkerchief in his breast pocket, wears dark gloves and carries a walking stick. He is wearing very much the same get-up, without the hat, in a photograph dated 1898.

In this last decade of the century, little girls too went nautical, as far as their top halves were concerned anyhow, the female version of the sailor suit consisting of a pouched blouse of navy serge, and a linen vest and square collar worn with a kilted skirt.

Dresses for small girls described as Knockabout Serge Frocks were advertised at the astonishingly low price of 1/6 each.[1] But it is not to be supposed that all little girls in the 90's were dressed so austerely. The same periodical described these startling toilettes for tots between the age of two and four:

Dress of sage-green velveteen finished round neck, sleeves,

[1] *The Child in Fashion*, D. Langley Moore, *et. seq.*

and foot, with black astrakhan; collar of cream guipure. Hat
of felt edged with astrakhan and trimmed with ostrich tips. . . .
Redingote of electric blue cloth with collar, cuffs and trimming
of golden beaver. . . . Nut-brown frize cloth dress with revers and
trimmings of mink. . . . Walking dress of olive green velveteen
with a grey cloth coat lined with plaid surah and trimmed with
bands of curled ostrich feather.'

A little girl in *The Child in Fashion* wears a dress (dating from
about 1892) which is made of dark crimson satin. The skirt
falls straight from a lace yoke. There is lace, too, on the sleeves
and round the long hem. The hat is a kind of pancake trimmed
with flowers. The utter unsuitability and impracticality of these
garments need not be stressed. Imagine how bedraggled the
curled ostrich feathers would soon become! It was as though
the fashions for little girls had flared up into a last blaze of
absurdity during the 90's, before dying down into a convenience and simplicity that has endured to present times.

Other mothers, as a result of Kate Greenaway's drawings,
favoured long muslin and silk dresses with high waists and
sashes, and large straw hats tied with ribbons for their young
daughters. This semi-18th-century attire was particularly popular for bridesmaid's dresses and for parties, and was certainly
becoming. Some fashion commentators considered it 'absurd
and inconvenient'—though it was less so, one would have supposed than those unwashable garments of sage-green velveteen
trimmed with astrakhan!

These various flights of fancy were, one supposes, more the
exception than the rule. The average girl-child wore a Sunday
dress of cream cashmere or white muslin stiffly starched, or
silk, with a sash, according to the season. In the summer, the
best hat would be of Leghorn straw with satin bows. For everyday there would be brown or cream holland, navy blue serges
and coloured prints. Over every dress would be worn the
inevitable pinafore. If the child's mother had a taste for bright
colours she might dress her in a green woollen Liberty frock
with a bright red jacket and a blue tam o'shanter.

With the dawn of the next century, children's feet were shod
in comfortable shoes with ankle straps, differing very little from
the shoes worn by present-day children, but in the last decade

of Victoria's reign, boots were still worn by both sexes, even in the case of little girls with summery frocks.

The author of *Left Hand, Right Hand!* relates a piteous story of how his sister Edith, then a little creature of five, relegated to a second place in the nursery by her brother's birth—both her parents preferring sons to daughters—tried to run away from home. 'Only the fact of her being as yet unable to lace her own boots, and of their being, as a result, so loose that farther walking became impossible was responsible for her capture and enforced return after an outing of three or four hours.'

In a photograph in 'The Scarlet Tree', the second volume of *Left Hand, Right Hand!* Sacheverell Sitwell is seen at the age of two, seated on a stone wall with a pug dog beside him. The little boy wears a coat very similar in shape to the kind of coat that a small boy would wear today, but with trimmings of fur on the collar and cuffs. On his head is another of those wide-brimmed Tom Kitten hats, this time of felt; like his elder brother at a nearly similar age he wears leather gloves and holds a little stick. No doubt under the coat he had on a little frock. At least that is how he is portrayed in the well-known portrait-group by Sargent of the Sitwell family which was painted in 1900.

By the end of the century a new personage had appeared in the nursery toy cupboard. The golliwog, in spite of its suggestion of plantation life, was created by an English writer, Miss Upton, who in 1895 brought out a children's book called *The Adventure of Two Dutch Dolls and a Golliwog*. The golliwog with his bright clothes, silky shock of hair and cheerful countenance was both exotic and appealing. A card game in which he featured testified to his success with children.

I wish I could do homage to the Teddy Bear in this book (I was in my own youth an ardent Teddy Bearphile, much preferring my family of bears to my one doll Isobel) but this charming toy which was to challenge the age-long supremacy of the doll, is beyond the confines of this book. The Teddy Bear according to the author of *Toys through the Ages* (Leslie Daiken) first made its appearance at the Leipzig Toy Fair in 1903.

Those little boys in the 1890's in their sailor suits spent a good deal of their time playing with toy soldiers. A very fine set of

English metal soldiers dating from about 1890, is illustrated in Leslie Daiken's book. It is an encampment set, and comprises cavalry and infantry, field guns, tents and trees. However if the children's nautical tastes were more than suit-deep, they could also play with a landing party of British sailors with a breech-loading field gun. The Crimean War was receding into history—the Boer War with its dissensions and disasters lay some ten years ahead. War was still a glorious game, to be a brave soldier a small boy's ambition. Unless, of course he preferred the role of cowboy, inspired to dreams of the Wild West by the spirited set of Cowboys and Red Indians, some of the former being on foot, others on horseback splendidly throwing lassoes.

The toy shops of the 90's must have been rich in these sets. Another one called a Boy Scout Encampment has boy scouts with moveable arms, a gate and hurdle and an entirely leafless tree. There were also jungle and farm sets. The familiar setting of nursery carpet, sofa and big round table could thus be transformed at will into a battlefield, a prairie or a jungle forest.

The earliest type of steam-drawn model locomotive dates from the 90's; the hand-carved traditional English rocking horse, whose fine head with white flowing mane, barred teeth and fiery eye is also illustrated in *Toys through the Ages* is early 20th century, so strictly speaking is beyond the limits of this book, yet the train, archaic as its shape would appear to a modern child, belongs to the future, the rocking horse to the past. Just beyond the scope of this book, too, are the little early 20th-century tin penny toys, the hansom cabs and buses (motor not horse-drawn) and the motor-cars of the 'Genevieve' type.

The turn of the century was to bring a new pleasure to children at Easter in the form of chocolate eggs (from the Continent). These superseded the very large, brightly coloured pasteboard shells, which in their turn had replaced the eggs covered with velvet cloth and trimmed with borders of lace that were the treasured possessions of an earlier generation. Models of saddles in the Army and Navy Store's catalogue, made to seat two children, reminds one of picnics and the out-door delights of summer, with their perennial appeal to children.

And so we have come to 1900 and to the end of this Nursery story. It is as well to bring it to a close now during 'that halcyon age'. It is, to quote again the splendid Sitwellian phrase, 'one of the great periodic calms of history'. It seems that this security and prosperity must endure for ever, becoming even more deeply secure and prosperous from year to year.

Alas! how many of those little boys in sailor suits playing on the nursery floor with their toy soldiers are destined to die on the battlefields of Flanders; how many of those little girls in pinafores will lose their young lovers! But no premonitory echo of the thunder of those guns that the future will make audible, penetrates into the cosy nursery; there is no sound more menacing than Nanny's 'Time for bed!'

They are living in the moment as children have always done and always will do as long as the human race endures. This is the miracle of childhood. 'They love an apple more than gold.'

Bibliography

❖❖❖❖❖❖❖❖❖❖❖❖❖❖❖❖❖❖❖❖❖❖❖❖❖❖❖❖❖❖❖❖❖❖❖❖❖❖

BOOKS CONSULTED

General

Children's Games throughout the Year	Leslie Daiken.
Children's Toys throughout the Ages	Leslie Daiken.
Toys of Other Days	Mrs. F. Nevill Jackson.
English Home Life	Christina Hole.
The Boy through the Ages ..	D. M. Stuart.
The Girl through the Ages ..	D. M. Stuart.
The Story of Medicine	Kenneth Walker.
History of Everyday Things in England	Marjorie and C. H. B. Quennell.
The English Interior	Arthur Stratton.
The Englishman's Castle ..	John Gloag.
Boys and Girls of History ..	E. and R. Power.
Article on *Horn Books* in '*Country Life*'	Sylvia Greves.
Popular Rhymes and Nursery Tales	Halliwell Philips.
Children's Books in England ..	F. J. Harvey Darton.
Four Hundred Years of Children's Costumes	Percy MacQuoid.
English Diaries	Arthur Ponsonby.

Middle Ages

Homes of Other Days	Thomas Wright.
A Medieval Garner ..	G. G. Coulton.

Medieval Panorama .. .. G. G. Coulton.
Medieval People .. .. Eileen Power.
Womankind in Western Europe T. Wright.
English Life and Manners in the
    Later Middle Ages .. A. Abram.
Social England in the 15th
    Century .. .. .. A. Abram.
Social England .. .. .. Traill.
La Vie Privée d'Autrefois Vol. 2. Alfred Franklin.

Tudor

La Vie Privée d'Autrefois Vol. 2. Alfred Franklin.
Society in the Elizabethan Age .. Hubert Hall.
The Elizabethan Home .. ed. M. St. Clare Byrne.
Elizabethan Life in Town and
    Country .. .. .. M. St. Clare Byrne.
Life and Work of the People of
    England (16th cen.) .. Dorothy Hartley and
    Margaret M. Elliot.
The Fyrst Book of the Introduction
    of Knowledge .. .. Andrew Boorde.
The England of Elizabeth .. A. L. Rowse.
Report on the Manuscripts of Lord
    de L'Isle and Dudley pre-
    served at Penshurst Place
    Vols. 1 and 2
English Costume in the Age of
    Elizabeth .. .. .. Iris Brooke.
Elizabethan Journal Vols. 1, 2,
    and 3 .. .. .. G. B. Harrison.
Witchcraft in England .. .. Christina Hole.
Haunted England .. .. Christina Hole.

Stuart

Repart on the Manuscripts of the
    Earl of Ancaster
The Lismore Papers
Memoirs of the Verney Family .. Frances P. Verney.
The Earl of Strafford's Letters
    and Dispatches Vols. 1 and 2
Lives of the Norths, 3 vols. .. Dr. Jessop.

BIBLIOGRAPHY

|---|---|
Some Thoughts concerning Education	John Locke.
Life and Letters of Mr. Endymion Porter	Dorothea Townshend.
Henrietta Maria	Carola Oman.
The Life-Story of Charlotte de la Tremoille, Countess of Derby	Mary C. Rowselt.

Eighteenth Century

18th Century London Life	Rosamund Bayne-Powell.
English Child in the 18th Century	Rosamund Bayne-Powell.
Some Thoughts concerning Education	John Locke.
The Scots Household in the 18th Century	Marion Lockhead.
The Domestic Life of Scotland in the 18th Century	Marjorie Plant.
Verney Letters of the 18th Century	ed. Margaret Maria Lady Verney.
Housekeeping in the 18th Century	Rosamund Bayne-Powell.
The Life and Times of the Rev. John Wesley	Tyerman.
La Jeunesse de Wesley	Augustin Leger.
Childhood a Hundred Years Ago (1876)	Sarah Tytler.
Divine Songs for Children	I. Watts.
Domestic Medicine	Dr. Buchan.
The Jerningham Letters	ed. Egerton Castle.
Letters from Lady Mary Wortley Montagu	
Emile	Jean Jacques Rousseau.
The Russells in Bloomsbury	Gladys Scott Thomson.
Diary of a Country Parson	Rev. James Woodforde.
Admiral's Wife	Cecil Aspinell-Oglander.
The Wynne Diaries	ed. Anne Fremantle.

Nineteenth Century

Dawn of the 19th Century England	John Ashton.
The Fairchild Family	Mrs. Sherwood.
The Stream of Time	Mrs. C. S. Peel.
Miss Weeton	ed. Edward Hall.

S   253

Elizabeth Ham ..	.. By Herself.
Praeterita	.. John Ruskin.
Early Victorian England	.. ed. G. M. Young.
Their First Ten Years ..	.. Marion Lockhead.
The Child in Fashion ..	.. Doris Langley Moore.
A House that was Loved	.. Katherine Kenyon.
Caroline Clive	.. ed. Mary Clive.
Lady de Rothschild and Her Daughters ..	.. Lucy Cohen.
Days before Yesterday ..	.. Lord Frederick Hamilton.
Happy World ..	.. Mary Carbery.
A Nursery in the Nineties	.. Eleanor Farjeon.
From Kitchen to Garret	.. J. C. Panton.
The Child in the Crystal	.. Lady Sybil Lubbock.
A London Child in the Seventies	M. Vivien Hughes.
The Lilac and the Rose	.. Lady Tweedsmuir.
Without knowing Mr. Walkley	Edith Oliver.
Dear Youth	.. Barbara Wilson.
Left Hand, Right Hand!	.. Sir Osbert Sitwell.
The Amberley Papers ..	.. Bertrand and Patricia Russell.
Diary of Lady Frederick Cavendish ..	.. ed. John Bailey.
Memoirs of Fifty Years	.. Lady St. Helier.
Our Fathers	.. Alen Both.
Our Mothers	.. Alen Both and Irene Clephane.

254

INDEX

Bute's, Lord, 'new little girl': 177

Breast-feeding: in Middle Ages, 8; story of Yde, Countess of Boulogne, 8–10; changlings and, 11; 16th-century French doctor advocates it, 41–2; popular belief about in 16th century, 43; alternatives to, in 17th century, 81; opinions of Rousseau, Drs. Cadogan and Buchan on, 126 and 126n; nursing difficulties in Clive family, 203–5; nursing difficulties in the Amberley family, 204; first break with tradition, 233.

Brief Introduction to the Skill of Song: 64

Bryan, Lady (Princess Elizabeth's governess): 52

Byron, Lord: 198

Cardigan, Lady: 118

Cadogan, Dr.: on children's diet: 126–7

Caldicott, Randolph: 242

Call to the Unconverted (Baxter): 102

Cambridge, Duke and Duchess of: 199

Canning: 198

Carbery, Mary (see *Happy World*)

Card games: 70, 150

Carlyle, Mrs.: 205

Caroline of Brunswick (Princess of Wales): 198

Caroline, Queen: 163

Carroll, Lewis (Rev. C. L. Dodgson, see *Alice in Wonderland*)

Carrots (Mrs. Molesworth): 242

Castle, Life in Medieval: 15–16

Cave, Sir Thomas and Lady, and family: trials of an expectant father, 119–20; Sir Thomas' congratulations on birth of a 'pretty lady', 121; more jocularity from Sir Thomas, 125; a 'House full of Bears', 164; Sir Thomas on his new-born son, 167

Cave, Miss (aged 6): 159

Cavendish, Lady Frederick (*see* Lucy Lyttleton)

Cecil, Lord David (quoted): 71

Changlings: 11

Charles I as husband and father, 72, 73; his letter to his brother, 93

Charlesworth Marion, (see *Ministering Children*)

Charlotte Princess: her death in childbirth, 174; despair of nation at her death, 198

Childbirth: in Middle Ages, 3–5; in 16th century, 40–1; birth of a 'goodly fat son' to Sidneys, 44; dangers and anxieties of, in former times, 117–9; childbirth less 'mortifying' in Turkey, 120; a midnight alarm in the Fremantle household, 123; confinements *en route*, 124; the Princess Charlotte disaster, 174; Mrs. Clive's confinements, 201; in Victorian times, 202, 204, 228–9

Child in the Crystal, The (Lady Sybil Lubbock): 236

Child in Fashion, The (Doris Langley Moore): 210–11, 212, 234, 235–6, 246–7

Child Marriage: in the Middle Ages, 31–2; in Stuart period, 73

Child Microcosmography, The (Bishop Earle): 90–1

Chimney sweeps, child, sufferings of, 194–5; in early 1860's, 220

China Toys (*see* Toys)

Christenings (*see* Baptism)

Christmas Box: 153

Christmas revelry: in 16th century, 70; in 18th century, 152; in early 19th century, 185; in Victorian period, 217–8

Chroniques de France: 12

Civil war: effect on family life, 73–4, 78

Cinderella: 101

Clarence, Duke and Duchess of: 198

Claderton, Henry: gives advice on begetting of sons, 75

the Fairchild family, 181–2; in Victorian times, 209; recommended by Mrs. Panton, 233–4; stodginess of nursery diet, 238, 243, 245

Diseases (*see* under Medicine)

Divine Songs for Children (Isaac Watt)

Dodgson, Rev. C. L. (*see* Lewis Carroll)

Dolls: in Middle Ages, 26; in 16th century, 60–1; a request for a 'Baby', 93; in 17th century, 98; in 18th century, 146–7; Princess Victoria's dolls, 182; in early 19th century, 183; another request for a doll, 184; a doll from Paris, 213; Victorian dolls, 218; penny dolls, 237

Dolls' houses; early examples, 98; and 18th-century Baby-house, 143–5; as collector's pieces and in toy shops, 146; Princess Victoria's doll's house, 182

Drums (*see* Toys)

Dudley, Lord and Lady: 97–8

Earle Bishop (see *The Child Microcosmography*)

Easter eggs; in 18th century, 141; in early 20th century, 249

Edgeworth, Maria: opinion of nurses, 162; *Moral Tales*, 185; as children's writer, 192

Education: in Middle Ages, 21–3; regard for learning in the 16th century, 60, 62; in 16th century, 63–5; in 17th century, 105–8; in 18th century, 154–7, 191–2; in 19th century, 224–5, 237, 241–2

Edward III's daughters: 23

Edward IV's family: education of, 21

Effingham, Lady: 41

Eighteenth-century interior: 130

Eleanor of Castille, Queen: 17

Elizabeth I, Queen: and John Stubbe, 46n; pitiful state of her wardrobe as a child, 52; her tutor, 57; her education, 63; life as a child affected by politics, 68

Elyot, Sir Thomas: 63

Emma, Children in (Jane Austen): 187

Emile (*see* J. J. Rousseau)

England of Elizabeth, The (A. L. Rowse): 47

English Children in the 18th Century (Rosamund Bayne-Powell): 142n

English Children in the Olden Time (Elizabeth Godfrey): 11

English Interior, The (Arthur Stratton): 38

English Schoolmaster (Cootes): 63

Epitaphs on infants: 77, 96

Erasmus: 39, 54

Erondell Peter: his dialogue between mother and nurse quoted, 48–50; quoted as showing status of Tudor mother, 56

Eure, Margaret and Mary: 85

Evelyn John: and political situation, 75; and his son Richard, 84, 103, 106; death of his niece Elizabeth, 85

Ewing, Mrs.: 242

Fabulous Histories, Designed for the Instruction of Children, respecting their Treatment of Animals (Mrs. Trimmer): 153

Fairchild Family, The (Mrs. Sherwood): 154n, 175, 181–2, 186, 192n, 194

Fairy Spectator, The (Lady Fenn): 153

Fairy tales: 101, 153

Fairy Tales of All Nations: 219

Falkland, Lady (*see* Lettice Morrison)

Fanshaw, Sir Richard and Lady: 73–4

Fenn, Lady (see *Fairy Spectator*)

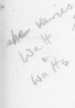